HYSTERICAL

HYSTERICAL

A MEMOIR

ELISSA BASSIST

New York

Hachette Books
Hachette Book Group
1290 Avenue of the Americas
New York, NY 10104
HachetteBooks.com
Twitter.com/HachetteBooks
Instagram.com/HachetteBooks

First Edition: September 2022

Published by Hachette Books, an imprint of Perseus Books, LLC,
a subsidiary of Hachette Book Group, Inc. The Hachette Books name
and logo is a trademark of the Hachette Book Group.

The publisher is not responsible for websites (or their content)
that are not owned by the publisher.

Library of Congress Cataloging-in-Publication Data has been applied for.

ISBNs: 978-0-306-82737-2 (hardcover), 978-0-306-82739-6 (ebook)

Printed in the United States of America

LSC-C

Printing 1, 2022

For my mom,

for Thea,

and for every other crazy psycho bitch

CONTENTS

INTRODUCTION

You don't have a brain tumor," the first neurologist said.

"You need new lenses," the first ophthalmologist said.

"You may have a sinus infection," the owner of the bagel shop said, along with my physician.

It was late February, three months after the 2016 election, and my vision had blurred.

This would accelerate into a wire-hanger-in-the-brain headache, and the headache would segue into a relentless sore throat, which would segue again, into a persistent stomachache, and then again, into a herniated disc, among other symptoms—so many that it got embarrassing. For the next two years I wouldn't have a life; I'd have appointments: with a psychologist or a psychiatrist or ophthalmologists or general practitioners or neurologists or a psychopharmacologist or a radiologist or an allergist or an ear, nose, and throat specialist or a gastroenterologist or a nephrologist or an orthopedic hand surgeon or an occupational therapist or a rehabilitation spine specialist or a physical therapist or a massage therapist or an acupuncturist or an herbalist or an obsessive-compulsive disorder specialist.

Each week I'd average two to three appointments and would take myself to each one alone, weighing a little less than I weighed before, and with a little less hair.

The diagnosis I'd receive over and over, second to no diagnosis, was Nothing Is Wrong with You.

I had what millions of American women had: pain that didn't make sense to doctors, a body that didn't make sense to science, a psyche that didn't make sense to mankind in general.

To make sense of it, to not die from it, to recover, I had to reach the origins of these undiagnosed ailments—and how they (and I) (and women) are misunderstood and mishandled. I had to backtrack to birth, to mine and to Eve's.

What I figured out is best expressed by my mom, who within ten minutes into any conversation says in her Southern accent, "It's a man's world."

The author and activist Caroline Criado Perez backs up my mom in *Invisible Women: Exposing Data Bias in a World Designed for Men*:

> Starting with the theory of Man the Hunter, the chroniclers of the past have left little space for women's role in the evolution of humanity, whether cultural or biological. Instead, the lives of men have been taken to represent those of humans overall. When it comes to the other half of humanity, there is often nothing but silence. And these silences are everywhere. Films, news, literature, science, city planning, economics. The stories we tell ourselves about our past, present and future. They are all marked—disfigured—by a female-shaped "absent presence."

These silences *are* everywhere. Many I experienced, but many I didn't notice. Sitting in cars, I suspected the seatbelt wasn't designed by a person with boobs. As a pedestrian, I noted that US traffic signs showed men walking (women were, obviously, at home, in triangle dresses, nursing their children or husbands). As I spent time in exam rooms as a sick woman, I stared at the medical wall art where female bodies were absent and male bodies—depicted as the human body, the universal body—were everywhere. When I scored a free trip to Israel and visited the Wailing Wall in Jerusalem, I faced what women have faced for centuries: far less of the Wall than men (the Wall splits women from men, and the men's spot is two-thirds of the Wall, so women squish together to talk to G-d as the men roam). In El Salvador, which bans abortion, seventeen women known as Las 17 have been imprisoned and sentenced to thirty years minimum for having miscarriages or stillbirths. In March 2019 history was not made when NASA called off its first-ever all-female spacewalk due to wardrobe malfunction: there weren't two spacesuits in smaller sizes (even in outer space there's a gender gap). Dogs are elected mayors (in Minnesota, in California, in Colorado, in Kentucky), while a quarter of human mayors in 2021 were women. "Woman" is defined in the *New Oxford American Dictionary*, Apple's default dictionary:

(1) *a woman got out of the car*: lady, girl, female; matron; Scottish lass, lassie; *informal* chick, girlie, sister, dame, broad, gal; grrrl; *literary* maid, maiden, damsel; *archaic* wench, gentlewoman; (women) womenfolk.

(2) *he found himself a new woman*: girlfriend, sweetheart, partner, significant other, inamorata, lover, mistress; fiancée; wife, spouse; *informal* missus, better half, (main) squeeze, babe, baby; *dated* lady friend, ladylove.

"Man" is defined:

(1) *a handsome man*: male, adult male, gentleman; *informal* guy, fellow, fella, joe, geezer, gent, bloke, chap, dude, hombre; (men) menfolk.

(2) *all men are mortal*: human being, human, person, mortal, individual, personage, soul.

(3) *the evolution of man*: the human race, the human species, Homo sapiens, humankind, humanity, human beings, humans, people, mankind.

(4) *the men voted to go on strike*: worker, workman, laborer, hand, blue-collar worker; staff.

In the beginning was the Word, and the Word was spoken by some guy, and the Word was "wench." Because men wrote the Bible and the five love languages[1] and the dictionary and the thesaurus,[2] forging the American lexicon, and as women "exit cars" and are romantic placeholders for other women, men vote and men strike; men are born good-looking and men are alive and men have souls and men are advancing. Men are the norm, and men are the ideal. Anyone who doesn't fit is invisible or irrelevant and may be ignored or mocked or scorned or silenced or erased or defiled or killed. Or a combination, which is how a wench or lady or chick or girlfriend or wife or spouse or ladylove can die from silence.

In *Doing Harm: The Truth About How Bad Medicine and Lazy Science Leave Women Dismissed, Misdiagnosed, and Sick* (2018), author Maya Dusenbery makes the connection: women are "at least twice as likely to have chronic pain conditions that affect 100 million American adults," and these conditions are "woefully undertreated and under-researched." Then there are "medically unexplained symptoms," the "latest label to be applied to allegedly hysterical symptoms," writes Dusenbery. She cites

---

1 The male Baptist pastor Gary Chapman wrote *The Five Love Languages: How to Express Heartfelt Commitment to Your Mate*, which became a best seller. Jeanna Kadlec, an ex-evangelical and author of *Heretic: A Memoir*, tweeted her read on the book, that the Languages, which include "words of affirmation," "quality time," "physical touch," "acts of service," and "receiving gifts," "were specifically designed to reinforce patriarchal gender norms."

2 Peter Mark Roget, in 1805. For this book I looked up synonyms for "victim" on OneLook Thesaurus, and the second on the list is "woman."

studies that show "up to a third of patients in primary care" and "up to two-thirds…in specialty clinics" have them. And "approximately 70 percent of [patients with medically unexplained symptoms] are women." Dusenbery also clarifies that some medically unexplained symptoms just "haven't been explained yet." This is because "many millions" of American women "experience long delays and see multiple health care providers before getting correctly diagnosed," and can wait up to ten years to be diagnosed with endometriosis. (Endometriosis "is thought to affect one in ten women," writes Perez in *Invisible Women*, yet "it took until 2017 for England's National Institute for Health and Care Excellence to release its first ever guidance to doctors for dealing with it," in which the "main recommendation" is " 'Listen to women.' ")

"I want you to understand this," warns author Alyson J. McGregor in *Sex Matters: How Male-Centric Medicine Endangers Women's Health and What We Can Do About It*. "If you are a woman, you are at greater risk of misdiagnosis, improper treatment, and complications in common medical situations."

If you're a woman, you're also at greater risk of mental illness. Depression is 70 percent more prevalent in women than in men. "About one in five women in the United States take a psychotropic medication, compared to one in eight men," Dusenbery writes. American adult women report a suicide attempt 1.6 times as often as men, and between 2007 and 2015, suicide rates among girls in their teens doubled. (2015 is the same year teenagers gorged on nine hours of media—sexist, misogynistic, violent media—daily.)

These statistics come out of a culture where men speak and women shut up.

As an only child of divorced parents who remarried other people, I called TV my fifth parent, and I was part of the first "always connected" generation of now geriatric millennials, so I know that men talk the most in films, TV, and streaming shows, and when women do speak, usually it's about men.[3] Men also report most of the news, even news that concerns women, like reproductive issues, gender-based violence, and harassment. And men founded and run our echo chambers (Facebook, Instagram, Twitter, Reddit, Snapchat) while pervading all levels of industry and government. Meanwhile, women's voices are squashed, attacked, and interrupted—sometimes with a woman's cooperation. During the 2020 vice presidential debate, not only did then senator Kamala Harris repeat (have to repeat), "I'm speaking," but also moderator Susan Page let Mike Pence speak longer, interject more, ignore her, and moderate the debate himself by asking his own questions.

Throughout history women like Harris have been rebuked or medicated for using their voices "inappropriately" by expressing sadness or anger or joy in ways that perturb others. My coming-of-age story took place in a culture that can't seem to handle women and their many, many feelings, where if a man doesn't take no for an answer, then he's just a man, but if a woman doesn't take no for an answer, then she's "psychotic." Also where a man on a dating app can get away with being unable to spell, but if a woman uses too many exclamation points, she's demented, or if she doesn't use enough exclamation points, she's a bitch. And where a man's silence means he's "uninterested," while a woman's silence is a matter of decorum. But if a woman is going to talk, if she has to, then what's most important is the desire she inspires, not what she has to say, and not what she takes issue with. Thus, a woman's voice is her cage, inside of which she must work the sound panel of her voice to be heard, and if I were a man, I could get away with that mixed metaphor.

---

3 Which is to say, most movies and shows fail the Bechdel Test—a test born from the comic *Dykes to Watch Out For* by Alison Bechdel—whose criteria are: a fictional work (1) featuring at least two women (2) who talk to each other (3) about literally anything besides a man.

What woman hasn't asked herself, in relationships as well as in the workplace, *What does it take to be heard when people don't want to listen to you?* And *why do words sound biblical out of men's mouths but naggy out of women's?* In relationships women are more likely than men to apologize and are less likely to say no. At work women are more likely than men to apologize and are less likely to say no.[4] And the unspoken rule for women in love is the same for women at work: less is more.

Society itself is basically a patriarchal livestream that blasts the same rule and other messages to girls and women: *Speak softer. Moan louder. Be pure. Don't be shy. Don't talk back. Don't tell. Don't say this (or that). Don't draw attention. Don't be difficult. Be pleasant. Be who everyone needs you to be.*

My self-esteem absorbed these messages that are subliminal until they are atomic, until I'd transmuted them solid and supreme and started saying them to myself and accepting them as my own. These messages became my filter, my philosophy and my personality, my every thought and basis for interaction (social, political, romantic, ideological, superficial), my pattern for behavior and inspiration to pick a voice so small and so nice and so normal that it's a medical wonder I could breathe—

I'd entered a feedback loop.

And what happens when the patriarchal livestream also blasts dead girls and ravaged women ad nauseam? "The single best predictor of rape," writes prolific author and professor of communication studies Julia T. Wood, citing a 1989 study, "is the circulation of...materials that glorify sexual force and exploitation," materials that declare their love to girls and women by degrading them.

---

4 Perhaps because standard chilly office temperature is based on male bodies in male clothing, which the *Atlantic* reported is lowering women's cognitive functioning.

Despite the rumors, it isn't so easy to just speak up. Since women are trained to disappear while being looked at constantly, we become our first and greatest critics and censors—so, speaking up for ourselves is not how we learn English. Instead, we're fluent in Giggle, in Question Mark, in Self-Deprecation, in Asking for It, in Miscommunication, in Bowing Down. These are all really different silences—we speak, but exclusively in compliments ("Your sexism is so well said") and in apologies and in all ways right. A typical conversation between women sounds like:

"I'm sorry."

"No, I'm sorry!"

"Don't be sorry! I am the one who is sorry."

"Oh, I'm sorry, you're right. I'm sorry."

"Please, the apology is all mine."

Since we barely exist, we must continue apologizing for existing, for our reason to be and feel human. Which can make sharing or even forming an opinion unthinkable.

Especially amid straightforward silencing. In the backlash to #MeToo, some people are questioning who deserves a voice, and arguing that since women have more of a voice than ever—

and since women comprised 26.7 percent of Congress in 2021 instead of 23.6 percent in 2019—

and since groups with 23.6 percent of women appear standard while 26.7 percent seems exceptional—

and since *Wonder Woman* (the first film) wasn't bad—

then we should shut up already. Or else.

Or else we're hysterical.

In 2017, former presidential aide Jason Miller called then senator Kamala Harris "hysterical" during a hearing over Jeff Sessions's collusion with Russia during the 2016 election. "I mean, she was asking some tough questions," Miller offered as proof, and all Republican men became erect from a man telling it like it is.

"Hysterical" means that a woman asked some tough questions. The centuries-old term can describe and discredit and dismiss anything a woman feels, thinks, says, or does. *She's not sick; she's hysterical.* Does she hurt? *She's hysterical.* Is she sensitive? *She's hysterical.* In love? *She's hysterical.* Is she direct? *She's hysterical.* Opinionated? *She's hysterical.* Hemorrhaging? *She's hysterical.* Did she do her job? *She's hysterical.* Disagree? *She's hysterical.* The label sticks—he's rubber and she's glue—such that a labeled woman and those around her will think one thought only: *Hysterical. Hysterical. Hysterical.*

Are we sick of the imbalance yet? I can say that at least literally we are.

And not to sound hysterical, but I almost died—from silence, from illness, from the Nothing Is Wrong with You diagnoses. From having a high-pitched voice that dogs can hear but doctors can't. From preferring to die rather than aggravate anyone or be a "crazy psycho bitch."

I'm a feminist (thank you) with a degree in women and gender studies and an "ERASE THE PATRIARCHY" eraser on my desk, and still. Still, I apologize to inanimate objects. Still, I smile while being insulted. Still, I tip cab drivers extra for not assaulting me. STILL, I wonder why my ex won't text me back. *(Is it because I said something wrong or texted too much?)* Still, I'm compelled to talk the "correct" amount, to verbalize my thoughts "sweetly," to regurgitate niceties that don't reflect my beliefs, to say "I'm fine" when I'm bleeding.

Still, it's not so simple to erase the patriarchy because not only do we live in one, it lives in us. Weeks before the 2016 election I saw bell hooks and Joey Soloway in conversation at the New School, where Soloway predicted the end of the patriarchy, and hooks laughed; there would be no end of the patriarchy. In part because patriarchy is our mother tongue and preexisting condition. Even now I flinch mentioning "patriarchy" for fear of being dubbed a "feminazi."

But my silence hurt me more than anything I could ever say. And it wasn't only that I thought I was going to die when I was sick (I was pretty sure I was going to die), but that I thought I was going to die with so much unsaid.

My illness, my *hysteria*, begged me to review how shrinking and muting myself threatened my body/mind/vagina/soul/life. To get better I'd have to break my own silences and get back the voice that was mine before the world intervened, and then use it again without regret.

I hope everyone who reads this will copy me.

BUT FOR NOW SHUT UP BECAUSE THE BOOK IS ABOUT TO START.

1

MEDICAL HISTORY

And the Oscar goes to…Casey Affleck, *Manchester by the Sea!*"
announced Brie Larson at the Eighty-Ninth Academy Awards. I
watched on my laptop in my one-bedroom Brooklyn apartment as
Casey Affleck, with a low man-bun, walked onstage, and Larson,
who'd won Best Actress the year prior for her role as a sexual assault
survivor in *Room*, hugged him and handed him the trophy—and I
couldn't do that thing: see straight. My right eyeball ached as another
accused harasser won an award for his art rather than be arrested or
otherwise disciplined for his (twice) alleged crime (that was settled out
of court for an undisclosed amount).[1]

Days later, the ache spread to my left eye. More days later, I couldn't
read my street sign at the crosswalk.

For what I'd guessed was eye strain from screen devotion, I
booked an appointment with an ophthalmologist on the Upper West
Side (not covered by insurance). Joan Didion's books were on display
at the check-in desk—this was, in fact, Joan Didion's ophthalmologist
(kismet, unintentional)—and the ophthalmologist's administrative

---

[1] Meanwhile, Brie Larson got flack for "the look on her face" and for being too
unenthused.

11

assistant handed me the first set of medical history forms I'd repeatedly fill out over the next two years.

Seated in the waiting room that looked like an art gallery, I told the form a little about myself.

Age/Sex/Location: Early mid-thirties/female/in my head

Race: White/translucent

Astrological chart: Virgo sun, Cancer moon, Scorpio rising

Marital status: Single. Like single-single, like assembling-IKEA-furniture-single single

Emergency contacts and safety nets: Well-to-do mommy and stepdad

Occupation: Freelance writer and editor working mostly for free; gig artist (dog-sitter, nanny, transcriber, barista); "artist"; artist; "unemployed" (per my dad)

Insurance: Medicaid, the law of attraction

Privileged: Yes

Medications: Yes

Do you agree to not get sick unless you (or someone you know) can afford it?: Yes

Do you agree to not make enough money in order to qualify for Medicaid and never make so much money that you won't (1) be eligible for Medicaid OR (2) be able to afford insurance?: I do

My eyes were dilated, tested, touched. Joan Didion's ophthalmologist recommended artificial tears and fish oil supplements, and he rewrote my glasses prescription. The ordeal was over.

One week later I picked up my glasses with the new lenses, tried them on, and waited for my eyes to adjust to Court Street in Brooklyn. They didn't. The prescription was wrong, or the lenses were, or my eyes, I couldn't tell, but at least I could begin panicking.

Back in the ophthalmologist's waiting room for repeat exams, I stared at framed landscape paintings I couldn't see and burst into public tears. *What if I never see another landscape?* I had taken landscapes for granted. I pressed the image of the landscape into my memory, just in case.

"The prescription's correct," the ophthalmologist assured me.

I revisited the glasses boutique. "The lenses are accurate," the optometrist assured me.

So, I met with new ophthalmologists and new optometrists with new hands, and I got newer prescriptions that were old after a few days.

Soon my eyesight didn't matter because I had another complaint: a headache. Actually, sometimes it was a headache, but most times it was a poltergeist trying to pry my eyes from their sockets.

I'd had headaches before, a few, and they were not like this one. This headache did not end.

A neurologist tried to categorize it. First, it was a migraine, classed as a "primary headache," the third most common and seventh most disabling medical disorder worldwide (forty-seven million Americans experience migraine, and 75 percent are women). But I didn't have typical migraine symptoms of nausea or seeing auras, so the neurologist reclassified my headache as "cluster headaches," also primary, also known as "suicide headaches," so nicknamed because the pain is off the pain scale, because the pain won't kill you but you wish it would. True to cluster headaches, my pain was one-sided and concentrated around my right eye but had spread and had a random beginning that suggested a random end. But my pain wasn't "enough" pain, although it was all-consuming, to be a cluster headache.

Other primary headache disorders the neurologist ruled out were "stabbing headache" (or "ice-pick headache"), "headache associated with sexual activity," "new daily persistent headache (NDPH)," and more listed in the infinite International Classification of Headache Disorders. That my headache was unclassifiable was its only certain characteristic.

To find the source of the pain, another neurologist tested my brain and my nerves and my gut (also called the "second brain"). I'd hoped for "brain tumor," just to have a name, any name. "Brain tumor" implied that doctors would come and get my pain and also take me seriously. Because if a woman is in pain that has no name, then no, she isn't.

The CT and MRI scans didn't show a tumor. To single out food allergies, the neurologist put me on an elimination diet, which has two parts, the elimination phase (stop eating everything you eat), and the reintroduction phase (start eating the food you eat again, one food at a time, to see which food, if any, causes symptoms). It takes five to six weeks that register as five to six years, and I found out I had no food allergies.

Next the neurologist looked for nerve compression via a nerve conduction velocity test. A nurse stuck electrodes on me that would send mild electrical impulses to the nerves under my skin to stimulate them and isolate nerve damage. "We'll start with a trial run. This won't hurt," the nurse had said, I think, though I'm not sure because she'd just electrocuted me. This was the first "wouldn't hurt" of thousands to come. *Wouldn't hurt whom, and wouldn't hurt how much?* The actual evaluation would have stimulated/fried nerves across every part of my body, like G-d stabbing Her fingernail into tangles of fibers until they smoked.

"I'd like to reschedule," I said, and then didn't.

Over the phone the neurologist put me on artificial energy (vitamins B-2, B-6, B-12) and wrote me prescriptions for military-grade magnesium and the headache medication of choice, triptans, which desensitize pain nerves and reduce blood vessel constriction in the brain. I took triptans in pill form and by self-injection with a prefilled syringe that I jabbed into my own thigh. The neurologist also prescribed sedatives. (Whenever I had a problem, whatever the problem, I was prescribed sedatives. Women like me receive sedatives for pain instead of pain medication for two reasons: hurting women are seen as "anxious," not "hurting," and medication treats the affliction, while sedatives shush the woman with the affliction.)

I swallowed the sedatives and felt better. So I swallowed more. *Even better.* I took just enough to sleep and just enough to be awake and just enough to sit still and initiate a time-lapse. Later I'd add to the mix and go through three thousand bottles of Advil and prescription-strength Advil and Advil Cold & Sinus, as well as multiple rounds of oral steroids that felt like snorting cocaine without having to snort cocaine, plus muscle relaxants and Benadryl I'd pop for nonallergy reasons. The pills took care of me, and because of the pills I'd be okay. *This is for my pain, and this, and this.* I'd do anything to relieve my pain, anything at all; I would have given blow jobs to Fyre Festival employees to relieve my pain.

"Are you better yet?"

"Get better!"

"I hope you're feeling better!"

"How are you?"

This is what well-intentioned people asked or said to me, to my face.

They expected me—and every other woman in pain—to answer pleasantly or exuberantly, with pain redacted.

I hated to be insolent, but I was not better or getting better or feeling better. The allegation of "better" lost its significance to a person in a pain that no one else was in, a pain no one knows unless it brings them to their own knees on their own floor.

"Have you tried going back to normal?" the same people would ask. "Or not feeling so sorry for yourself?" Like that which didn't kill me must be gotten over without further ado. Like I was unfun to hang around and could I please stop that now?

They suggested "relaxation" and "juicing" and "showering" and "going agog at the splendid majesty of the sunrise sky" or whatever—

"Could it be that you don't *want* to get better?" they wondered out loud, implying I was doing this to myself and making a choice, an ugly choice, living with pain I decided to have.

I didn't want to talk about it anymore with the feeling-fine. What they were really doing with their questions was putting my pain out of their minds by suggesting it was all in my head.

I must not have wanted to get better when during my annual physical that fall my primary care physician said what we pray they'll never say. "Hmm."

She was doing a breast exam, and my breasts were lumpy.

"Which is probably nothing to worry about," she said and referred me to radiology for an ultrasound.

Days later a male technician smeared goop all over my chest and moved a wand in circles as he watched the attached monitor and pressed down without pity. He lingered over one spot, pressing harder and harder for longer and longer—probably nothing to worry about.

The male radiologist joined us. "I want to biopsy this," he said. "You shouldn't worry about it."

Once alone I used a roll of brown paper towel to sop up the goo and then scheduled the biopsy for as soon as possible.

The earliest available appointment was in one month. I had to *maybe* have breast cancer and not worry about it for thirty-one days.

My mom has had breast cancer three times. I was in eighth grade; I was twenty-eight; I was thirty-two when she told me about the small malignant tumor in her left breast. But apart from that she kept her cancer from me, and I wouldn't have known she had cancer if I didn't, actually, know. She wore blond wigs or head coverings day and night, and not once did I see her bald scalp. She washed everyone's laundry and went to work and prepared every meal. She also downplayed or withheld specifics: the third recurrence was "a molecule of cancer," and her double mastectomy was "like going to the drive-through" and dropping off her breasts without leaving her car. ("Drive-by mastectomies"—an extensive surgery of body-part removal downgraded to an outpatient procedure—are routine.)

My grandmother, my mom's mom, had pancreatic cancer in 1966, and no one told her. Doctor's orders. As if to name her pain would cause her more. My grandmother would ask my mom what was happening to her, but my mom was told not to tell her, out of love. In turn, my grandmother, out of love, would ask my mom, age fifteen, to go into her bedroom and close the door so in the living room my grandmother could cry out from pain she didn't understand. (Male doctors refused her morphine, claiming that she—although dying—would become addicted; instead, they severed her nerves twice.)

"It was not mentioned," my mom says now about her mother's illness.

My mom worshipped her mother, a brown-eyed brunette with glow-in-the-dark pale skin like me. I wasn't told about my grandmother's pain until I was sick, years after I'd written a short story about a woman who tries to drown herself in her bathtub—not to kill herself but her pain, to be dead only to end her dying—which my grandmother had tried. (This is a family secret because the act was "out of character," because my grandmother was "strong.") How did I write that story without knowing about my grandmother's suicide attempt? How did I know without knowing? I just did.

"This will feel like being at the dentist," the male radiologist said about the fine needle aspiration, moments before the biopsy.

For most minor procedures on and in my lady parts—procedures that feel anywhere from painful to there-are-no-adjectives-to-encapsulate-how-painful-this-is painful—I'd pop two or three Advil half an hour beforehand, which doctors suggested if they remembered. But for a biopsy, aspirin-like medications (e.g., ibuprofen) are forbidden, so I was stone-cold sober.

"You may feel some discomfort,"[2] the male radiologist said as he shot me in the right boob with local anesthesia, then shot me again in

---

2 Similar to "you may feel some pressure" or "you may feel some cramping" or "you may feel a small pinch" or "your pain shouldn't be causing you any pain" and other phrases that people-not-in-your-pain say that almost never match the actual feeling or reaction.

the boob with a hollow needle that sucked out boob innards, and then shot me a third time in the boob to insert a stainless steel grain of sand as a marker for future radiologists (in case the biopsy disclosed cancer cells).

"LIAR," I'd wanted to yell. I've been going to the dentist my whole life—for cleanings, retainers, mouthguards, headgear, braces, teeth-pulling, wisdom-teeth removal, and gum surgery in which the top layer of my soft palate was snipped off and stitched onto four spots above my teeth where the gums had receded to the root from grinding—and the dentist was not like a breast biopsy at all, not at all.

Nor was the post-biopsy mammogram—an archaic process that pancakes one breast at a time—like the dentist.

The male radiologist, who did not have to sleep with boobs or walk with boobs or travel with boobs, also did not prepare me for the coming days and weeks where I'd have to hold my bleeding boob to stand or move in any way, or if I were on the subway, sit and fold over onto my thighs and stifle feral noises.

My lump was benign. It sits in my chest with the stainless steel grain of sand at its heart, and once a month I do a self-breast-exam to see if it's grown bigger than a golf ball. It hasn't yet.

The male radiologist could have told me to put my boob on ice or at the very least acknowledged the difference in our chests. I would learn—not from the mouth of any doctor but from reading books by women—that the institution of medicine rarely acknowledges sex differences that show up in every human organ, tissue, and cell, and in most diseases. This disregard begins in medical schools. Caroline Criado Perez writes in *Invisible Women*, "Medical education has been focused on a male 'norm,' with everything that falls outside that designated 'atypical' or even 'abnormal,'" so medical students "learn about physiology, and female physiology. Anatomy, and female anatomy." Just like how

there are "executives" and "female executives"; "presidential candidates" and "strident hags who are running for office for some reason."
Most medical school curriculum hardly integrates sex- and gender-
based medicine; AARP found that "most medical schools and residency programs don't teach aspiring physicians about menopause,"
despite every cisgender woman eventually going through it ("nearly 80
percent of medical residents admit that they feel 'barely comfortable'
discussing or treating menopause").

This bias enters medical research, which often excludes women.
Perez quotes article after article that states some version of "Female
bodies (both the human and animal variety) are…too complex, too
variable, too costly to be tested on. Integrating sex and gender into
research is seen as 'burdensome.'"

(Note: when medicine says "female" and "women," the institution
has a smaller group in mind. "Woman" often means "white, cisgender"
woman, which does not represent all women, not Black women, Indigenous women, women of color, trans women, nonbinary people, people with uteruses, pregnant women, menopausal women, incarcerated
women, immigrant women, uninsured women, working-class women,
women in shelters, fat women,[3] or disabled women, even though differences in race, history, age, class, and circumstance alter a patient's
treatment and treatment options.)

What the male radiologist didn't say said it all: that millions of
women are in unexplainable pain because a woman's pain just isn't
important, and that if men had to experience a woman's pain, only
then would a woman's pain be a matter of life and death, and attended
to. Male artist Pablo Picasso once explained, "Women are suffering
machines." Like women are well versed in living with pain and are
bred for pain, for giving birth when birth splits us open.

---

3 The most popular medical advice for women, regardless of issue or fact, is to lose weight.

In all modesty, a woman's pain is a lot to bear; who can bear it but women?

Women report less pain than they bear. In her essay "The Pain Scale," author Eula Biss rates her pain a three, and her father, a physician, says, "'Three is nothing.'" To Biss, a three is "mail remains unopened. Thoughts are rarely followed to their conclusions. Sitting becomes unbearable after one hour. Nausea sets in." Sonya Huber, in *Pain Woman Takes Your Keys*, rated her chronic pain lower than it felt so she'd "be manageable"; she grapples, "If I rate my pain a two or a three, do I mean that I thought about death only two or three times in the past week?"

Whenever I was asked to rate my pain, I sensed the trick question. The "right" answer involved a lot of subtraction: *My pain is killing me, which is "ten" out of ten—*

but my pain isn't that bad unless it actually kills me, so it's a "nine"—

but I shouldn't exaggerate, so "eight"—

and I should subtract my feelings about my pain—

and subtract for emotion in general and to account for gender stereotypes—[4]

and subtract again because I don't want to be unreasonable or unoriginal or pessimistic—

and subtract again just to be safe—[5]

and subtract again so that I'm not outside sympathy and shrugged off, and can get the help I need—

Three.

---

4 A Yale study revealed that young boys' pain is taken more seriously than young girls' due to gender stereotypes like "girls are more emotive" and thus dramatize their pain in "cries for attention."

5 McGregor writes in *Sex Matters*, "The more vocal women become about their pain, the more likely their providers are to 'tune them out' and prescribe either inadequate or inappropriate pain relief medication."

Whatever number my pain felt like, I was always going to say it felt like a three.

And if I weren't white, then doctors would hear "zero."[6]

The pain in my boob was a three. And my next symptom was also a three. That winter my throat was a California wildfire. But I was slow to go back to doctors because I thought that they thought I was hassling them with my afflictions. So I hydrated with over-the-counter cold medication and herbal resistance remedies with high Amazon ratings.

In spring I caved. The three-month sore throat called for four specialists over as many months: a general practitioner, who then referred me to an allergist, who tested me and told me I didn't have allergies and then referred me to an ear, nose, and throat specialist (ENT), who stuck swabs all the way up my nose until I swear she touched brain, and then an herbalist (not covered by insurance).

The ENT guessed that my sore throat came from my stomach and from the bottles of painkillers I'd pounded for the headache, which had torn up my gut and resulted in acid reflux. (This is common, when taking too much pain-relieving medicine causes more pain.) She recommended over-the-counter acid reducers, and I tried one after the other, and each made the hollow organs of my digestive system weep. (This is also common for women, when the treatment causes havoc.) Most medication didn't agree with me not because I was abnormal (my working theory) but because I was typical, *because*:

1. most medications aren't tested on women;

---

6 Dr. Nafissa Thompson-Spires resisted a hysterectomy for her unlivable endometriosis because of its history: in the mid-nineteenth century, the "father of gynecology" carried out his "groundbreaking" experiments on Black women based on the false premise that Black people don't feel pain, which endures today as doctors provide even less adequate and even less appropriate treatment to Black women.

2. most medications, if tested on women, aren't tested during the four phases of the menstrual cycle, and some drugs may hit differently at different times;

3. both over-the-counter drug dosages and prescribed dosages for "adults" are based on a man-size person with a nonmenstruating body (who is seen as "human" and "universal"), so women take inappropriate dosages;[7]

4. women are overmedicated and prone to an adverse drug reaction.[8]

The ENT recommended seeing a hypnotherapist and getting an endoscopy where she'd insert a long tube into my body through my mouth to see my throat, esophagus, and stomach in detail—

Instead, I booked an appointment with an herbalist and hoped Western medicine would lose my number.

The herbalist had slipped on a broken wineglass and torn her Achilles tendon at her baby shower, so we had to meet over FaceTime. Off the bat she asked, "Do you track your period or use a period tracking app?"

Not one MD asked me about my menstrual cycle beyond when my last period was, which I never knew.

"Download an app now," she said.

Out of apps named Flo, Eve, Glow, and Life, I downloaded the free app Clue, and as I tracked my period with technology, the herbalist brewed many hundreds of dollars' worth of teas and tinctures that I boiled or dripped onto my tongue, along with a shot of apple cider vinegar before breakfast and a shot of sauerkraut juice after dinner. But

---

7 A friend of mine was prescribed Ambien in 2007 and was prescribed so much that she woke up in the bathtub choking on water after falling asleep; in 2013 the federal Food and Drug Administration recommended cutting Ambien dosage in half for women.
8 "Nearly twice as often as men," according to 2020 research on adverse drug reactions from the University of California, Berkeley.

the teas and tinctures had the same effect as pills and put me in two alternating states at every time of the month: suicidal and diarrhea.

Throughout the summer my throat was sore and now my stomach felt as though some part inside of me had given up.

Finally I shat blood. That is to say, finally my latest problem was bad enough where I could call it a problem and ask for help for my problem. Blood clarified that I wasn't making up another symptom.

"What if nothing is wrong with you?" asked the gastroenterologist at our appointment. She ordered blood work to confirm nothing was wrong and called me the next day.

"Are you hallucinating right now?" she asked.

I didn't think so?

She said I had hyponatremia, a fatal condition of low sodium in the blood. Hyponatremia happens to marathon runners and to young people who take MDMA at raves and drink so much water that they die (water drowns their cells through swelling).

Symptoms include confusion, hallucinations, fatigue, abdominal cramps, and drowning from the inside out.

Blood sodium regulates the water in and around cells, and normal sodium levels are between 136 and 145 mmol/L (millimoles per liter). Hyponatremia occurs when the blood sodium level goes below 135 mmol/L. The gastroenterologist intercepted my level at 125 mmol/L. Drastic declines are lethal (my good friend's colleague physically dropped dead from a quick decrease), and gradual decreases like mine make a person sick over time.

"If you start to hallucinate, then go to the ER," the gastroenterologist said. "That means your blood sodium has dipped to a point where it would be terminal."

She made an appointment for me the next morning with a nephrologist who dealt with kidney diseases, and that night I monitored myself and tapped 911 on my phone to have it there if I forgot numbers—

But! My landlord had me call 911 the day before to report a robbery I witnessed in my building—

and I didn't want to call two days in a row and seem unbalanced. Better to just wait and see if I died, like the many women who don't report their own heart attacks or strokes for fear of being called stressed-out hypochondriacs.

To raise my sodium, the nephrologist put me on a no-water diet. Every day I was starving for water and had to walk in 90-degree heat and humidity to urgent care to have my blood drawn. I walked very, very slowly since I couldn't spare the sweat and felt catlike to still be living.

2

HYSTERICAL WOMAN

Stop me if you've heard this one: "hysteria"—the diagnosis for over-dramatic, attention-seeking people with uteruses who have too many volatile feelings and lie about their bodies hurting.

In the nineteenth century, if a woman had an unidentifiable ill-ness, then her diagnosis would be hysteria. Today, if a woman has an unidentifiable illness, then her diagnosis may be hysteria. For exam-ple, endometriosis has a "long history of being pathologized as phys-ical expressions of emotional distress," writes Dr. Elinor Cleghorn in *Unwell Women: Misdiagnosis and Myth in a Man-Made World.*

Women have been diagnosed with hysteria for everything from being barren and failing to marry, to having a miscarriage or meno-pause, to having unexplained physical pain or an actual disease, to displaying emotion or speaking.

Hysteria has been considered a medical condition, a mental condi-tion, an emotional condition, and a spiritual condition (specifically a satanic possession). It's been conceptualized as a brain malady, witch-craft, and a metaphor to contain anything and everything that men can't tolerate or explain in women.

Hysterical women are "sick" but only in the hysterical woman's imagination. Or hysterical women are sick in a mysterious way that is inexplicable and annoying. As late as 1980 the American Psychological

Association removed "hysteria" from the *Diagnostic and Statistical Manual of Mental Disorder*, the mental illness bible.

Although no doctor called me hysterical to my face, a few specialists conveyed what today's mindbody doctors theorize, which echoes part of the hysteria diagnosis but without the sexism: that the mind transcribes emotions on the body in the form of intense pain along the nerves. An acupuncturist first said "mind" and "body" in the same sentence to me when she poked me every few days for my headache. At the beginning of each appointment, before the needles went in, she and I chatted about my chronic pain; then she counted my heartbeats and read my tongue.

"Are you angry?" she asked me at our initial session.

"Yes," I said, without thought or mercy.

She asked how often I was angry.

"All the time."

She asked who made me angry.

I started at the top: "My dad," then went down the list.

She noted this on my chart and asked me if I'd expressed my anger.

I laughed, like this was an option. Like anger did not have to be extracted from my mouth like wisdom teeth.

This appointment was after a text exchange with my dad, a Texan who owns three pistols and had left me and my mom for Houston when I was two years old. He'd called me to see how I was feeling, and I didn't call back because of how I was feeling. Then he texted me, "We have a 24 hour call back window and I am expecting you to call," as if he were an automated student-debt collector. I replied with facts about his phone calls, that he didn't make them enough. "You can call me, too. Works both ways," he responded, now like a teenage boy. Usually I'd apologize or change the subject or say nothing (but think about saying something for many months), but the pain made me text, "You're my dad. Be a dad." Which was the most emotion I'd shown him in the history of our thirty-year relationship. He had not, in my memory, ever been a dad. And ever since my adult friends began having kids, I believed that a man who turns a woman into a single mother and a child into a fatherless daughter is a bad hombre.

He didn't respond.

The acupuncturist looked at me with the eyes of a mother and suggested with a straight face, "What if caged fury is contributing to your physical maladies? What if your headache has something to do with your voice and with what you haven't expressed?"

What if? I thought as I lay on the table and she needled near my tear ducts to move energy out of my head. She put more needles in my eyebrows and in my scalp and in the fleshy web of my thumb and in my knees and in my feet; she twisted each needle to activate the meridians that channel energy and fire up the nervous system, and I tried very hard to time my gasps with the gong soundtrack.

Forty-five minutes later she plucked out the needles, and I left with a black eye and clarity.

"The startling fact was this," wife and mother Joan Didion realizes in the essay "The White Album" about her ongoing mysterious disorder that "was not really in my eyes, but in my central nervous system": "my body was offering a precise physiological equivalent to what had been going on in my mind" during the '60s and the Manson murders.

Women often hear that their body is offering a precise physiological equivalent to what's going on in their mind. We're also more likely to hear that our physical—actual, real, clawing—pain is "psychosomatic" or "stress" or "hormonal,"[1] and while men will receive

---

1 *You're just having your period*, my then boyfriend said to me years ago when I was not having my period but was peeing blood. For days I'd been peeing flames and sweating while freezing. I rode the 6 train alone and cross-legged for almost one hour to the Mount Sinai emergency department (where a friend interned) on the day I lost my health insurance. Distracted by a fever and the inability to urinate with the nonstop urge to urinate, I autographed intake forms and waited to be awarded a prize for surviving the previous few hours. A young and unfortunately attractive male MD saw me and my pee, and with a raised eyebrow commented that I must be having fun. I had

physical tests, women are more likely given a psychiatric diagnosis—even for strokes and irritable bowel syndrome—and a prescription for psychotropics.

The day after the 2016 election I swallowed a mood stabilizer.

Several months before my vision changed, I got off the waitlist to see a psychologist at a neighborhood center for mental health (covered by insurance) to talk about what had been going on in my mind in 2016. The potential repeal of affordable health care, the comeback of swastikas, the planet aflame, the loss of reproductive and civil rights, and more, so much more. A presidential candidate had just said, "Grab 'em by the pussy. You can do anything," about women, and I was going through every psychological stage at once. Denial (*What is happening is not really happening*). Shock (*Is what's happening* really *happening???*). Confusion (What *is happening?*). Disbelief (*Really? Seriously?*). Melancholia (*Everything is dry, withered, spent*). Acceptance (*American voters don't give a shit about women and fully support a misogynistic racist homophobe with transphobia who sexts Nazis*). The future had teeth, and life was a slap in the dick, which was what I started calling my vagina so it wouldn't get grabbed. There was something I kept forgetting: how exactly to be whatever alive is. The third worst part of the day was going to bed, waking up was obviously first, and a close second was the rest of the day.

Part of the intake process at the neighborhood center was a psychiatric assessment by a psychiatrist who could prescribe medication if so inspired. I asked nicely to skip this, but the bureaucracy turned me down.

---

had a UTI, a common sex injury for women—WebMD says a woman's lifetime risk of getting one is 1 in 2—courtesy of my boyfriend, but now I had a kidney infection from waiting too long to treat the UTI. The MD prescribed antibiotics and told me about different sexual positions to prevent future UTIs. The antibiotics gave me a yeast infection.

The psychiatrist and I met in a claustrophobic room furnished and decorated for very small, sad children, and she went through the standard inventory.

"Do you feel sad or irritable?" she asked me, pinpointing symptoms and their severity.

"Yes and yes," I said. She circled my answers in the packet in front of her and asked me to assign numbers to my sadness and irritability. Then she read through the rest of the questions, which I heard through a filter of depression. "For more than two consecutive weeks have you noticed changes in weight or appetite? Does the biological fact that you must eat, for sustenance, to locate food, purchase it, prepare it, taste and masticate and swallow and digest it—pro forma, three times every twenty-four hours, daily, in perpetuity—seem batshit?

"Do you sleep too much or too little? Are you exhausted from giving your all, yourself completely, to the men of the world?

"Do you look out of the window, dolefully, regularly?

"Has no email ever found you well?

"Is no 'sorry' sorry enough?

"Are you not 'you'? Do you suspect you're not the main character? Is 'hurt feelings' your entire personality?

"Do you believe that other people have reasons to feel the way you feel, but you don't?

"Do you have any family history of feeling anything at all?

"Does every silver lining have a cloud?

"Can you not find a reason to live except to keep yourself alive?

"Are you powerless to answer these questions because the room is melting?"

My every answer was *YES, YES, YES*. Through the walls it must have sounded like the psychiatrist and I were going down on each other.

Whatever I was feeling that led me to psychologists and psychiatrists, I began to feel it the first day of sixth grade, an epoch when language can't touch experience, when things are not so sayable and most unsayable of all are feelings. Unlike fifth grade where I had hobbies other than my feelings, in sixth, as I changed into skirts and bras and makeup to appeal to the middle-school male gaze, my heart felt like a bomb on my lungs.

The bomb detonated one spring day in the sixth-grade hallway. My boyfriend dumped me via handwritten note, the beta text message, that he delivered in front of a crowd. Without reading it but knowing what it said, I burst into hydraulic sobs and fled to the girls' bathroom to tear out my hair (which was cut in the shape of "the Rachel").

At home I curled up on the cream carpet in my bedroom to dehydrate from crying-snotting. I cried before bed, in broad daylight, in malls (that's how teenage girls prefer to do it, all out). I'd been jolted square in the spirit, in the dead center of the Mariah Carey CD. *But where is the blood?* I journaled. *The severed something? The gaping bodily hemorrhage?* There was visceral pain—the size, shape, texture of pain—with no injury.

When I was twelve, as far as I knew, "depression," "anxiety," "antidepressants," "therapy," "no," and "female masturbation" were fictional and among the many conversations I never had. The Feeling, as I named it, didn't give up and could not be burned off. It came with me everywhere, to class, to lunch, to Claire's in the mall, to the weekend, to sleepovers. There was no place to run from it and nowhere in the body to hide. It was in my tear ducts, and everyplace else, too, in my cells and in the seconds, and in the spaces between cells and seconds. It was just *this*; *this* every moment, nothing but *this*. The Feeling had one mode, and that mode was Dead Pet. The Feeling doubled when I or others ignored it or me, tripled every time it was misnamed ("drama"), quadrupled when minimized. Soon the Feeling was bigger-deeper-realer than anything, and it would only get grimmer and grimmer, I just knew. I just—

went out of my mind.

And I went out of it one afternoon after the meanest middle-school girls executed a three-way calling ambush on me, and I headed straight to the kitchen pantry, to a footstool, to the butcher knives, to the biggest one, and placed its serrated edge on the knot of veins at my wrist—

This knife, I'd thought as one of the shadowed millions caught up in the Event of Self, *will say what I can't*. I wanted to act out my feelings, and to end them, and to show the world what I felt. And I needed the world to know without me having to say it. And to take me extremely seriously. Call me crazy, but I'd hoped to light myself on fire to prove I was burning.

If I said how I felt, then how would I sound?

"I WANT TO DIE!" I'd shout at my mom a lot, duped by what my own mind could make of my life. She'd tell me to shhhhh, and that my life was just a phase, that nothing was wrong. She, unaware of what went on in the pantry and unable to fathom it or even to fathom fathoming it, said I was "simply hormonal" "and emotional" "but normal" "but sad"; and "sadness," as everyone who is "jazzed" most of the time knows, "is temporary."

Coming down with feelings—and the systemic shutdown of those feelings—is natural. But my feelings, the Feeling, had a name: major depressive disorder. I wouldn't discover it for seven more years of having it and holding it in. (Nor would I discover that although it was mine, the Feeling wasn't personal or about unheld hands or the fact that we can never control our hearts.[2]) The National Institute of Mental Health says it takes, on average, over a decade to ask for help. *Just to ask*. For me, "I need help" was more than a sentence; it was an act. An act of admission and alienation. An act of telling a secret and sharing a shrouded, stigmatized [I-don't-know-what]. It was initiative and persistence and patience, three words the depressed haven't heard of. It was trial and error and hanging in there. It was waiting and waitlists

---

2 Heartbreak bumped clinical depression to the front of the line of my life, but unrequited love or a breakup cannot cause clinical depression.

and payment and insurance and scheduling and rescheduling ("today" wasn't fast enough, but also who cares about anything at all?). It was having something in me that maybe I didn't. It was trying to tell the difference between me and everyone else. It was understanding myself and making myself understood. (Plus, the one time I called the suicide hotline I was put on hold, a long hold, only to be hung up on.) So for seven years I didn't ask. And meanwhile suicide rates went up and up.

When I was twenty-one, George W. Bush was president, and I scored my first prescription behind my parents' back. It was for an SSRI, or selective serotonin reuptake inhibitor, if you're nasty.

It was my singular act of teenage rebellion. My mom and her Arkansan side of the family did not believe in: premarital sex, mental illness, premarital sex, antidepressants, premarital sex, that the popular birth control I took to clear up my moderate acne prevented pregnancy, street drugs, talking about any of this, party drugs, and premarital sex. My family, like other "normal people," would get "depressed" when a celebrity couple broke up and would think of a mass shooter as "mentally ill," but otherwise, if the topics of mental health and medication came up, they were extinguished instantaneously, as if someone had breathed fire, as if actual psychological issues—having them, discussing them—were contagious and socially transmitted and could be inhaled and cause everyone within six feet to also ruminate unhealthily.

One summer break home from college I asked a thirtysomething cousin for the name of a doctor, any doctor, because the Feeling was back. Then I drove to an out-of-the-way male internist (a man who specialized in internal organs and body systems) and not a psychiatrist (a person devoted to the diagnosis and treatment of mental disorders), and it was like seeing a regular doctor and meeting in a regular exam room.

"What brings you in today?" the internist asked me.

"I feel like I'm dying."

"Can you be more specific?"

"I can't be happy," I began without breaking eye contact. "And I feel like since I can't be happy, then I'll be profoundly unhappy. If that makes sense. Like I don't even want to feel better? Like, if nothing else, at least there is this: to be gutted, and engulfed," I said, turning the conversation into a poem. "Like for fun I envision my funeral the way I'm encouraged to envision my wedding."

Without hesitating the internist prescribed Lexapro, a hot new SSRI at the time, and assured me that most terminal sadness responds to designer chemical shortcuts that stimulate complex brain operations and require only swallowing.[3] "Do you have any questions?" the internist asked.

Hundreds. *What does it mean to take and to need medication? Did I require it? Will drugs ease me back into myself or turn me Stepford? And if I become someone I'm not, will I finally be happy? Productive? Will the past be the past? Will I think beautiful thoughts; will I become whole? Or able to say "Fuck it"? Will I have a truer understanding of the relative importance of all things? Will I be able to leave my room more or ask questions out loud?*

"No," I told him. "No questions."

I paid for the visit and the prescription with my allowance.

Twelve years later, when I was thirty-two and at the neighborhood center in Brooklyn, the psychiatrist recommended medication based on my psychiatric assessment.

"Not to brag," I said, "but I've taken medication before, many times."

---

3 It's "estimated that four out of five prescriptions for antidepressants are now written by physicians who aren't psychiatrists," writes Maya Dusenbery in *Doing Harm*, proving the point that "while women may truly have a higher risk of depression and anxiety disorders—for cultural or biological reasons or some combination of the two—many have argued that the difference in prevalence rates is at least partly a consequence of overdiagnosis in women and underdiagnosis in men."

"Tell me about that."

"I almost starved to death on Lexapro, almost walked into incoming traffic after missing one dose of Effexor, almost jumped out the window on Prozac."

What I didn't know and wasn't told, and what my body had to find out for itself, was that some people (usually women) on any given medication may experience any given special effect:

healing, numbing, nothing;

the feeling of being overmedicated but nowhere near medicated enough;

looking almost the same but haunted;

identifying more with infants than their mothers;

the likeliness to hum the Arcade Fire song "My Body Is a Cage";

loss: of mornings, nights out, days, years, hair in clumps, courage to email, life.

Now, whenever a doctor mentions medication, in my head Whoopi Goldberg says her famous line from *Ghost*, "Molly, you in danger, girl." Which is why I'd tried to opt out of seeing the psychiatrist. (But I didn't try too hard because I didn't want to be difficult, and because obedience can eclipse the gospel of intuition, and because no one would listen to me, not even me.)

I said no to the drugs. But then the psychiatrist—professional, credentialed, specialized, playing G-d—had one question for me, "Do you want to be happy?"

"Tell your doctor right away," said the mood stabilizer's instructions, "if any of these unlikely but serious side effects occur," and the paper unfolded into a gothic novella about unusual or severe mood changes, thoughts of suicide, unusual bleeding, yellowing of skin or eyes, Stevens-Johnson syndrome (a rare and potentially deadly rash that spreads, blisters, and sheds the top layer of skin), and headache.

"Many people using medication do not have serious side effects," the bottle reassured, beyond "nausea, anxiety, trouble sleeping, loss of appetite, sweating, yawning, non-serious rash, abnormal dreams, dizziness, and headache."

The bottle also reminded me that my doctor prescribed this medication because she "judged that the benefit to you is greater than the risk of side effects." The bottle further seemed to intuit "the prescriber wooed you with the un-promise-able promise of happiness and said this is your only option if you care to be happy, which you do, don't you?"

My mood stabilized after one month. I couldn't see and had a headache after three months. After one month with the headache, I told my psychiatrist right away about it. Her outgoing voicemail message said (as I recall), "The office will be closed during your personal crisis and will reopen after your memorial service. If this is an emergency, please hang up."

Ophthalmologists had suggested I stop the mood stabilizer, but once I was able to reach my psychiatrist (who was in the office Wednesdays only), she disagreed. And I agreed with her, because if ending the headache meant feeling like Sylvia Plath again or chancing a mental breakdown that attends titrating off a drug, then I would choose the physical pain. I would choose the physical pain as long as it was a choice.

I chose the physical pain for six months.

Every chronically sick person reaches a point in her sickness where she crowdsources help because her doctors are sick of her shit and she is sick of theirs. The mother of a teen I babysat emailed me about her psychopharmacologist. Her what? I googled it: a psychopharmacologist is a combination psychiatrist-pharmacist-physician who understands "pharmacodynamics" (what medications do to the body) and "pharmacokinetics" (what the body does to medications), and charges a month's rent for a forty-five-minute conversation (not covered by insurance).

In her office the psychopharmacologist had a miniature marquee sign displaying the message "IT IS GOING TO TAKE SOME WORK."

"I've had a headache for six months," I told her, knowing this was impossible to believe.

She believed me instantly, as if I were a human person. "It's the mood stabilizer." She ordered a genetic test named GeneSight that confirmed it.

"You have a genetic mutation that doesn't allow your liver enzymes to break down medication well," the psychopharmacologist explained. "You're genetically vulnerable, a rarity," she said, "a slow metabolizer of many medications" and "unable to regulate and maintain serotonin levels in the brain and periphery." SSRIs and the mood stabilizer increase serotonin in the human body, but not in mine. "With little or no serotonin acting on receptors of the muscles in your head and neck, headaches are happening and your eye muscles cannot contract, which is blurring your vision," the psychopharmacologist added. "The headache may or may not come back once treated."

I braced myself to taper off the first mood stabilizer and titrate onto a second, one that treats nerve damage.

"You'll feel better soon," she told me.

It was one year later, when I was headache-free, that the gastroenterologist diagnosed me with hyponatremia. I called the psychopharmacologist in a controlled panic. The nephrologist had said that the second mood stabilizer can lower blood sodium and cause hyponatremia, typically within the first three months. I'd been on it for twelve.

Now I was experiencing a rare side effect of a second mood stabilizer that I was on to remedy the rare side effect of the first mood stabilizer.

The nephrologist and the psychopharmacologist directed me to taper off again. As I did, and as my blood was drawn daily, I gained one or two NA (sodium) points, and my blood sodium returned to normal, and my sore throat and stomachache receded to memory, and I'd been sick for one year and six months.

To help with withdrawal from the second mood stabilizer I started an SNRI (serotonin-norepinephrine reuptake inhibitor), a class of antidepressant that also treats nerve pain, and this time it was a happy ending, which I won't get into.

3

CRAZY PSYCHO BITCH

Historically, expression has been called "illness" in women, and women who spoke or laughed or wept in public, women who couldn't keep their words or feelings to themselves, were mocked as sick and/ or mad. Expressive women were madwomen whether or not they were mad or ill or mentally ill. And they were drugged all the same.

Not to be dramatic, but after every breakup I was prescribed antidepressants. My very first illness was mental, so I was familiar with prescriptions because every time some straight, white cis guy left and took with him all meaning, a doctor said, "There's a pill for that."

Antidepressants are "the new (and obviously preferable) lobotomy for women dealing with trauma," pitches Caroline Criado Perez in *Invisible Women*.[1] America has a history of prescribing pills to traumatized, anxious, depressed, "too emotional," and loud-mouthed women. Most opium users were women by the late nineteenth century, after doctors injected female patients with morphine to relieve everything from menstrual cramps (nice) to morning sickness to nerves, so uterine and ovarian problems led to opium habits. Today,

---

1 They're also a new and preferable nullifier: women who report sexual assault may be asked if they're on any consciousness-altering medication such as antidepressants.

medication has been institutionalized at a sacramental level world-wide with women two and a half times more likely to be medicated than men.

So when the university psychologist asked in my inaugural therapy session at age twenty, "What brings you here today?" I didn't know where to start, didn't know just how many reasons there were, or that there were so many reasons from the personal to the systemic.

"A system of society and government in which men hold the power and women don't, and also the internet," I wish I'd said.

Days earlier www.thefacebook.com informed me via university library Ethernet that the love of my life was in a relationship with someone else, and I'd signed out of myself and did what really forlorn actors do: found a nearby wall and slowly slid down it, knuckle in mouth, head in hand, face arranged in despair as I projectile sobbed over the Shakespearian betrayal. *Here was my torch; pictured there was his girlfriend.* I'd hung on his line, so to speak, holding, indefinitely, breaking, until it was Facebook that said we were never, ever getting back together.

Classmates watched me or didn't see me, texting about Michelangelo as I hugged my knees to my abdomen and rocked back and forth on the floor until the library announced it was closing. Life was, by sleight of heartbreak, dogshit. I managed to function, sort of, outwardly—like, I could walk if I felt like it, but I didn't feel like it.

This is just being a person, I'd romanticized, *a woman, a hungry woman.*

But no one called me a hungry woman.

"She's a crazy psycho bitch," I'd overheard one classmate say.

Back at the dorms I saw posters for a place called Mental Health Services, and I needed help—

but for *what*? For *this*? For crying a lot? Over a boy? For acting my age and genus, twenty and human? For wanting and needing? To be loved? Because I felt crazy for feeling how I felt?

"I'm in love," I told the university psychologist. "Unreciprocated," I added and didn't stop for the full session.

Oh, to talk! And the other person, an employee, had to listen, had to help, had to solve everything.

"Is there anything else you want to talk about?" she asked me months later, regarding the clock. "You talk about boys an absurd amount."

It was true that I consistently failed my own Bechdel Test. But I was raised to talk and think about boys above all, to have boys be my response to *How are you?*

"More than is normal?" I asked, thinking of the medical history form I'd filled out to see her that had me circle my title: Miss or Mrs. or Ms. *Is not married* or *is married* or *was married*. My relationship status was my identity.

"What is normal anyway?" she asked.

The university psychologist diagnosed me with depression.

If I had lived in other centuries, the Greeks would diagnose me with having a uterus—"the origin of all disease," according to them—and would say it caused me to behave erratically, i.e., to have emotional outbursts. The Egyptians, who were the first to use the term "hysteria," would use the term on me to explain my behavioral disruptions, i.e., my emotional outbursts. Medievalists would label me "diseased" since I didn't conform to traditional, quiet femininity—i.e., I had emotional outbursts. Renaissance men would call me a witch and behead me. By the nineteenth century I'd be a "nervous" hysteric, and anything could flag me as such, like having an emotional outburst. During the nineteenth century I'd be certifiable; author Rachel Vorona Cote writes in *Too Much: How Victorian Constraints Still Bind Women Today* that "madness was used to label and manage dangerous, disruptive femininity" like mine. In the late nineteenth century the male neurologist and psychotherapist Dr. Freud (who wrote about "Hysteria" and his patient "Dora,"[2] whose main symptom was losing her voice) would

---

2 The name Dora came from the Greek "Doron," which means "gift." Freud called his patient Dora because the man who raped her first groomed her by giving her little gifts.

deal with me the way the university psychologist did—with talk therapy, treating me using my own voice. He'd also hypnotize me into an emotional outburst and get me to admit some repressed weird sex stuff. By the early twentieth century "hysteria" as an allegation would be back in fashion, and while I'd be called hysterical for emoting publicly, I'd also catch the label for being a suffragette. In 2017 Tucker Carlson et al. would say I was hysterical for criticizing the sex pest President [BLEEP].

Today, my ex-boyfriends would diagnose me as a crazy psycho bitch (CPB), a trope, an ex-girlfriend who "has been scorned by a past lover, maybe trapped in unrequited love" or "wants something she can't have," observes the critic Kennisha Archer about the CPB who appears in American thrillers[3] and horror movies and in every heterosexual relationship. Urban Dictionary, "the people's dictionary," defines a crazy psycho bitch as having, among other things, "emotional instability in romantic relationships," which "is often, but not always, found in conjugation with daddy issues." Urban Dictionary elaborates that if a man "is unfortunate enough to date [a crazy psycho bitch], she is likely to behave in irrational ways. She will be incredibly clingy and she will become deeply distraught and/or enraged over the slightest incident."

I have daddy issues. I behave in irrational ways and become deeply distraught and/or enraged. I *am* a crazy psycho bitch.

And because I am her, I know the CPB is obsessed and overzealous, needy and stubborn, aggressive and sexual. She's also beautiful but psycho, sweet but psycho, driven by trauma but psycho. And in the

---

3 "I won't be ignored, Dan," Glenn Close's character tells Michael Douglas's character in *Fatal Attraction* (written by a man, directed by a man, nominated for six Academy Awards), a thriller about a male publishing house lawyer who cheats on his brunette wife with a blonde slut who gets pregnant and wants more than a one-night stand so she boils the lawyer's daughter's bunny.

strict definition of CPB, the bitch is crazy, and not only crazy, but psycho, pathological.

Slapping "the label 'crazy' [on] any socially inconvenient behavior," writes Cote in *Too Much*, like acting actorish or having an emotional outburst where you humiliate no one but yourself, means the "boundaries between emotional intensity and diagnosable illness are always collapsing" and are also "rearticulated by hegemonic masculinity" as "conditions unworthy of distinction, significant only as symptoms." Vocal, dependent, sentimental, irrational, neurotic, imbalanced, insane, hysterical, psycho, melodramatic, theatrical, hormonal, oversensitive, overemotional, unwell, unstable, fragile, irritating, infuriating, manipulative, vindictive, mendacious, clinical. These blur together in the indiscriminately applied label, until women who feel and express feeling are associated with madness and sickness, until "vocal" is a symptom.

I couldn't help but wonder in college: Did I have a chemical imbalance, and were my emotions diseased? Or was I just an emotive woman living in a man's world where the "talkativeness of women has been gauged in comparison not with men but with silence," as Dale Spender femsplains in her book *Man Made Language*, and so there are no "outspoken" women, just women who speak and women who don't? Could it be both? Depression and discrimination?

It could! A woman can have it all.

And a woman doesn't have to be ill or depressed to be called either and be discarded or medicated accordingly. "I broke up with her because she's crazy" has justified millions of unconscious uncouplings, including mine. With one word a boyfriend or doctor or male politician can dump/scar/make fun of/curtail the rights of an ex-girlfriend and also dismantle feminism. Anyone can use the language of mental illness out of context to stop a woman's voice dead in its tracks: Call her "insane," and then any rational expression is predetermined to be irrational. Call her "mad," and whatever she says can be voided, and no one has to listen to her anymore. Call her "crazy," and then it's as if she said what she said because of emotions, not thought. Call her "hormonal" and convey *Shut up, you're embarrassing yourself.* Call her "emotional" so we don't get a female president. Call her a "psycho" and render her a vulnerable and voluble woman with a death wish to die alone.[4]

"How can it be that so many people's ex-girlfriends are crazy?" the famous online advice columnist Sugar asked rhetorically in response to a man's anonymous letter about dating a "self-absorbed crazy" girl. There's no national statistic or study on crazy ex-girlfriends, but it seems that so many of us are "crazy" because it doesn't take much to be "too much." I've been called crazy for wanting to communicate and for seeking closeness; for trying to understand a man's feelings and behavior and for expressing my emotions through crying or yelling, a few times in public; for texting multiple times in a row without a response and for actually texting more than that. Too many times I put myself out there and said what I meant and—

"That's psychotic," good men said to me for experiencing my experiences and thinking my thoughts and being desperate enough to express them and other crazy-sounding opinions (especially about Taylor Swift and airborne misogyny and traditional gender roles; some women have only one thing on the mind, and that is "rape culture").

Any conversation can become a diagnosis.

Every woman I know has been under similar fire, has also sat mutely as some guy gets philosophical on her ass and theorizes with abandon about devil's advocacy after brushing off whatever she says just because he doesn't like it or understand it or want to understand it. A friend of mine was called "a raging lunatic" for objecting to the idea that Dr. Christine Blasey Ford's soft voice indicated she was "lying or insane." Another friend was "pretty hysterical" for asking her boss

---

4 Men cannot be crazy psycho bitches. The horror-thriller-dramedy *American Psycho* is about a legit psychotic man, Patrick Bateman, but real-life men revere him because as a psycho he can be as violent and disgusting to women as some real-life men wish they could be.

not to permanently hire a contract worker who had harassed her for romantic and sexual attention (my friend's concerns were dismissed as way out of proportion). A third friend, well, all my friends have new anecdotes every day.

It isn't that the lines between women and men are down indefinitely. The "social invisibility of women's experience is not 'a failure of human communication,'" clarifies academic feminist Joanna Russ in *How to Suppress Women's Writing*. The social invisibility of a woman's experience "is a socially arranged bias persisted in long after the information about women's experience is available (sometimes even publicly insisted upon)."

I must sound nuts. Because the bias, like "crazy," works. Reducing women to the psychological gets *results*. Being called a crazy psycho bitch or any variant kept me quiet while keeping me crazy. It also kept me in pain, which kept me powerless. Among the first conversations I left behind were those in which I could be branded crazy or psycho or a bitch. It was just easier to suppress moods and sorrows and my personality, easier to yell less and ask for less and settle for less and be less and to censor my wanting and want less. And I tried to suffer less— invisibly or with a smile—to not provoke or inconvenience or frustrate anyone, ever.

4

WHO GETS TO SPEAK AND WHY

Is there any productive way to speak without seeming unhinged? "What becometh a woman best, and first of all? Silence. What second? Silence. What third? Silence. What fourth? Silence," wrote male rhetorician Thomas Wilson in his 1560 book *Arte of Rhetorique*. And if not silence, then the right words in the right way with the right tone at the right moment.

When I was sick, I socialized exclusively with doctors, pharmacists, employers, and deliverymen—and I wanted something from all of them. At each medical appointment, I wanted an actual diagnosis and a prognosis and a strategy and a cure and alleviation and also each doctor's unconditional love. But I didn't say that. I said, "Thank you." Because if I did speak, I spoke in "the good female patient voice": the pleasant and accepting and grateful voice, the voice that wasn't too assertive or too blunt or too cold, the voice that didn't ask too many questions or follow up too frequently, and especially the apologetic voice. With every doctor I was just so sorry. I apologized for my unshaved legs.[1] I apologized

---

1 I apologized even though leg shaving was invented by Gillette to sell razors to women while men were at war, and I apologized because even a woman's hair has been pathologized;

for bleeding all over the hallway when I hemorrhaged after a blood draw (and I tried cleaning up the blood before asking for help). I apologized for crying and for bothering and for confounding. I may as well have set apology reminders on my phone. I did not think to apologize; apologies were not conscious, not willing—they just were, and I just did. G-d, I hated the sound of my voice. Even my inner voice was shrill.

Everyone hates the sound of a woman's voice. The "nominal problem is excess," writes author Jordan Kisner in "Can a Woman's Voice Ever Be Right?" "The voice is too something—too loud, nasal, breathy, honking, squeaky, matronly, whispered. It reveals too much of some identity, it overflows its bounds. The excess in turn points to what's lacking: softness, power, humor, intellect, sexiness, seriousness, coolness, warmth." And that's just for white women. There's also "too Black" and "too blue collar" to be credible and audible.

I began hating the sound of my voice at five years old, when I was ride or die for *The Little Mermaid*, the 1989 Disney classic about a teenage fish-princess who had everything but wanted more, so she signs away her best-in-the-world voice for long legs to pursue a boy with a dog. For ten thousand hours I memorized each song, and each song was my gospel. Especially the banger "Poor Unfortunate Souls," in which the octopus witch Ursula sing-splains how human men aren't impressed by conversation and avoid it when possible.

I wanted to sing full-throttle like Ariel and then stop speaking for a boyfriend like Ariel. I would not blabber or gossip or say a word! Besides, at five I had my looks, my pretty face, and I would never underestimate the importance of body language.

---

in *Plucked: A History of Hair Removal* Rebecca M. Herzig writes, "Late-nineteenth-century criminologists, alienists [the former term for psychiatrists], and dermatologists" asserted "an association between heavy hair growth and mental illness. This association was not novel; hairiness has long been considered a sign of lunacy." Sane women are hair-free, and my mental health was in question when my legs looked like a man's.

*   *   *

Anyone who grew up watching TV shows on a television in the 1970s, '80s, and '90s grasped at least three things: Men have a voice. Women have a body. Mentos are "the Freshmaker."

I was born the year the original *Ghostbusters* premiered (1984), and whenever I turned on something—TV, VHS, radio—the male voice was talking, coming out of everywhere as the mouthpiece of humanity, the soundtrack to existence.

"An analysis of prime-time TV in 1987 found 66 percent of the 882 speaking characters were male—about the same proportion as in the '50s," writes Susan Faludi in her tome *Backlash: The Undeclared War Against American Women*. Recent analyses by Martha M. Lauzen, a professor of film and television at San Diego State University who has tracked women's employment in filmmaking and television since 1998, shows the percentage hasn't really budged.[2] Men even talk the most in rom-coms, billed as "chick flicks" made for women and starring stick figures known as women. And in 2016 the *Ghostbusters* reboot was dubbed a "controversial comedy" (and instigated a coordinated boycott) because it starred women (and thus ruined adult men's childhoods).

My mom and stepdad have a television hooked to cable in every room in the house, and around the kitchen table are three chairs and a television. The three of us watched TV together during dinner, in a loud silence, and watched TV separately after dinner. Before bed the upstairs televisions switched to late-night TV talk shows, which men have hogged since the invention of television in the 1940s, and men's jokes were the last thing we heard before falling asleep.

At dinner we were glued to *Entertainment Tonight* or TV news that starred white men who barked at each other and a few blonde bombshells. (Brunette women did not address the public about current

---

2 The "percentage of top grossing films featuring female protagonists declined precipitously from 40 percent in 2019 to 29 percent in 2020."

events.) Then, like now, mostly men reported the news, and the news stories were mostly about men and were backed up mostly by men as experts and sources, anointed as thought leaders to tell us all the truth. Star news anchor Chris Cuomo[3] might have reported on the heyday of executive producer Harvey Weinstein,[4] which legal analyst Jeffrey Toobin[5] would then corroborate.

(If and when news outlets did talk about women, they didn't have anything nice to say. In my thirties my Democrat parents said in unison, "We don't like Hillary Clinton," repeating the cable news they ate for every meal. In 2016 and 2020 election coverage, female presidential candidates received less coverage than men and more negative coverage than men, and much of the criticism came down to voice and how men can and should raise their voices but women need to calm down.)

"WHO GETS TO SPEAK AND WHY?...IS THE ONLY QUESTION," wrote Chris Kraus in her 1997 epistolary cult novel[6] *I Love Dick*.

Offscreen, in real life, men also talk and talk. Perhaps because of the feedback loop, the dance craze sweeping the nation, the process by which viewing goes from a static activity to a metabolic one. The

---

3 Cuomo used his media sources to help his brother, former New York governor Andrew Cuomo, stave off and fight sexual harassment allegations. CNN fired Chris days after he was also accused of sexual misconduct, and in March 2022 he filed an arbitration demand for $125 million from CNN ($110 million designated for "lost future wages," which, wow).

4 Needs no footnote.

5 Legal analyst for CNN, lawyer, and author who masturbated during a Zoom video meeting with the *New Yorker* staff and WNYC radio, believing he was off camera and muted. He was suspended from CNN for eight months and then reinstated.

6 Also known as a "novel," a nonmemoir, a feminist manifesto, a cultural lambast, an art experiment, and autofiction-cum-autotheory. The novel was coadapted by Joey Soloway and playwright Sarah Gubbins for the small screen in 2017 and was written by all women and gender-nonconforming writers—and was canceled after one season by Amazon Studios. The head of Amazon Studios, Roy Price, who was notorious for canceling female-driven vehicles, resigned in 2017 after an accusation of sexual harassment.

feedback loop gets us where not even G-d can find us; it drafts our understanding of how people should be, then our borrowed beliefs, in a mind-body alchemy, turn into behaviors. That is, boys talk more than girls in three-quarters of Disney's princess movies—and boys speak more than girls in the classroom, and men speak more than women in work meetings.

"In group settings men are 75 percent more likely to speak up than women," says Dr. Meredith Grey in season 12, episode 9, of *Grey's Anatomy*. (If you're anything like me, then everything you know about the medical establishment—and hooking up—you gleaned from nineteen seasons of *Grey's Anatomy*.) In "The Sound of Silence" Dr. Grey (who is assaulted to the point of being physically unable to speak in this episode) stands in front of a group of interns and asks a question. The male interns take up most of the room and raise their hands to answer. Not one woman raises her hand. Each looks scared to speak. This scene could be any classroom or meeting or drinks with heterosexual cis men, who, per evidence ad infinitum, are actually "too much" because they speak the most and the loudest and the longest; they spew the most Wikipedia pages and unsolicited comments and stories; they say what a woman is on the verge of saying or repeat what a woman just said (but with more confidence or rudeness); they take more credit and interrupt more (but call it "cooperating"), then perhaps apologize, sincerely or not, and justify themselves, at length.

Meanwhile, women use their voice to help men use theirs. Studies on the female voice found that female-identifying speakers tend to serve up conversation in warm tones that embolden everyone else to speak.[7] "A trans woman friend of mine recently explained to me how the technique for training your voice to sound more feminine has

---

7 Sociolinguist and professor of linguistics Janet Holmes cites research that "men tend to contribute more information and opinions, while women contribute more agreeing, supportive talk, more of the kind of talk that encourages others to contribute."

a lot to do 'with speaking less or asking more questions or deferring to other people more,'" writes author Melissa Febos in her collection *Girlhood*. Because the discipline of desirability is also the discipline of submission.

As a kid I believed women just didn't talk that much. Or shouldn't. Or couldn't? But once I grew out of *The Little Mermaid* and my fantasy of silence and sailing away from my family as a royal child bride, I had a new ideology about a girl's voice: it should sound like a boy's.

In fifth grade to be a tomboy was the tits, and to be "cool" was to be "down" with what boys said and liked. The secret code to being one of the guys—whose approval I sought because the universe said I needed it—was to suppress or erase all signs of girlhood. To graduate girldom, I watched *South Park* and memorized *Pulp Fiction*, wore Umbros and Adidas, read R. L. Stine and Mark Twain, listened to Dre and Snoop, leveled up in math classes (aka boys' classes), wallpapered my room with posters of sports I wasn't allowed to play, camped outdoors and peed standing up while camping, liked guys who'd liked Green Day before Green Day sold out, talked in drag and cursed like a dickhead, and masked my true tastes, point of view, and attitude to align with boys' tastes-POV-attitude.

I'd keep experimenting. In middle school I reverted to being girly and a drama queen—but also depressed because my voice was so nails-on-a-chalkboard, so full of so many feelings there wasn't room for anything else; it sounded like a tampon if a tampon talked. I'd made a huge mistake, so in high school I joined the speech and debate team, and once more spent every effort to talk like the boys, because when boys talked, everyone listened. Boys' talk let them be understood, and their voice existed for only themselves. (Even today's automated speech recognition technology, like virtual assistants and voice transcription, is more likely to respond to the white male cadence. About voice recognition in cars that don't recognize women's voices, one male VP of voice technology suggested women fix their voices "through lengthy training" to "speak louder" and to "direct their voices towards the microphone.")

After school I'd talk to myself in the mirror in my own lengthy training, rehearsing a chiller but louder and lower voice, a voice that was sensible and cocksure and won video games and masturbated into a sock.

I wasn't born into the wrong body. I was born into the correct body in the wrong world.

In this world Margaret Thatcher took voice-lowering lessons to deepen her pitch to sound firmer and more powerful and as if she had a cold and a penis in order to be taken seriously. Elizabeth Holmes faked a baritone to attract investors and scam them. A National Public Radio cohost told me that several radio women take voice-lowering lessons and that producers tweak women's timbre and enhance their bass on air—all due to listeners' complaints. Since the male voice is the voice of every generation, a lot of us find ourselves speaking with it (the average woman today talks in a deeper voice than her mother and grandmother), retuning our voices to put us in league with self-described gods.

With my less-feminine voice I became speech co-captain and spoke at graduation, about *The Simpsons* and *Zen and the Art of Motorcycle Maintenance* by male author Robert M. Pirsig, and was the sole girl to be nominated for the end-of-high-school superlative "Most Likely to Be Successful" (I lost to a boy).[8] At last I had a voice; it just wasn't mine.

When asked about "the heroine's journey," Joseph Campbell, the originator of "the Hero's Journey," purportedly said, "Women don't need

---

8 I was also nominated for "Best Hair" and "Biggest Flirt" and lost both (to a blonde girl and an accused slut, respectively).

to make the journey. All she has to do is realize that she's the place that people are trying to get to."[9]

My male high school speech coach coached me to wear my hair curly during male-dominated competition. "It's sexier," he said in an empty school hallway. I hadn't yet realized I was the place that people are trying to get to.

I realized in college.

In college I underwent a change, like a second cycle, but instead of changing from girl to woman, I changed from subject to object, from person to place. A deeper voice didn't fly—it was in an unfuckable octave, and men couldn't hear me (again) or, it seemed, didn't care to.

So I grew another. At parties I spoke in a combination of high pitch, vocal fry, uptalk, and broken sentences that curled. A "sexy baby voice." Men liked this voice. It was horny yet nonconfrontational. It was defenseless and signaled that I must be protected and coddled and burped.[10] Actual research shows that this higher voice coming out of a female body is perceived as more agreeable and much hotter. Vocally and weight-wise, infancy is apparently a woman's sexiest time.

---

9 Campbell purportedly said it to Maureen Murdock, his student, after she showed him her alternative to his narrative paradigm and patriarchal hegemony: "the Heroine's Journey," which addressed "the psycho-spiritual journey of contemporary women." In 1990, Maureen Murdock published *The Heroine's Journey: Woman's Quest for Wholeness*, and her website summarizes the concept: "The Heroine's Journey begins with an Initial Separation from feminine values, seeking recognition and success in a patriarchal culture, experiencing spiritual death, and turning inward to reclaim the power and spirit of the sacred feminine. The final stages involve an acknowledgement of the union and power of one's dual nature for the benefit of all humankind. The Heroine's Journey is based on the experience of fathers' daughters who have idealized, identified with, and allied themselves closely with their fathers or the dominant masculine culture. This comes at the cost of . . . denigrating values of the female culture. . . . If the feminine is seen as negative, powerless or manipulative the child may reject those qualities she associates with the feminine, including positive qualities such as nurturing, intuition, emotional expressiveness, creativity and spirituality."

10 Pro tip: A woman should need saving so that men can save her.

The anti-voice is so adored that voice assistants like Siri and Alexa default to feminized voices based on retrograde stereotypes of subservience. "I'd blush if I could," Siri says to sexual commands, while Alexa responds flirtatiously when verbally abused. ("Men Are Creating AI Girlfriends and Then Verbally Abusing Them" is a headline I read recently about "chatbot abuse.")

Artificial-intelligence-powered voices don't yet have the porno mode that comes standard in real women, in me, which was part of my college realization.

Sophomore year I wanted to join the university speech and debate team, but there wasn't one, so I auditioned for the only play with an open casting call, *The Vagina Monologues*. I'd hoped for "Narrator" but was cast as "The Woman Who Loved to Make Vaginas Happy," also known as "The Moaner." I acted with no previous acting experience and orgasmed with no previous orgasming experience. But, as a woman, the sounds were on hand for me—you know the sounds—I was born with them on the tip of my tongue.

For three evenings over Valentine's Day weekend, the sounds came out with a soul, and I fake-orgasmed in the campus nondenominational chapel, groping for nothing.

Near the pulpit, I did "the clit moan"—a soft "yum" sound—and then "the vaginal moan," a crescendo from far inside the throat. Under spotlights and candelabras, in the black pantsuit I wore to high school speech tournaments and now with a black corset underneath and cherry red tie, I gave a surely-you-jest laugh for "the elegant moan," then flashed a look of quiet surprise for "the WASP moan," then screamed *OY VEY* for "the Jewish moan." For "the Irish Catholic moan," I fell to my knees, crossed my chest, and looked heavenward to beg, "Forgive me, G-d, forgive me, oh, G-d, please, forgive me." In the silver cast of the organ, I spread my arms and yodeled for "the mountaintop moan," cooed and gurgled for "the baby moan," dropped to all fours and panted for "the doggy moan." Above me the stained-glass windows twinkled as I did the rest: "The uninhibited militant bisexual moan" (a series of grunts). "The machine-gun moan" (an impression of lawn sprinklers, *uhn-uhn-uhn-uhn-uhnnn*). "The tortured zen moan" (lustful *om*s, fingers twisted into mudras, a down-dog pose). "The diva moan" (operatic). The specialized "Washington University in St. Louis moan," for which I whipped off my black plastic-frame glasses, inserted just the tip into my mouth as I slammed myself against an imaginary wall and pretended to bang a ghost, while crying out, "I have a test! I have a test! Hurry up, I need to study!" For the denouement, "the surprise triple-orgasm moan," I slid my glasses back up my nose, ever so slowly, like a librarian or a porn starlet impersonating a librarian, telepathing *Let's do this—*

But never mind that one.

I "came" twenty-seven times each night to stadium-style applause from eight-hundred-plus people, including my mom and stepdad, who, after the final curtain call, walked down the aisle with a dozen red roses.

I got good at changing my voice, as if it were outfits. For Halloween that same year I went as a cheerleader—the union of toddler and slut—and wore a big bow in my hair and encouraged everyone around me. Again I was acting: squealing like a baby while wearing next to nothing like a skank, and I wasn't either. Men must have popped so many boners at simply the idea of me. But it felt like a curse, almost, the way the legs of my voice could spread or shut, the way I could sound helpless and open to suggestion and to being walked all over and ignored everywhere but the bed and the crib.

"Sorry to interrupt," a student, a male student, my male student said to a female student in the class I was teaching as an adult woman thirteen years post-college.

After he interrupted her, he corrected her opinion, and she and I exchanged identical just-punched looks.

"When a woman does speak up," Dr. Meredith Grey continues in voiceover in the same *Grey's Anatomy* episode, "it's statistically probable that her male counterparts will either interrupt her or speak over her."

I called out my male student, lovingly, and the next day he emailed me for calling him out. He "just wanted to take a quick second" to tell me why he interrupted "that other student." "There was a reason for it," he wrote. He "felt like we were getting dragged off topic quite a bit," and he "could feel that we were really slipping behind schedule." A former student had told him "how much fun it was to do the pitches and I wanted to make sure we had time for that." In the next paragraph he concluded, "So that was why I [interrupted]. I was trying to help you. But it obviously didn't come off that way so I apologize."

I didn't reply, didn't point out that he'd come to class thirty minutes late, didn't ask why he didn't take notes and instead smiled at me for three hours, didn't correct him about how we weren't off track because people are allowed to talk in class, didn't remind him that I can teach my own class by myself, and didn't yell at him—a white guy—about his pitch, a satire about slavery. Saying or doing any of the above, my colleagues and I agreed, would've made things worse.

Right now women are being interrupted— or undermined or spoken for or misinterpreted—in classrooms across the world, if they're lucky to be in one.

"It's not because [men are] rude. It's science," Dr. Grey says about interrupting women. "The female voice is scientifically proven to be more difficult for a male brain to register."

It isn't only because of systemic sexism that women are hard to hear; it's science.

Except it isn't. The fictional Dr. Grey's scripted dialogue is pseudo-scientific and likely based on the oft-quoted study "Male and Female Voices Activate Distinct Regions in the Male Brain," conducted by all men using all male subjects and described as men versus women arbitrarily (it could have been described in any number of ways, like lower pitch versus higher pitch).

Whether women are harder to hear (we're not) or people just don't want to hear women (it's this one), the onus is on women to be heard.

At my medical appointments, before I spoke up in "the good female patient voice" with doctors (who may be among the hardest of hearing the female voice), in my mind I was following a flowchart titled "Should I Ask a Question?"

If "YES," then an arrow pointed to "How should I ask it?" This led to "WAIT" and pointed to "But first, what do I need and do I really need what I need?" If I really needed what I needed, then there were considerations of timing and mood, then picking out the perfect words and the perfect tone.

Once again I thought I might work around sexism by speaking like men—like female hummingbirds that avoid harassment by bearing plumage resembling male colors—by being more stoic and reserved, more even-toned and even-tempered, and all while pain reminded me of itself. But when I was stoic and reserved and even, it appeared "everything was fine"—

But if I was in tears, then I was "hysterical"—

But then again, if I wasn't in tears, then no one believed in my pain the way I did.

As my mom would say, "A woman can't win for losing."

My choices, which led to my doctor's choices, were subject to audit by both parties.

If only I could move my voice into the impossible right sound that is likable and pleasing, educated but not snotty, and that grew up in a suburb, then moved to a city, then moved back to the suburb.[11] It doesn't protest too much and knows not to whine or sass.[12] It's tuned in to others and makes everyone else's life easier. If it were a size, it

---

11 In *Detransition, Baby*, a novel by Torrey Peters, the protagonist had "been in a lesbian relationship with a trans woman named Amy…who became so suburban-presentable that when she spoke, you imagined her words in Martha Stewart's signature typeface."
12 "Black women in particular need to be a little 'sassy,' but not too aggressive, lest we are not seen as feminine," writes *Washington Post* columnist Karen Attiah in her op-ed "America Hates to Let Black Women Speak." "Black women especially have to be seen as tough, but we aren't allowed to be angry, even if our anger is justified in a country that too often silences us."

would be a size small. And it admires jokes but doesn't make any.[13] The right voice has been sad before but never depressed, is emotional but isn't going to talk about it, asks for help without asking for help, is optimistic and fakes health when sick,[14] and has an astrological chart of Sagittarius sun, Gemini moon, and Cancer rising. The ideal is not girly but not yet womanly—it should be more like a man's, with notes of gravitas, yet not manly or masculine.

But, really, nothing is nicer on a woman than her silence.

---

13 This is "the humor gap," as described by *Scientific American*: "Men want someone who will appreciate their jokes, and women want someone who makes them laugh."
14 Women are like rabbits, for most rabbits "have, in their skill set, the ability to pretend that they're healthy even when they're quite sick," writes Susan Orlean in "The Rabbit Outbreak." "It's sort of the inverse of playing possum, but done for the same purpose, namely, to deflect attention from predators, who would consider a sick rabbit easy pickings. As a result of this playacting, rabbits often die suddenly—or what appears to be suddenly—when, in fact, they've been sick for a while" but pretending otherwise.

5

GIRLS VERSUS BOYS IN CONVERSATION

The problem of voice is resolved online, where we can voicelessly communicate nonstop. And the internet, unlike life, is a void that demands to be filled by anyone, by women, by me. America Online, Gmail, social media, smartphones—new modes of contact and new floodgates are being invented and opened all the time, and if they were not, then I'd be fine today.

For me, the internet was a classic long con: give a girl the tools to express herself, and then punish her for expressing herself. Because Ursula in *The Little Mermaid* was right; men dote and swoon and fawn on a lady who's withdrawn. That song was about *life*, about relationships, about heterosexual relationships.

When I grew up to be an adult woman and freelance writer, my first pitch (to the now defunct feminist vertical of Salon.com) was about *The Rules: Time-Tested Secrets for Capturing the Heart of Mr. Right*, a you-need-help book written by two married women that became a blockbuster best seller and a lifestyle with lifestyle coaches. I interviewed one such coach about the romantic legality of funny women, and she verified that a woman cannot be funny and date men simultaneously. As it happens, out of the thirty-five Rules for dating heterosexual men, almost one-third pertain to a woman talking less:

"Don't Talk to a Man First (and Don't Ask Him to Dance)"
"Don't Stare at Men or Talk Too Much"
"Don't Call Him and Rarely Return His Calls"
"Always End Phone Calls First"
"Don't Tell Him What to Do"
"Let Him Take the Lead"
"Don't Open Up Too Fast"
"Be Honest but Mysterious"
"Accentuate the Positive"
"Don't Discuss the Rules with Your Therapist"
"Be Easy to Live With"

Dating rewards the woman who keeps her thoughts and feelings (and desires and needs and negativity) to herself.

Obviously, *The Rules* was very stupid! Or was it forged in timeless truth and imprinted indelibly on popular thought? It was, for sure, controversial—maybe it was useful; maybe it was antifeminist—yet because of the book an unreported horde of women married men. Because what says *hard-on* like a disempowered woman who won't or can't challenge you, who doesn't ask for what she wants and forfeits social and sexual status and power?

Rules, mating rites, and Disney set up a binary of good speech versus bad speech in the game of women versus men in love. For a woman, "good" is "less" and wins her the love of a man. "Bad" is "more" and guarantees a hetero woman will die alone.

I did not want to die alone. I wanted to die with/for/over a man. I wanted what I wanted according to heteronormative scripture:

a girl is born in love with a boy before meeting him;

a girl should spend her life in relationships because only through
    a boy does a girl know herself and feel alive;
women don't have the right *not* to love men;
life is not worth living without a man.

These lessons started in the home. My family's business was a bridal registry and high-end gift store, and for forty years my mom, aunt,[1] and uncle sold china, silver, flatware, crystal, and art glass to aspiring breeders in Denver's shopping district until the store went out of business in 2010. My mom bought me my wedding china at a discount so I'd have it when I needed it: sixty-five-piece flatware, twelve place settings, twelve crystal wineglasses, oversized serving forks, a wine decanter, platters, a Waterford vase—"a fabulous set," she said.

I wasn't even in a relationship. I was actually recovering from my "relationships" in college.

The first guy I wanted to marry/die with/for/over was my best friend freshman year of college who inked his name and hometown on my left black Chuck Taylor low-top, and I decided I loved him very much. It was love (I thought) because:

he called me all the time—once I counted how many calls in one
    day (eleven);
I scrolled through my digital photos and saw that every photo was
    of him looking at me;
during finals I helped him study for his exams instead of study for
    my own, which was how my mom defined love: *caring about
    someone more than you care about yourself*;
glossy women's magazines commanded I view and value myself
    in terms of how men viewed and valued me, so when this

---

1 My mom and aunt look like sisters, yet it's my uncle who is my mom's biological brother, which raises a question I'd rather not ask.

man said that he wished I played a musical instrument, I took piano lessons.

He and I talked about everything except us. We could hold hands the entire cab ride to the airport for summer break but not mention one word about it or what it meant or how we felt about it or each other. It was one of those things two people did but didn't discuss. Although I loved him (I thought) I couldn't even tell him that I liked him since I shouldn't talk first or too much, should not call or open up, should sit back and let him take the lead, should be mysterious and positive and easy-breezy and quiet and cool and not inflict the worst on him: dialogue.

Besides, he didn't like me like that. I was his friend; he was my crush; he was also his long-distance girlfriend's boyfriend.

Though outside the realm of plausibility, I met someone else. It would be true unrequited love that rendered my friend a rough draft.

The spring semester of my sophomore year, one cloudless day in early April, I sat on the quad to watch boys play Frisbee with their shirts off, and one senior boy I saw in slow motion.[2] He was a dark-haired hero with black plastic-frame glasses, deep-set brown eyes, and a silver lip ring. And his ears were pierced, both of them. His was another level. He was also an undeniably talented Frisbee player, advanced yet humble, and his play charged the atmosphere around me, which was a reflection of his character, I could tell—I could tell tons about him yet did not notice the Frisbee game was over and he'd sat down right next to me.

It was a magic afternoon. I picked blades of grass as he leaned back on his palms and tilted his face toward the late afternoon sun and talked to me about raising kids in a world where the price of polymers was tripling; for fifteen minutes, he speculated adorably about

---

2 People you see in slow motion go on a pedestal so high that their position creates the distance between you and immunizes you from reciprocal affection—and you're the one who put them there and defined them by their distance.

impending climate-driven apocalypses—which is to say, he mentioned having children to me.

Up close, he was a thousand times hotter than when he played Frisbee topless. I squeegeed grass between my fingers, squinting through some sunbeams and hallucinating sex when he said something about *schmucks* (we were both Jewish, serendipitously Jewish, with divorced parents who gave us computers whenever we wanted)—it was something his grand-mother had said, that the plural of *schmuck* isn't *schmucks* like most people think, the plural is something I don't remember, but from then on we shared a private knowledge.

Things were intense. So I got up to leave. But he yanked my Dasani water bottle from my bag and hurled it. He liked me! He was being uncer-emoniously mean. It was playground logic,[3] not even slightly cryptic.

I picked up the Dasani and hit him on the shoulder with it and then ran away.

He chased me—

and caught me—

and unscrewed his own water bottle and poured water on me, all over me.

Our two-person water fight ended outside the dining hall with me soaked and winded up against a rough brick wall and with him pressed against me. Breathing together, we shivered. Droplets rolled down the bridge of his nose as he stepped back and said, with a bit of a pant, "Hey, we don't hang out anymore."

"We've never hung out," I clarified.

"Oh," he said. "We should."

We hung out for one month.

Semesters earlier, our college was invited to participate in some-thing called social networking, and in spring 2005 I received an email

---

3 Which is the prelude to most stories of domestic and emotional violence, sexual assault, and harassment.

from www.thefacebook.com saying, "[Future Ex-Boyfriend You'll Name Fucktaco in Your Memoir] has asked you to be in a relationship. Confirm you are his girlfriend."

I confirmed, then I printed the confirmation.

Before he graduated and moved back to Colorado (we were both from Colorado, which united us, primordially), he asked me if he could tell his Jewish grandmother that he had a Jewish girlfriend.

"I do," I said. "I mean, yes."

That same month a friend emailed me another invitation, this one to a new email service powered by Google. "If you haven't already heard about Gmail," gushed the pitch, "it's a new search-based web-mail service." It was invite-only for beta testers, and I invited Fucktaco, gave him his @gmail.com so we could stay in touch while I backpacked through Western Europe for the first half of the summer along with every other white liberal arts collegiate with an art history credit.

Most of my time in Europe I spent in European internet cafés. Gmailing was the gutsiest move I'd ever made. I typed all day and into the night, sharing text instead of saliva and rubbing words until the words orgasmed. My in-box was *It*. Real living was on the screen, and I dreamed of staying inside.

If I wasn't writing to him, or checking my email at the top and bottom of every minute, then I was planning what I'd write or reviewing what I'd written, losing not my virginity to him but my agency.

For one decade Fucktaco went with me everywhere: Western Europe, junior year of college, post-college in San Francisco, grad school in New York; before, during, and after other relationships, and sometimes before and after. We were "together," off and on, forever. Or so it seemed because after Facebook launched in 2004 and Gmail in 2005, there was Gchat in 2006, the first iPhone in 2007, and the rest is history. Each new tool opened up unforeseen ways to express, think, feel, emote, disappear, manipulate, wedding-plan, devastate, and obliterate time, space, and the ability to move on and not contact someone. There I was and would be, in an empty corner, face illuminated by the screen, attempting to breathe through it, to squeeze blood from plastic. And there he was and would be, replying instantaneously.

One year after we met, a chat box appeared in my Gmail window, and he had a green dot alongside his name.

"Let's have a mechitzah at our wedding," he messaged me on Gchat. He was talking about a partition that Orthodox Jews use to separate men from women. We were Jews but not Orthodox, but I didn't say no.

"I would like to own a piano," I typed back, since we were making plans and I'd taken two semesters of piano.

"Upright or grand?" he asked.

"Grand. I don't know. Upright."

I wanted a library and to alphabetize books by author, so I told him.

Seven minutes later he typed, "haha can we have one with a rolly ladder?"

He kept typing. "And then, on weekends, I could go out and get the paper in my bathrobe, and we could look at the headlines and disinterestedly complain about the world."

"Oh please, please, please!" I begged. "And we'll need comfortable chairs and love seats, for reading to the kids."

Our kids.

"No question," he said.

"And they'll have poor eyesight, a great flaw, like their parents."

"No, no. Great eyesight," he argued.

"But teeth. Straight teeth," I said, changing the subject.

"Teeth, of course." Teeth and eyes and kids.

"Do Jews have godparents?" I asked.

"No, I don't think so. Do you think you could continue your writing career if we moved to India or Nepal?"

I could. It could go this way: *We move to India or Nepal and get married.* My thoughts went that far, that fast: *him in his bathrobe, me continuing my career, hooded monks chanting as we lived together abroad, me and him, our upright or grand piano, our well-read kids with poor (or great) eyesight and also teeth, without godparents.* All that was missing was body heat.

I never expected anything more than the physical enactment and reenactment of our chats that I considered an ongoing script we were cowriting and both rehearsing for our in-person visits and lifetime together. *When* could we move to Southeast Asia?

Two years after we met, he Gchatted me about throwing himself in a lake "to avoid our wedding." Alongside our chats ran Google links like:

Negative Thoughts »
Children with Anxiety »
Child Anxiety »
Child Behavior Problems »
Writing a Novel »
Example of a Cover Letter »
Really Short Stories »

Our first breakup (of millions) predated Gchat and was the second I returned from Europe. I was in Colorado for the rest of the summer, and for our reunion I drove to his mother's house, met his mother, and watched *Family Guy* on the sofa with his brother while he lay on the floor at my feet.

After a few episodes, he said he was tired, and he yawned—*no*—
then walked me to his front door—*no, no*—
then out the door—*no, no, no*—
to my car.

He walked me to my car and didn't kiss me.

Fucktaco@gmail.com would not do this. Fucktaco@gmail.com would kiss and fondle and mount me.

Angrily I drove home to email Fucktaco@gmail.com about how angry I was.

He didn't reply instantaneously, so I called him. We talked briefly about what I wrote in the email, and the more I talked, the less he did.

Later I called him again, this time casually, just to say hi, just to talk, and I listened, very casually, to his outgoing voicemail message, and after the tone, I spoke with utmost casualness about how we were "bashert," soulmates in Judaism.

He didn't call me back.

So I texted him (why not?) and emailed him my every thought about *Buffy the Vampire Slayer* and fumed against the dying light of my screens.

"Don't send another text," friends@gmail.com said.

But because I could, I would. As long as I could, I would. But not before crafting draft after draft (one with periods, one with exclamation points) and soliciting feedback and line edits from everyone I'd ever met.

Emotional dumping isn't a conversation, but with more ways to communicate, I was getting worse at it. I could share and overshare, could profess what I would never, could talk too much about how much I was feeling, and feel, wrongly, that I could tell anyone everything and go against centuries of women barred from doing that.

"Don't send the email," friends@gmail.com pleaded.

But I'd pass out if I didn't...just...say...this...*one*...thing.

I'll just do what makes me feel good, I thought. *Even if it makes me feel bad.*

It wasn't only that my heart had shit for brains. Or that I had separation anxiety. But that the screens had my soul by the throat. Google and Verizon and Facebook and Apple unrolled 3,144,823 new mediums and put them at my disposal, and I should say and do nothing? Like him?

"Don't send that message," friends@gmail.com texted whenever they sensed I was on the verge.

But I would have sooner felt bad about messaging than not message. I would say anything but nothing.

Whether it was the freedom or the dopamine withdrawals or too many Rilo Kiley deep cuts—my thinking switched from "it's she who holds her tongue who gets her man" to: *When a woman falls for a man, she should tell him things, literally all the things, especially the sad things, things that will expose her, because she hopes that he will feel closer to her and know her better than anyone else on Earth, which will reserve them for each other.*

But it was always too much and never enough.

I was just asking to be ghosted. And I reacted to ghosting by lying in the fetal position for hours, spooning my phone, and staring into the dark to another dark. Were there any unread emails or texts? Any unmissed calls? There were not. If someone died each time I checked, there would be no one left.

The punishment went beyond the action, into a kind of torment that technology facilitates. Like, at any moment Fucktaco could reach out (anticipation!) but didn't (agony). Or the phone *would* ding and deliver a mild shock that sailed from the blood in my hand's veins directly to my heart—the phone was no longer noiseless, unlit, black as hell; the phone was magnanimous! I'd cradle and thank the phone for its validation, its mercy. Then I'd open my messages and see I'd received an alert from Bed, Bath & Beyond that my mobile offer for 20 percent off one item in-store was expiring soon. I tried and failed to remind myself "this is just the phone" and "that is just the computer," as opposed to life and death.

Ghosting exhorted me to review what I'd done to deserve it and to cross-examine myself. *If I hadn't sent that one text, then everything would be okay.* It always came down to that: I'd said too much; if only I'd said less.

When Fucktaco wouldn't talk to me, still I kept in touch with him, stayed looped in to what he was doing and thinking and saying, courtesy of social media, where he told me everything without communicating with me. Because in efforts to optimize conversation, Silicon Valley has obliterated it, and in its place is a virtual hell with nine echo chambers of dead-end communication that binds human beings who need never speak to each other.

I did what anyone with Wi-Fi and a pulse would: cyberstalk to be in an eternal one-sided conversation with my once-future domestic partner who was now an avatar I followed, a specter who lived and whose life I could only search.

One day junior year, months after break-up-via-ghosting, I found what I was looking for, the end of the world. Fucktaco was "In a Relationship."

"In a Relationship" has at least twenty-six mutant interpretations and insinuations. The more online I was, the more I could read the signs that spun nearly every sentence into something to translate. (Plus, when you're heartsick and in front of a screen, the facts are whatever you guess they are.)

Updates relationship status to "In a Relationship" = Your ex is dating someone else only to hurt you.

"Likes" an old post = Your ex is stalking you—not because they want to date you but because they have nothing else to do.

"Likes" multiple old posts = A form of flirting that's also a form of torture that's also a blend of passive aggression and active aggression.

Follows you or refollows you or doesn't unfollow you = A reminder (eternal) of a relationship that ended or that never was. On the ghost ship that didn't carry the partnership, you'll wonder (agonize) What Might Have Been *if only [this]*.

Watches your Stories = Remote virtual observation that handcuffs the viewer to the viewed, and it means "I like you" or "I hate you," but not "I love you."

Watches your Stories but doesn't "like" or comment on posts = Your ex does not even care about you enough to unfollow you.

Comments with an emoji = Despite whatever deranged thing(s) you said or did, and regardless of how long two people like you have been apart, you can and will meet again.

Comments in full sentences = A marriage proposal is not out of the question!

Updates relationship status to "Single" = Your ex wants to get back together. This ex might as well have jizzed on your face.

An alert = Says, "I love you." Or rather, in an alert one can hear "I love you." Or rather, an alert is a lot like love, a lot like rescue; it sets off a paranormal sensation that's deeper than seeing or hearing or thinking, and it can be enough. (Whatever the alert says is irrelevant; one grows attached to alerts and not to what they relay.)

Replies instantaneously = A grand romantic gesture, which says, *I am into you, as into you as you are into me. I read your words with the fervor in which you composed them, and I invest proportional time and energy by hitting "reply" as often as you hit "send." You get my undivided attention; I listen when you "talk," hang on your every letter; what you say means something to someone who hears you, and feels you, and values you. It goes without saying that I am building a shrine to you, just as you are building yours to me.*

Types "oh" and "um," and/or is idle for minutes at a time = This is awkwardness that is so awkward it is awkward online, a space zoned to eliminate awkwardness, which means your ex never stopped loving you, not at all.

Response rate changes = Maybe due to no service or a dead phone or the signal or the satellites, something radioactive and staticky, or being stranded somewhere or being flayed alive or (worst case) over you.

Ellipsis appears that signifies someone is typing and then disappears = Time to call therapists in your area to see if they accept your insurance in order to discuss what could have been typed and deleted.

Inevitably, Fucktaco would change his status back to "Single" and reach out to me again, directly or indirectly, because he could. He might "orbit" me if he didn't actually want to talk to me but also didn't want to not contact me, so he'd bear witness to me through social media by publicly liking my content. And I'd "talk back" via subliminal message by surveilling and reacting to his posts. He might also "breadcrumb" me. He might text, then stop texting (eliciting in me weeping and shadowboxing), then text beyond reason (as if he could now be said to experience emotion—like, what a twist) and even send radical texts like, "I am sorry," but then disappear (refusing dialogue and my existence), and then, when I'd least expect it, text (something like, "Mmm...baby you put the sexy in dyslexia") and keep texting (because I was not to come too close nor wander too far) but then text more robotically, such that I had to load the hours with texts of my own—until he'd COMPLETELY *vanish*, and EVERY SINGLE TIME I'd get sucked into his texting or not texting (which was it going to be?); but if he left me alone (but really this time), and if I left him alone (BUT REALLY THIS TIME), and if I could turn thoughts about him into plain, dead-end thoughts, and if consciousness became manageable again, then he'd sense it and know I was over it—which is when my phone would light up. And it would rip me so wide apart so quickly that it'd yank me into a future where there was a house to call a home, and only guardian angels could stop me from replying.

Also inevitably, he would ghost me again. I learned, over time, to fight silence with silence, to sit tight until he contacted me again so I could ignore him (and make him want me).

Even our silences had nothing in common. His silence was the most preferable (the most convenient, the least bloody) manner to convey information, e.g., fuck off. My silence bestowed or returned control (power, the upper hand) and was the one way to save face after I'd said too much. I'd just wait for him to text—wait so as to not appear forlorn or berserk, wait with no alternative to waiting until he was ready for me to talk (but not over the word limit or the cycle would begin anew) and resume our wedding plans. (A woman who breaks her silence is unattractive and feeble, and it should not ever be done.) (But it will be done.) (And there is no one to blame or hate but the woman.)

I just...needed him to want to talk to me. I was on my knees for a ding. (I expressed myself exclusively to these ends, which led to the traditional happy one, me and him. But expression itself was not an end, and my "love me" voice did not speak for me.) Thanks to the cloud I could scrutinize my every word and everyone else's every word, which I could use to circumvent saying the wrong thing and to score a response and leave my mark. I'd noticed Fucktaco used particular words a lot, so I used those same words, since male words are the only words. Once he messaged me, "The second I told you [about certain Facebook] pix, I knew you would decide that [the woman in the photo with me] was my girlfriend or lover. NB: not the case. And WTF with the unilateral blocking! I am going to block you back." From then on I'd say things like, "It's not a unilateral decision!" and "You have made this a unilateral decision" and "I guess this is a unilateral decision." I typed with his vocabulary to hint we had a lot in common even during emotional warfare.

(If you compound a woman's conditioned suspicion of her own voice with the online imperative to express yourself 24/7, then the strangest shit will come out.)

As I used his words, I used the same number of them, too. For every one of his texts I had three to five replies in mind but held back to match him, so if he gave me an inch, then I'd take a mile, then compress it into an inch. As the poet Elizabeth Bishop wrote, "Half is enough."

My inclination stretched back millennia, to the part in Plato's *Symposium* in which male playwright Aristophanes spoke about the genesis of human nature, love, and pairs when the Earth was considered flat and human beings were spherical with four arms, four legs, four ears, two sets of genitals, and two faces looking in opposite directions on one globular head. Over time, these humans grew strong and arrogant, and they attacked the gods. To weaken and punish them, Zeus cut each in two, and then Osiris and the Nile gods brewed a hurricane to disperse the pieces across the world. Once scattered, each incomplete human sought its other half. When a set reunited—recognizable by their twin pain—they weaved and wrapped and smushed (fucked), to reconnect, to draw two halves back together.

I had wanted to be part of the set, two-cum-one.

This matching is also known today as mirroring, or people-pleasing—repeating another's words or opinions neutralizes conflict and is the origin of love and gets people to like you. And women live to be liked (and must be liked to live). So, I parked in Fucktaco's throat to cement myself in his thoughts so that I could touch his heart through my fingers and his words, and never get ghosted again.

But in the process, he cemented himself in my thoughts. I'd watch a movie and see it through his perspective, or read an article and think four ways about it: Would he like it or not, and how would I tell him about it and when?

A male psychotherapist and complex trauma expert named Pete Walker coined the term "fawn response" as a type of stress response. "Fawn types seek safety by merging with the wishes, needs and demands of others. They act as if they unconsciously believe that the price of admission to any relationship is the forfeiture of all their needs, rights, preferences and boundaries." Yeah. Yeah yeah yeah yeah. The fawner exits her self and her voice. Or rather, her voice serves the listener and not the speaker and then everything comes to depend on who is listening.

Just be you, I'd remind myself whenever I'd exchange myself for Fucktaco.

Who's that? I'd ask myself, especially if Fucktaco, and the Fucktacos who came after, wasn't there to tell me.

"We are as much made of words as we are of flesh and blood," writes critic Alexandra Schwartz. And to Virginia Woolf, women and men "need different sentences to contain the shapes of their experience." In writing my sentences like his, I bent the shape of my experience. In fawning, I didn't say what I meant so often that I didn't know what I meant to say. Did I really care about what I said I cared about? Were my favorite books really my favorites? Did I even like Fucktaco? Instead of an Aristophanes pair, I was like Echo the Greek nymph, whose punishment for having "no door on her mouth" was to lose her voice and have it replaced with the reverberation of others' words.

Whatever I did, it worked, and I'd get what I wanted, a date. After many rounds of ghosting, breadcrumbing, etc., there would be one email that would lead to emailing, which would lead to planning a visit and a date at a restaurant with appetizers and an exchange of oxygen. Each date was the same date. Italian, Japanese, Mexican—once seated, as people, in person, we were at a loss for words.

> **Fucktaco**: Would you be interested in more water?
> **me**: Yes, more water, thank you.

"Conversation" would go on, but when he'd talk, I'd hear very little of what he said because I was planning what I'd say and who I would be. When I'd talk, my words were defense mechanisms, and none of what I said relayed any of what I felt. His face reminded me of a sad emoticon as I'd try to talk the same way we did online, to feel all the same things but verbalize them, but what I'd get out was, "EfhΣyaœ!iuøh≈gy9π*du°au¥blarf†."

In person I was just a body and not embodied, which was one problem among hundreds.

Back at our computers our avatars twiddled their thumbs, waiting for us to return to our screens and remind them of a relationship we'd never know.

"So much of the time I thought we were in love or could be," I told Fucktaco over Gchat, five years into our [whatever]. I told him this in an interview I published online titled "The Exit Interview." Staying in touch for years without real communication drove me to it, to get replies through an art project; I had to interview him to get him to talk to me, and I had to speak as a writer since I couldn't as a woman (a writer can be bold, direct, unapologetic). And he would deliver himself to an audience and not to me, as if he needed the endorsement of publication and my voice as text that would be edited to hear me and answer my questions.

"That fact," of staying in touch, "made me think you loved me, or could love me, circumstances permitting," I said in the interview. Staying in touch was love granted as attention, wasn't it? Love meant never saying goodbye. Right?

I'd thought so. The first time I tried to tell Fucktaco I loved him, years into staying in touch, I'd lost my phone in a bar while grind-dancing with a stranger, so I couldn't text "i <3 u" and let the hands handle what the mouth couldn't.

To speak "I love you," I went to his house on one of my visits.

Fucktaco opened the door, and with my voice I said, *"I'm in love with you"*—aloud and in italics, with the preposition "in" that escalates everything.

I was in love with him. I thought I was in love with him. I thought I should be in love with him. Because I was born in love and only through him did I feel alive and know myself and I didn't have the right not to love him and life wasn't worth living without loving him and I cared more about him than I cared about myself and I had only one adventure to choose from and it had been chosen.

"No," he said, "you're not," and closed the door.

Like he knew my feelings better than I did.

Later on Gchat he told me he thought I was joking or was saying "I love you" to mess with him. He didn't take me seriously, he said.[4]

---

4 If we had continued the conversation, I imagine the Gchat to be:

me: How do you feel now that you know I was in no way joking?

The next time, with the next boyfriend, I couldn't say, "I love you"; I could say only, "I opposite-of-hate you."

Maybe I didn't love Fucktaco, just as he didn't love me, because he never knew me, the me that split in two when I talked online and to him.

Many women writers describe splitting between person and persona, between private and public self. Adrienne Rich experienced the split in college, "between the girl who wrote poems, who defined herself in writing poems, and the girl who was to define herself by her relationships with men." Anne Sexton split as a wife and mother: "All I wanted was...to be married, to have children. I thought the nightmares, the visions, would go away if there were enough love to put them down. I was trying my damnedest to lead a conventional life, for that was how I was brought up, and it was what my husband wanted of me.... The surface cracked when I was about twenty-eight. I had a psychotic break and tried to kill myself," because she wasn't herself.

bell hooks was able to think back critically about splitting in her memoir *Talking Back: Thinking Feminist, Thinking Black*: "In reflection, I see how deeply connected that split is to ongoing practices of domination (especially thinking about intimate relationships, ways racism, sexism, and class exploitation work in our daily lives, in those private spaces—that it is there that we are often most wounded, hurt, dehumanized; there that ourselves are most taken away, terrorized, and broken)."

Practices of domination played out through my relationships with men—men I existed for, felt I couldn't exist without, and so I

Fucktaco: I knew, on some level, that you loved me because you had told me so, a lot, in other ways.

Fucktaco: Were you expecting me to say it back? When you said you loved me?

me: Not at all. I expected maybe you would say something else, something very enigmatic, something that would mean you loved me, too.

didn't exist myself. And some of them, like Fucktaco, were less men than holes in space I turned to every time I was lonely, that bathed me in spotlight, fantasies that responded after I'd made myself empty enough.

Fucktaco and I would never break up for good and would never not text. That's what I thought. It wasn't going to end. Because communication devices will keep perpetuating splits and ongoing practices of domination. And will continue to be open-ended and to consist of dead ends. The attention economy will forever run on emotional reactions that outsize circumstances and will forever turn molehills into mountains and will forever appear to ease the hysteria it agitates.

Taking the time and effort to communicate straightforwardly will be unsexy, always. Every day social media will replace conversation with broadcasts, and every day we'll confess at the same rate we repress. Character limits and limitless timelines and consolidating platforms and newer methods to provoke an ex-girlfriend so anyone and everyone may call her crazy and take his feelings out on her will abide.

Communication tools will hijack thought and behavior and will render "I love you" harder to say than "I hate you." Communication itself will remain a serious action that no one knows how to do anymore. Smartphones will inhibit me personally from saying what I most want to say, how I want to say it—

because it's the lifeblood of techno-patriarchal-capitalism. And most important—

Sorry, what was I talking about? My phone dinged.

6

WHY I DIDN'T SAY NO

Mhmmm," I moaned the moment his tongue touched my swimsuit area. "OmmmuhhAH-Mmm-mmm," I whimpered, sounding and acting how women supposedly sound and act when touched. "DO NOT STOP," I shouted in a composite of thousands of voices that rushed through actresses wearing bras in bed into me. "Mygodmygodmygod, just like that," I said, because it has to be said. "THERE, right THERE." (But where, exactly?) "THAT'S THE SPOT," I squealed knowingly, knowing not a thing. Then I asked for it harder, HARDER. And FASTER. I asked for it to the left, then to the right. I moaned in eight octaves. I manically called for Jesus. I cranked my volume to 11 and reverberated like Cinemax women who orgasm easily and ceaselessly—I had something stuck in my throat, and it was someone else's words, like "amazing" and "holy fuck." "Uhhhhhh," I groaned, to express *Is this ever the best*. Eventually it was time for a loud gasp, then a sigh, and then to go quiet, oral-sex-struck.

Would you believe he didn't applaud?

A star was born—or rather, the right kind of woman, a girl who'd learned early on how to be a woman. But nobody told me to do this; nobody had to. It was automatic, my first impulse.

To prepare for my future, to get in shape to be a whore for men, I watched TV and subscribed to *Cosmopolitan,* "the international magazine for women," and found tips and tricks that promised we can all be beautiful if only we memorize forty-two sexual positions and let men finish our sentences for us. In my childhood bedroom I sang along to lyrics like "all you ladies pop your pussy like this" while I pored over articles that, if honestly titled, would have been:

"Independence Schmendependence, 'One' Is the Ugliest Number"
"Opinionated? Go Fuck Yourself"
"Silence Is This Spring's Must-Have Accessory!"
"Your Horoscope: Bottomless Disappointment for Mature
    Communication"
"'I'm Attracted to My Dealbreaker'—A Real Woman's True Story"
"EXCLUSIVE: Expressing Yourself Is Masculine"
"QUIZ: How Vexing Is Your Voice?"
"ADVICE: Single Out Those Who Oppress You and Worship
    Their Cock"
"BONUS: 69 Tips to Take Up Less Space Until You're Literally
    Invisible"
"SCIENCE SAYS: You're Crazy"
"Equality! The Only Joke Women Can Tell"

During stolen moments with premium channels that made heat come off the screen I studied women who hurled from darkness quivering and quaking, writhing and undulating, and arching and convulsing while they got spanked, slapped, rammed, and reamed, and in answer they cried the earth-shattering word "yes" in all its synonyms: *Yes! Yes? Yep, oh yeah, okay, sure, uh-huh, affirmative, aye, of course, positively, absolutely, you bet your life, why not, no doubt, MORE, oh G-d amen.* (Only cold-hearted shrews withheld sex; every other woman was a fanatic of dick and all it could make her do.) With my face almost pressed up against the glass, getting as clear a picture of sex that a teen girl who should ask for it harder and faster could handle, I mouthed along, my heartbeat moving south of my heart and into my swimsuit area when a man or a vampire took a woman by force and she broke herself against him.

"Let's talk about intercourse and female masturbation," my parents never said to me. "Intercourse" and "masturbation" were difficult words to verbalize, much less do to (on?) myself.

"Why does the man go to the bathroom inside a woman when there are toilets everywhere?" I asked my mom in elementary school about the love that was made (sex). She didn't correct me or explain, ever, and I kept my virginity so I wouldn't be a urinal.

Our second sex talk was months before I left for college, during dinner. "I am going to have sex in college," I told my mom and step-dad, after pausing the TV.

"No," my mom argued. "You are not."

"Yes, I am."

"Yes, she is," my stepdad intervened.

"Then she's not going." My mom left the table and went into the pantry.

One might say I got my uncontrolled extreme emotions from her. Also, my life was affected by her loss—her mother died when she was seventeen; she had two divorces and three miscarriages; in her womb I went from triplet to twin to me ("my one, my only," she says). If ever I did something she herself wouldn't do, she'd ask, "Do you not love me?" Or say, "I don't know what I did besides love you so so much and give you everything you've ever wanted." She took my existence personally, and in her Southern, Jewish mindset, sex came after marriage, never before, and although spelled differently, "sex" and "love" were the same.

(My dad and I had zero sex talks and almost as many real talks.)

I didn't lose the deformity known as virginity until I was (DO NOT LAUGH) twenty-two years old. I was a virgin other virgins mocked, a girl who'd nicknamed her vagina Sleepy Hollow.

Playing my first game of Never Have I Ever in college, I volunteered first since I had never ever done more than most.

"Never have I ever tried mustard," I said.

"Never have I ever given road head," the freshman who went next said, letting me and the room know that I had grown up wrong.

But no girl I'd ever met got near herself or felt anything other than disgrace for her body and all it could or couldn't do. We weren't raised by wolves; we, as a society, pretty much pretend the clitoris/vulva/vagina isn't there, and like society, I pretended and would continue to pretend until someone else discovered my clitoris for me and did what he wanted to do with it that I would pretend to like.[1]

Even though I ignored myself the way I was meant to for two decades of my life, I could tell you how my sexual debut would unfold. I, a chastity-belted nerd, and he, a more fascinating, way more likable male demigod, would meet-super-cute, and feet would get swept, and we'd fall in True & Perfect Love after a prolonged will-they/won't-they

---

1 "The clitoris has been contested, debated, ignored, demonized, and mythologized in medical discourse since antiquity," and it has been maligned "as a pathology" and "misrepresented, suppressed, and even completely omitted from anatomical and gynecological literature until very recently," writes Dr. Elinor Cleghorn in *Unwell Women*. "The tale of the clitoris is a parable of culture," according to Professor Helen O'Connell, Australia's first urologist who is a woman. In 2019, Twitter banned ads using the word "vagina" to promote the book *The Vagina Bible: The Vulva and the Vagina: Separating the Myth from the Medicine* by Dr. Jen Gunter, relegating and reinforcing "vagina" as an unutterable word instead of an anatomical term, while Delta Air Lines showed edited versions of the film *Booksmart* to exclude the word "vagina." Though Delta put "vagina" back after complaints, a lot of people remain committed to ignorance about women and their bodies. In response to the survey statement "Most women get their periods at the first of the month," 40 percent of Republican male voters said it's "true" or they were not sure. Even the *Oxford English Dictionary*—"the principal historical dictionary of the English language," from which most other dictionaries derive—defines the clitoris as "a small, sensitive, erectile part of the female genitals at the anterior end of the vulva." Wrong. So wrong. The clitoris is an organ, part external and part internal, and the only organ whose function is pleasure. And it isn't "small"— internally it ranges from seven to twelve centimeters long and has twice as many nerve endings as the penis.

courtship. Then, as boyfriend-girlfriend, we'd wait for it to rain to kiss in it, which would designate that night as "the night." Soaked to the core, we'd seek sanctuary inside (location TBD; a turret?) and get out of our wet clothes in a striptease-off, which would be the prologue to some unforgettable fireplace foreplay wherein our every feverish sigh, body quake, etc., would say what words could never, like that we knew one another on a soulmate level, that we'd united in past lives and would reunite in future ones, that we were emotionally synced and fated. With everything in place spiritually, the demigod would possess me, and I would submit, voluptuously, would give everything of myself, would *get lost unto it* in a carnal interrogation that would build and build to a physical struggle, a tangle, a catalogue of sexual practices (some standing) that'd ignite a blind fury. The Lotus, the Jellyfish, the Inverted Jockey—we'd do all the positions. The Reverse-Reverse Cowpoke, the Flip-Flop, the Blessing and the Curse, and whatever else was left. We'd do things to each other we couldn't spell, and he'd whisper Pablo Neruda into my vagina. If there happened to be a French maid's uniform nearby, I'd dress up. My years as a child gymnast would pay off as my legs did the undoable while he'd bore into my flesh, passion 100 percent unbridled, until I'd beg for mercy (seared to the bones, ravaged) and collapse next to him on the broken bed. Trembling and recuperating from our simultaneous orgasms, we'd lie together for hours, our designed-for-one-another limbs entwined in soaked sheets, our unquenchable hunger quenched.

In a nutshell I pictured that I was in store for some crazy fucking.

Because if done right, sex should be a furious, raw, rowdy, athletic, transformational, professional encounter where two people lose their minds while celebrating each other's bodies. Done right, a man would "take" me, and I'd surrender (and nimbly indulge his uncontrollable primal biological urges with lewd acrobatics and ear-splitting affirmations, no matter how fake or uncomfortable or anatomically unrealistic).

"What woman understands by love is clear enough: it is not only devotion, it is a total gift of body and soul, without reservation, without regard for anything whatever," the male philosopher Friedrich Nietzsche wrote in *The Gay Science*, which media baked into the rest of us, along with male philosopher Søren Kierkegaard's observation that "when a girl's love is not self-sacrificing, then she is not a woman but a man."

Total, unreserved, oblivious, charitable gift of body and soul is what real relationships, real fireworks require, and real girls sacrifice themselves for love, or else they are men.

My first legit, offline boyfriend and I did meet-cute. Junior year of college, 2006, in the backyard of a house party, I was standing alone, drinking whatever had been mixed and ogling the hottest guy of all time balancing on top of a giant concrete pipe from the construction site across the street. He had an audience, and when he jumped down, he—through serendipity—jumped down beside me.

Standing together was an opportunity of a lifetime. His epic act, my tortoiseshell glasses. "You must skate or surf," I said, to impress him.

"Both," he said. Like a touch from G-d.

I nearly sprained myself from yearning and couldn't tear myself away, though he'd already left.

We re-met-cute the next spring, on a playground near the dorms. I was in the air this time, on a swing. The skater/surfer who could have been a model/actor in a toothpaste/vodka commercial stepped out of nowhere, approached my swing of all the swings on Earth, and said, "Hey."

His mouth probably had hundreds of positive reviews on Yelp.

I failed to speak, or forgot to, or didn't speak as a strategy, to let him be captivated by my silence, which worked because he smiled.

I was breathless. He was breathtaking, literally.

Out of every word I knew, I picked the best: "Hi." In the language of love (English), "hi," if spoken by a girl, means: *I will crucify myself for you, for a glance, for a scrap, for you to rescue or destroy or define me.*

Soon I worked out his schedule and knew where he'd be when he'd be there so that I could be there, too, dressed sacrificially. (To be stalked was the ideal scenario, but no one was interested, so I stalked instead, which is feminism.)

In the basement of another party I spotted him. I danced ecstatically very nearby, inviting his gaze toward my rhapsodic rosebud body—I imagined that's how the voiceover narration would describe me, if there were voiceover narration. But his gaze did not move, so I drank a lot more and then sauntered over and delivered the line I'd rehearsed: "Remember me? From the swings."

He remembered.

When we first kissed, we kissed until sunrise, until there was steam on our clothes.

Beginning of senior year we made out again, and then again, also again, then once again but with feeling, and one fine morning he told me that he'd hang up his chick habit and spurn all other girls for me. My feeling was, basically, euphoria that love happened per my wildest prayers.

Our relationship played out like a montage. *He let me pop the zits on his back and I brought him five tacos on Taco Tuesdays and he made me grilled cheese after midnight and we dressed up in a couples' costume for Halloween (the Morning-After Prom Date) and met for five-minute breaks during class under the same oak tree on the quad where we'd sit face-to-face, me on his lap, our arms and legs squeezed around each other in a posture of eternity.*

I still dream of it.

One day, because they loved each other very much, a group of researchers combined "script theory" (*human behavior fits script-like templates*) and Adrienne Rich's theory of "compulsory heterosexuality" (*heterosexuality is the default and mandatory sexual attraction*) to develop the "heterosexual script" in prime-time television (*how men, women, and the undead date, commit, and fuck, which forms viewers' expectations of dating, committing, and fucking*). A male protagonist's dating profile might be *6'0, forceful, verbose, always correct, power-hungry, commitment-phobic, sexually prolific, emotionally vacant.* A leading lady's dating profile might be no text and all photos of wedding dresses, chastity belts, aspirational babies, tits, and ass.

"What counts is what the heroine provokes, or rather what she represents. She is the one, or rather the love or fear she inspires in the hero, or else the concern he feels for her, who makes him act the way he does. In herself the woman has not the slightest importance," said film director Budd Boetticher about mainstream film's squaring of a woman's visual presence with her inclusion in the narrative, as quoted by Laura Mulvey in "Visual Pleasure and Narrative Cinema," the essay where she debuted the term "the male gaze."

In any script, a man experiences desire while a woman ignites desire and must be desirable (and accuse and absent herself if she is undesired). A man is guided by his desire, and by a primordial brutality, some innate yet conditioned virility that's more bestial than conscious, and it commands, *Take from a woman's body the gratification that is your right, and she will be honored and not whine.* She won't whine because a heroine is a good sport who goes along with whatever. And because she knows her body is for giving and her sexuality is not for her, and if she isn't good in bed, she'll implode.

The screen whispers to viewers like Cyrano2.0, and real women like me mainline the concept until the supply runs dry (it never runs dry): that in ourselves we have not the slightest importance and what counts is what we provoke or inspire or elicit that motivates someone else's action. The rest of the dating population also assimilates and echoes the heterosexual script in unison, without asking why, instituting an Ouroboros Effect of eternal return, until our voice and desires are not wholly our own, are not strictly biological, and do not come from within the body alone.

"That's not what women want," a man said to me after we saw *Magic Mike XXL* in theaters on a third date in 2015. "Women want their hair pulled," he said.

My argument killed his erection:

Let's say a man pulls a woman's hair because he saw an actor pull an actress's hair and the actress gasped in pleasure. *She's going to love this, all women do*, the man thinks as he pulls, and the woman gasps, in pleasure, or in pain, or because she's seen something, too, or because she's had a legacy shoved down her throat before she can learn what she desires, or because she wants to be "normal." (She "should" be "normal"; she "should" "want to," even if she doesn't, just as he "should" pull because it's "normal," and all shocks become "normal" sooner or later, then "natural"). But a gasp is a gasp is a gasp, and through repetition, the action escalates, and maybe the man thinks it's kosher to choke the woman after seeing a waxed starlet from RedTube take it with gratitude, so he pulls or chokes, and she gasps—bound to the performance (perhaps forgetting or never knowing it's a performance). In lieu of being turned on, she turns on, her gender both an amplifier and a gag, and then straight sex's call-and-response ensues: the woman yells, "Fuck Me, Polo" every time the man says, "Marco," using words pushed between her lips, words that men have written so that other men may enter a woman's body through her own mouth. Plus, conforming can be comforting, if not survival, to see oneself among the televised elite, our generational gods. So she summons the hundreds of bodies she's seen onscreen humping against shifting tableaus since only by reenacting them can she hope to be seen and heard, to prove to the man that she exists. *I'll give it to him*, she thinks, *whatever it is, and give it to him so good that he'll think I'm great. That I'm someone.* She cries out, "MORE," as if to whisper, *I was here. Am here. Let me stay here, forever.* Her reward is recognition of her sexuality, and eventually perhaps she pulls her own hair, to please him.

"In conclusion," I told the guy on what would be our last date, "no one knows what women want, not even women."

Being socialized is almost like being gaslit into mental illness. Or, to be literary about it, like nineteenth-century Bovarism that conflated the real and the imaginary, which scholars pitched as a pattern of mental illness. ("Psychosis": a severe but common form of delusion that impairs thought and emotion such that fantasy is the reality that counts.) The term Bovarism comes from the book *Madame Bovary*—

Of course Bovary was a Madame. And of course Bovarism ends in tragedy. And of course *Madame Bovary* was written by a man.

Madames are socialized differently, and the difference is akin to razors: women's razors aren't as sharp, and they cost more.

Since I was raised as a girl and gazed into screens as if they were mirrors and maps, plotting experience through fiction and furnishing my inner life with it, true to the feedback loop, I devoured and digested the role of Woman whose life hinges on her sexuality and whose love takes the form of mute devotion, and I regurgitated it.

I was terrifically excited to notch my immaculate bedpost with my college boyfriend, to join mind, body, and soul until he ran out of orgasms.

One winter afternoon of senior year, three months into our relationship, I gave him a Tonight Is the Night monologue outlining the plan to rename Sleepy Hollow:

> dinner at a restaurant
> action movie
> It.

Dinner at a restaurant: He bought a twelve-pack of condoms, and I dressed up in my Seder clothes, and he opened the door of his unwashed white truck for me and drove us to a Mediterranean restaurant with menus written in cursive and décor that resembled the bottom of the sea as depicted in a cartoon, and we squeezed into a raised booth with a linen tablecloth and awaited the everyday's transmogrification into the everlasting.

Action movie: We picked the latest James Bond and hand in hand watched the suited secret agent set out on a mission to earn his license to kill by defeating a weapons dealer in a high-stakes game of poker at Casino Royale (directed by a man, written by three men, edited by a man, produced by men, based on a novel by a man, starring one man Daniel Craig and some models).

It: Back at my apartment, we opened a box of wine and lit too many scented candles, and I gave him my practiced come-hither, devirginize-me look. This Was It.

(After It, I took a photo of the condom sagging in the trash and memorialized It by placing the torn turquoise condom wrapper in a shoebox.)

I wasn't miffed or surprised when It felt like being in an accident the first few times, or the times after that, too. He'd slam himself into me then work into his factory-set motion: fast and hard and every which way that invented, stylized women scream they want it.

"Relax, relax," he'd say, this strong-sweaty-panting-thrusting-unrelenting-anonymous maniac in the place where a boyfriend should have been.

Relax, relax, I'd berate myself mentally while he'd pound and grind against me, unaware of me, at the dead center of me.

Let this be over quickly, I prayed as I waited and waited for him to experience the greatest pleasure known to mankind. (My ache, his state of grace.)

If I cried, he might say, "Should I keep going?" and in my head I screamed, *No! Stop!*, but it came out quiet and ragged, as if ripped out, and like this: "Keep going."

So he did.

Because the words he wanted to hear seemed to be the only words I knew how to say. And because I would not say what he didn't want to hear if it made me harder to desire, harder to love. Also because women should act like accommodating sex kittens watering at the mouth for dick and use our own voices to ask for it, to say *yes!* in a thousand languages, to beg G-d for it. And because what was important to a man was the only important thing, and I did not want to ruin my boyfriend's experience of me.

If he ever thought to ask, "What do you want me to do to you? What do you like?" I'd think, NAPE OF THE NECK, INNER THIGHS, NIPPLES, LIPS, EARS, BUTT, CLIT. I was in an advanced-level women's sexualities course and could rattle off my seven erogenous zones at breakneck speed for an exam. I could talk-the-talk but not fuck-the-fuck. Well, I couldn't talk-the-talk either.

I'd think also, *What a stupid request for information I couldn't answer at gunpoint.* What I wanted was for him to want to stop hurting me without me having to ask, and to take crying as a sign and as a way to communicate and as a request to relent. I wanted him to be a hero and rescue me from him. And I wanted him to hear what I didn't allow myself to say. I wanted to be telepathic.

But I settled for him to keep going, to show his love for me in how he hurt me. Because when he first said he loved me, facing me under pale moonlight, somewhere trumpets blared, confetti exploded, a chorus of angels sang, "Hallelujah," and my heart ejaculated—so if he said he loved me while hurting me, then I'd consent to be hurt.

"The cult of love in the West is an aspect of the cult of suffering," Susan Sontag leveled in the collection *Against Interpretation*, noting the two-thousand-year-old Christian conflation that exists today, like in rom-coms that advertise love as a temple, a higher law, an addiction, a psychosis, an otherworldly and socially constructed biological necessity and eternal torment. Or like in other rom-coms that teach us if women suffer enough, then everything works out.

I'd gloat to my friends, on the rare occasion that I saw them, "We're violently in love"—a common saying, romantic, a heated sentiment. The word "passion" comes from Greek and Latin words that mean "suffering," and indeed, "love" and "suffering" share terminology, phraseology, symptoms, and metaphors: Love cuts deep, and first cuts are the deepest. We cry, tremble, burn. We're wounded, sore, aching, undone, damaged, destroyed. We're in need of relief, of a fix, of a cure, of a reality check.

Sontag later clarified: "It is not love which we overvalue, but suffering."

I saw two gynecologists for help.

"My vagina is broken," I hypothesized.

Although under oath I would've said, "Love has an analgesic effect, and my empathy reaches a pitch where if sex feels good to my boyfriend, then it feels good to me, although it really feels like I won't survive it."

The first gynecologist, the father of a friend, recommended more sex, a nineteenth-century recommendation based on curing hysteria, in which intercourse (as well as birthing babies and orgasm) can remedy any woman's problem and also remedy any woman with a problem.

"Women come in and say the same thing," the second gynecologist told me. "That something feels not right in an unclear, uncertain way, like regularly getting the wind knocked out of you or being stabbed." She was talking about a penis in a vagina.

"It's psychological," she said about my vagina. As in my pain wasn't actual or so serious, and my symptoms were not symptoms but illusions, and I wasn't a reliable reporter of what goes on in my own body.

I was being dramatic, anxious, neurotic. I was overreacting, confused, sensitive. I was seeking attention, dramatizing my pain, acting crazy, acting like a baby, being ridiculous, playing victim, crying wolf, making too big a deal, making things up.

She suggested destressing, meditation, medication.

I asked for an immediate solution.

She brought out a device. She called it a vaginal dilator and handed it to me.

"Put it in," she said.

"I'll try it at home," I said.

"Let me help," she intervened. "I'll show you," she said about the stiff, opaque silicone, medical-grade dildo that she held with my vagina as her field of vision.

She lubricated it and pushed it in, and I went momentarily blind.

"Please take it out," I said. "I'll use it later. Another time."

"Relax, relax," she instructed. "You're expecting it to hurt. Let me glide it a little . . ."

I scooted miles away. She'd just reached into my body and punched, and she spoke to me as if I could trust her.

"Fine," she said, with concern. "Take one with you. We have different sizes."

"I should get the large," I said.

"I tried the small on you."

"The small then, please."

She prescribed the vaginal dilator nightly, to lifelessly dangle in me for ten to fifteen minutes while I listened to soft instrumental folk CDs. Whatever was wrong could be solved, possibly, by starting my last semester in college with a prescription ghost dick.

"Consent," I'd believed, was an uncomplicated yes/no articulation and action. And I was guilty of consenting.

I was guilty as well of "choice," one word containing many: faith, expectation, the chaos of the heart, inculcation, self-consciousness, surrender, and free will. I was guilty of choice and consent on nights I told my boyfriend I didn't want to have sex, but then he'd give me the silent treatment, and since I preferred not to be frozen out or to fight (it wasn't worth the fallout or the shame or the retribution), I'd say, "Never mind—I want to."

Sex was the right thing to do. And since women are anyway doomed to please, I'd wear the white flag as a short skirt, cornered into willingness. In no way resisting, I chose to want what I didn't.

Like in *Sixteen Candles*, when Caroline tells the Geek she enjoyed the sex she wasn't conscious for. That was her choice, her cognitive dissonance, her knowing that her thoughts and her words didn't agree, so she pushed agreement through her actions, once she was awake. Not to mention that "lying" can be classified as "being nice," and women should, above all, be nice. So I lied; I chose niceness. I said, "I want to."[2]

There's an official Faking Orgasm Scale for Women (FOS) to measure lying about sex and pleasure. Women fake because of "Fear and Insecurity," "Fear of Dysfunction" (women want to have, or to be regarded as having, a bomb-ass pussy), "Altruistic Deceit" (prioritizing a partner's feelings over her own), and "Sexual Adjournment" ("to end sex," or to "end unwanted sex," as though the exit to sex is to abandon ourselves, body and brain, to dishonesty). Among millions of sex studies, a few about female pleasure address altruistic deceit, unearthing that women feign satisfaction (or absence of pain) to satisfy men, that the impulse *to please* is more overwhelming than *to be pleased*. Or pain-free.

You asleep? my boyfriend might ask. *Babe?*

I knew what was next. *Babe?*

I can't now, I said, and with a smile, I apologized. *In a few days?* I bargained.

But you said you would, he argued.

When I would plead, he would plead.

---

2 Women are twice as likely as men to lie, sometimes up to "twice every waking hour," according to a British poll by an insurance company. The poll cited rationales like to "make someone feel better," to "not get in trouble," and because "life is complicated." If I'd been polled, I would've written in my answer: *Because everything I say must be perfect, not truthful, for someone to see I can be perfect*. And I would've added a part two: *To connect—emotionally, genitally, metaphysically—because isn't this what we all want? To be liked? To avoid misunderstanding, which leads to fatal loneliness, and to avoid the unavoidable (heartbreak) by whatever means necessary, by saying anything?*

I will, I swore. *Later. I'm sorry. I'm sore from last time. I'm really sorry. Forever sorry.*

I was at a loss for even the wrong words. So, I tried to sleep.

Can't we try now? Babe?

And he tried.

Don't be mad, he said, as warm semen trickled down my inner thighs, coating and staining them.

Out of all the positions women attempt, "feeling safe" isn't always one. Still, I slept beside him every night until graduation, by choice.

In "Trigger Warning: Breakfast," an anonymous graphic artist writes about cooking her rapist breakfast just the way he liked it the morning after. *If you cook eggs medium well, toast golden brown, and bacon extra crispy, then it isn't rape and didn't ruin your life* is the logic, ingenuity, and self-talk in a rape culture. Social psychologist Shelley E. Taylor says that women under attack will "tend and befriend" rather than "fight or flee"; women have done so for centuries. Scheherazade may be the original, the woman who, aware that the king marries a new virgin every day and beheads her the next morning, exercises a self-saving loophole: storytelling. She narrates *One Thousand and One Nights*, and it works—he's happy; she lives; they live together happily.

Rather than fight, women blabber and take care. Rather than flee, women anticipate and manage a man's feelings, assess a man's needs and recalibrate. We are guilty of consenting.

He and I never said, "It's over." We allowed postgraduation distance to do its work—or I should say that he emailed me from abroad confessing he'd cheated with four different women while we were together, and I'd worried I had syphilis.

While checking for syphilis, a third gynecologist asked me when I had given birth.

I said, "???????????"

I had never been pregnant.

She said that my cervix was ruptured like a new mother's.

Together we figured out that my boyfriend tore a tear, which must have ripped open the more he had sex with my body.

Your cervix is ruptured, she had said, but she meant *Your boyfriend ruptured your cervix.*[3]

"You'll feel some pressure," she said as she resumed the exam. But I didn't feel a thing, not for many years.

Like anyone, my boyfriend was born, he grew up, he was sucked into the milieu that doesn't listen to women and will tune out any cue of being told something they don't want to hear. My boyfriend came to me straight from the locker room, but I don't mean he was in a locker room—I mean the locker room is *in him*.

"What's a little locker room talk, after all?" former president [BLEEP] once asked.

Worst-case scenario? Incels, or involuntary celibates, are a tribe of white, heterosexual, sex-starved male supremacists who sometimes go on shooting sprees to punish women for saying no to them. As if the worst act a woman can commit is to say no (rude, unexpected) or to weep (manipulative, emotional terrorism), while the worst act a man can commit is mass murder, because violence is his only means of expression. To start somewhere: Columbine High School—the deadliest high school massacre in American history at the time and nine miles away from my middle school. On April 20, 1999, the doors of my eighth-grade science classroom locked us inside; we were

---

3 My educated guess, putting my college degree to use, is that, in part, I rarely if ever reached the state of sexual excitement, comfort, and nonpanic that would've prompted my brain to tell my vagina to elongate and my cervix to lift, which is what the brain and vagina and cervix do when aroused, to accommodate [whatever your pleasure].

in "lockdown," a term we hadn't heard until two guys at a nearby high school felt rejected and murdered twelve of their peers and one teacher. Incels Wiki (est. 2018) reports that shooter Eric Harris called himself an incel, and in his final journal entry wrote, "Right now I'm trying to get fucked and trying to finish off these time bombs. . . . Why the fuck cant [sic] I get any? I mean, I'm nice and considerate and all that shit, but nooooo. I think I try to [sic] hard."

Subsequent nice and considerate and unfucked mass shooters felt inspired by Harris and Dylan Klebold. In an act of "War on Women" for "depriving me of sex," twenty-two-year-old Elliot Rodger murdered six people and injured fourteen in 2014 in Isla Vista, California, and he wrote in a 141-page manifesto that surfaced online in the aftermath, "Those girls deserved to be dumped in boiling water for the crime of not giving me the attention and adoration I so rightfully deserve!" Attention and adoration that our culture—which dumps make-believe girls in boiling water and represents women as servants to male lust—promises men. If I listed all the domestic terrorists who imitated Harris, Klebold, and Rodger—boys and men who are made murderers by the circumstances women have put them in—I'd never stop, if only because they keep going.

Incels aren't outliers. Many men[4] do not like or expect to hear no, so many women don't say no. A woman who dates men is in that War on Women, and it's called femicide, a hate crime in which women are murdered because they are women (every day in America three women on average are murdered, and almost one-third are killed by an intimate partner; specifically, more than an estimated one thousand wives, girlfriends, exes, and love interests are murdered annually for telling men no). Ninety-eight percent of mass shootings since 1966 have been committed by men, usually by white men, often after

---

4 BUT NOT ALL MEN.

women rejected them romantically.[5] Which makes "no" the hardest word. Especially when refusal and failing to speak up are ways of asking for it. And when "no" has translations, like "convince me" and "try harder" and "I don't mean what I say" and "I want to but just can't vocalize it" and "you know what I want better than I do."

Author and sociologist Tressie McMillan Cottom, in her collection *Thick*, adds that Black girls never have "no": "If one is 'ready' for what a man wants from her, then by merely existing she has consented to his treatment of her. Puberty becomes permission."

"No" expires at the back of women's throats on purpose. The disease to please is our birth defect, and then we're brought up to be obliging, reassuring, and noncombative. To refuse is "demanding," "hostile," and "hideous," and we should not hurt someone else's feelings by expressing our own. Our empathy also alerts us to the adverse effects "no" may have on another person, and the more important someone is to us, the tougher it is to pronounce "no." Love itself can exorcise "no" from any woman's vocabulary.

And even if we do say no, some people don't hear it and instead hear something that sounds *crazy, psycho,* and *bitchy*.

When "no" is unavailable—or isn't allowed or produces a noise that offends men's ears—something has to fill its void. With other men, in place of "no," I've said, "Ha ha ha ha ha" or "Thank you, I'm sorry, but I'm not up for another drink, I'm so sorry," only to come back from the bathroom to find another and to drink it because it's inexcusable to not drink purchased drinks. The first man to take it too far ripped off my pants when I wasn't looking, and I said, "Wait, I have a tampon in." (I didn't.) Samantha Gailey, at age thirteen and naked

---

5 All statistics cited here are underestimates. More incidents go unreported because dead women and girls can't speak and because survivors don't want to be "victims" and because shame and fear can silence anyone about anything.

in Roman Polanski's Jacuzzi, said she had asthma (she didn't) and wanted to go home for her inhaler.[6] I've pretended periods, fake boyfriends, and diarrhea rather than say no. After a guy I met on Hinge asked me, "What scares you?" and after I said, "Karaoke," and after he dragged me, literally, to a karaoke bar, I managed to say, "There's my subway stop," before he threw me (passionately) against a gate so hard it flew open, and I fell backward on concrete, and he fell on top of me, à la a rom-com based on an Ayn Rand novel.

"What is rape culture?" the original ghostbuster Bill Murray asked me when I worked as a writers' assistant for an award show in which he was being honored. He had lived his entire life without having to know. Bill (he'd asked me to call him Bill) and I and two friends were drinking whiskey in the restaurant of a Four Seasons, and I was talking about rape culture to impress him. He was seated across from me but moved to sit next to me to listen to me explain, "In your films, the women are only and always your love interests." He held my hand and didn't argue, and it would've been the best date if it had been a date. After infinity drinks he asked to swipe through my Tinder, and he messaged strangers that I was too good for them. We drank until last call, until the fluorescent lights gave away everyone's age. At the elevators, Bill Murray picked me up off the floor. My two friends grabbed my feet, and the three pulled and debated where I was going: to his room with him or to mine without him. The next morning I woke up next to the two friends who would not let me say yes to a celebrity.[7]

---

6 Jeffrey Toobin (*Jeffrey Toobin*) reported in the *New Yorker* that Samantha testified she had further explained to Polanski, "'I had to get out because of the warm air and the cold air or something like that.'" Toobin continued, "Polanski wrote [in his memoir] that 'she said she'd stupidly left her medication at home.' He encouraged her to join him in [Jack] Nicholson's swimming pool instead, which she did. After a few moments, she left the pool and went inside to the bathroom."

7 The woman who had my job before me worked on the show the year Bill Cosby was honored. (The honor was taken away after he was convicted of sexual assault in 2018.)

As Anne Carson writes in "The Glass Essay," "Girls are cruelest to themselves."

Why didn't I just say no? That's the question everyone asks.

And it's a really good question.

She told me, "Cosby was walking with some show people, and I was alone walking toward him. He saw me and said, 'Hello,' excitedly and that he missed me. Then he hugged me and pressed his cheek to mine and whispered, 'I miss you,' in my ear. I said, 'I miss you, too,' though I'd never been introduced to him or met him." She said she missed Bill Cosby because she didn't know what else to say.

7

EMPERORS WITHOUT CLOTHES

My plan was to graduate college with a degree in English literature and a dual minor in creative writing and women and gender studies, to forget college boyfriends and unbirthed babies, and to move to San Francisco to work for free for white male geniuses lacking boundaries in independent publishing and see where the sausage was fictionalized.

Although I studied women in school, to me and everyone else the best voice was male and white, and genius was gendered. Growing up I'd named my pillows after dead/old/older literate men with big type-writers, and I practiced conversing. And if any male authors had had a church, I would've worshipped there.

Through my stepbrother's wife's brother's now ex-girlfriend, the summer I graduated I got an internship at a tutoring center across the street from an independent publishing house. And through Craigslist, I got a bedroom in a converted two-bedroom apartment in Cole Valley, near Twin Peaks and a few blocks from the Upper Haight, up many hills.

I interned two days a week. My main responsibilities were to take out the trash and improve youth literacy. It was not hard to be the best intern. In the back offices I helped organize writing workshops by filling in spreadsheets, which paid in experience and exposure (to the literati, to being a part of something, to Big Names who knew mine for one second).

To support my intern habit I applied for other jobs—I bottled perfume for a perfumer, fact-checked travel guides for places I hadn't been, modeled SEE eyewear for free pairs, applied kids' makeup for a Learning Channel commercial that I didn't see because no one in San Francisco owned televisions—and at one point had seven simultaneously.

I hadn't lived in a city before, and the city smelled, and I smelled of the city. I was a bit lost in a different way during each moment of every day—until a blessed afternoon when the workshops coordinator mentioned my favorite anthology, which (I didn't know) was compiled at the independent publishing house across the street. I'd bought the first and second volumes from my college bookstore and read both cover to cover, awed, because each page delivered on the promise of art and celebrated the possibilities of language: to heighten feelings and to give the brain a boner.

"May I sit in on an editorial meeting?" I asked the workshops coordinator.

He said yes, and I peed a little.

Weeks passed.

Then the editor of the anthology organized a meeting with my intern class that consisted of ten or so college students and recent college graduates. We sat at a big table in the tutoring center, and he asked everyone to go around and introduce themselves, say where they went to college, why they care about youth literacy, and how they pay rent.

During my turn I described my sublet bedroom. "It's separated from my roommate's by a glass door, and she talks to me through the wall like there's no wall at all."

The editor laughed, and a million angels got their wings as the introductions finished, and the editor asked which intern had hoped to attend the editorial meeting for the anthology. We all raised our hands.

A few of us showed up. Walking into the independent publishing house across the street was as awkward as entering a party, early, uninvited. The staff—with their remarkable cool and curiosity about how syntax might show a reader what it's like to be alive—must have wondered what I, an intern from across the street, was doing there. I felt too seen in the way no one noticed me at all.

I walked past their desks and down the stairs to the basement, which looked like a house basement, with two tan suede couches, a drum set, and bookshelves filled with literary journals and magazines (I actually ran my fingers along the spines), and an oriental rug that knew the shoes of writers famous in my heart.

The selection committee was comprised of the editor and a group of local high school students. The first half of the meeting we read—fiction, nonfiction, comics, etc., in the most prestigious and popular literary journals, magazines, websites, and books—and the second half we discussed what we read and argued for what we read to be considered for the anthology. The meeting lasted a couple hours, only a couple hours, but what a couple of hours.

"How would you improve meetings?" the editor asked the interns who showed.

I spoke first. "You could use more lamps."

"Okay. What else?"

We hadn't discussed or argued for anything written by women. So far the most prestigious and popular literary journals and magazines and websites published mostly white men and were edited by same. I said as much, and also said—I said this out loud—"No vagina left behind in 2008."

He laughed. That's how easy it was to win the day.

The conversation foreshadowed a Real Job in the Real World as a Real Adult, and since I was in my very early twenties and anything was probable, I wrote a three-page proposal for a full-time managing editorial position working on the best-selling American anthology. (In fact, the woman whose perfume I bottled told me to do this—I would not have thought of it on my own.) Sometimes all a woman has to do is ask. And then a man will do math in front of her to show her that what she's asking is a joke. He could offer me the job for a third of the salary I proposed and would give me other projects to make up a living wage.

Every time the editor asked if I knew how to do something, I said, "Yes." Even though almost every time he asked if I knew how to do something, I had no idea how to do it.

"Do you know how to proofread?" he asked.

Nope. "Yes," I said aloud.

"Do you how to design books?"

Not at all. "Yes," I said.

"Do you know what 'stet' means?"

What? No. "Of course."

What I did know was that the editor could not stand the word "no," nor could he stand critics; he said so in an infamous interview. He said "no" was for wimps and pussies, which cemented my distaste for "no" in the workplace, as well as my distaste for being a critic and for criticizing—men especially, him specifically.

The one year I lasted in the independent publishing house—as a managing editor, an assistant editor, an associate editor, a research coordinator, a designer, a proofreader—can be boiled down to one day. The day we moved the desks around.

The business next door closed and left behind several desks. My colleagues (most of whom were men) and I competed to take what we could get, and I couldn't get anything. I'd been sitting at the intern table or the built-in desk under the bookshelves that served as a wall.

"Why don't you sit at the front desk?" the president asked me. "That way you can be around to receive the mail, direct traffic, and field phone calls," she said.

"But I'm an editor," I clarified, as in not a receptionist.

In the end I took the one desk in the basement, next to the Ping-Pong table.

That night, like most nights, the staff left together and locked the doors. Another way to put it: they forgot about me and locked me in the basement. When the door to the basement wouldn't budge, I texted the sole employee who'd given me his number. He replied that he was already settled into a bar, so he texted the publisher who lived nearby.

I'M NOT SCARED, I thought.

The first twenty minutes I looked through the junkyard of first editions in cardboard boxes. The next ten minutes I lay down on one of the couches donated by a best-selling writer and cycled through possible reactions to have when the door was unlocked. The final ten minutes I did lunges.

Then there was a jangle of keys and the publisher at the top of the stairs.

"Sup," I think I said, so cool, so chill, so not mad.

The publisher's face looked more annoyed to unlock the basement door at nine p.m. than my face looked annoyed to be locked in it. Of course I wanted, as women are charged with wanting, to make a scene. But "feminine rebellion was visible, if at all, as personal pathology," as Ann Douglas sums it up in the introduction to *Minor Characters*, Joyce Johnson's memoir about the women poets who dated the Beat poets.[1]

Other days I'd wanted to make other scenes, but why would I make a scene about the basketball games in the middle of the work day that only the male editors played, or about uneven publishing ratios and male writers taking up almost every page?

---

1 I published this line in an essay on silencing for an online magazine, which was fact-checked by a male fact-checker, and in a meta-move, he flagged it as wrong facts. He corrected me: Johnson is a "novelist," and the book is about something else. But I had read the book and studied it in grad school, where Johnson—a memoirist, poet, and novelist—taught me.

For the anthology I read everything published that year to find the best of it, and in the basement I maintained a vast library of mostly male writers. (Print was dying, sure, but certain voices were deader than others.) There was fiction by male authors who put on haloes before they wrote and drew a crowd to watch them think. There were reissued classics by male authors about men and for everyone, required reading in grade school and college. There were too-long books by male authors who wrote women into death or marriage and described them thusly: *She's beautiful but can't see it. She's not like other girls her age. She's evil/psychotic/heaven. [Extremely detailed yet medically impossible description of breasts.] [Extremely elaborate metaphors of how impossibly thin/pure/wanton she is.] [Extremely explicit, lyrical, impossible love-making scene.]* There was nonfiction by white male authors who wrote as "we" and wrote for all but actually wrote to and for each other, wrote also about humanity without questioning their own, and imbued themselves with the sovereignty to organize and influence public opinion and feeling.

These men, I thought, *must not go to sleep hearing a voice repeat,* "Can't."

What must it be like to not hear that voice?

It got very *The Devil Wears Prada* in the independent publishing house. The editor expected his employees to mirror his writing style, and we weren't to use exclamation points, italics, or all caps. Writing could not be "cute"; "cute" was "the kiss of death." There is a single space after a period, and whether it was a good day at work or a bad one depended on that single space. Typos, misspellings, errors were capital offenses, or so it seemed.

As part of my job, which was my living and my life, I wrote in his voice, in his syntax, in his POV, with his rules that I adopted as my own because not doing so gave me a little headache, and because he piped through my every sentence (still, right now), and shouted in my ear (literally, figuratively) patriarchal copyedits, policing my writing to police my ego. I abided, and his grammar lent me his superiority over fools who ended sentences with prepositions—and if I didn't write like him, then the writing was amoral, and I should be fitted with the Scold's Bridle.[2]

I'd do as I was asked and write in language that sterilized and was hostile to my own, and I'd do it until it felt innate and wrong to do otherwise, until it was a kind of faith I kept that contained me.[3]

"We're not reinventing the wheel," the editor would say to me in a raised voice whenever I wasted his time with a mistake.

Five years later the editor, who is also an author, made minor headlines for allegedly using a woman's story as his own. He wrote a novel about social media that received a critical orgasm, and a woman writer claimed his novel appropriated her memoir (published one year prior) about working at Facebook. She posted on Medium noting specific parallels on the plot and paragraph level, and called out the difference in critical reception. She wrote, "Society makes assumptions about women that make us guilty by default: our work is supposedly minor, less valuable, and limited to the personal, where the work of a white man is presumed to be 'universal,' 'essential,' and relevant to all." In an interview on the site Jezebel the memoirist mentioned the bright side of the alleged plagiarism (which the editor/author denied):

---

2 A medieval face mask and iron cage for the woman who nagged, gossiped, talked back, or talked too much, with a bridle that locked onto her head and a piece of metal with spikes that went into her mouth so that every time her tongue moved it'd be lacerated. This could be used in the home (there was a hook by the fireplace) or portably in town.
3 Women writing as per their male overlords is so common it's cliché. In the 2015 *New York Times Magazine* feature "The Women of Hollywood Speak Out," Maureen Dowd interviewed over one hundred women and men in every level of Hollywood about its gender disparity. "Female writers," Dowd wrote, "told me they are used to hearing things like 'Can you insert a rape scene here?' or 'Can they go to a strip club here?'" from male executives who enlist women to help them tell the stories about women that they want to tell. Male characters will go to a strip club, and we can insert a rape scene—if we want to work and not get in trouble or be accused of personal pathology.

it illuminated "how the industry is working to suppress women's writing and exalt men." Posting on Medium, she said, was less about the novelist and what he did (or didn't do) than about bias and the assumption that her book "was not important, because how could a woman writing about technology be important?"[4]

One month before the anthology went to the publisher, the "Yes" and "Maybe" pile had only a few pieces by women. I called a special weekend morning meeting to scour over fifty publications for more.

The issue was that men wrote "the best." Men wrote on Big Topics, including but never limited to technology, alcoholism, numbers, politicals, smartscience, sportsball, war, raped women, the ways we live now, and everything that's "serious" and thus outside a woman's wheelhouse, above the glassed ceiling's pay grade.

Men wrote "fiction," while women wrote "chick lit" (or "thinly veiled nonfiction," because women have no imagination). Men's writing was "writing," and women's writing was "women's writing." Men wrote "nonfiction," and women wrote "women's nonfiction, which is cookbooks." (Wikipedia made this official in 2013 when editors, around 90 percent of whom were male, relocated women writers from the list of "American Novelists" to the subcategory "American Women Novelists," since subgenres are where women's words—their romance fantasies, their musings, their doodles—belong.)

In women's writing, girls and women wrote only about boys and men (and marriage and motherhood) (and sex and gender and trauma) (and midwifery and gardening) (and mood swings and bleeding out one's insides twelve times per year as the potential for human life unsticks from the walls of one's organs) (and weight gain, weight loss, the art of the nag, dating as competitive sport, real-housewiving, divorce, bondage, magic, work/life balance) and oppression, and THAT'S IT.

---

4 The memoirist has since deleted her Medium post.

And when women writers were not doing calligraphy between chores, they were conserving their energy to defend the claims of victims of sexual violence and harassment.

Women further disqualified themselves from the best by writing personal essays—or "cathartic narratives" or "humiliation screeds"—that excluded acclaim, skill, or forte. "The best" was not "confessional" or "raw" or "navel-gazing," which defined women's writing and signaled that women wrote without revision or published diaries or scribbled for the attention, to trade their secrets for affirmation they didn't deserve.[5]

(The weekend morning meeting was actual days before the personal essay boom, sparked by Emily Gould and her cover story in the *New York Times Magazine*, which I alphabetized in our anthology library after staring for many minutes at the cover of a young woman in a spaghetti-string tank top lying on an unmade bed where maybe she wrote or maybe had sex.)

At the independent publishing house (and elsewhere) male writers and male editors sometimes published using female pen names and pen names of writers of color to cover the fact that so few actual women and fewer actual writers of color were published. They weren't being exclusionary—women and people of color just didn't write as well, and also that some men want the truth to be what they invent so they can keep saying whatever they want, believing they know how everybody thinks.

---

5 In *How to Suppress Women's Writing*, Joanna Russ clarifies what the sentence "She wrote it" really means and what it becomes: "*She wrote it but look what she wrote about* becomes *She wrote it, but it's unintelligible / badly constructed / thin / spasmodic / uninteresting, etc.*, a statement by no means identical with *She wrote it, but I can't understand it* (in which case the failure might be with the reader)." Behind it "lies the premise: *What I don't understand doesn't exist*," and Russ compares this to "Sylvia Plath's 'hysteria' which came 'completely out of herself' " and from no one or nothing else.

Writing was the worst if it had a vagina. To one anthology meeting, I handed out photocopies of a short story by Mary Gaitskill to consider for the collection. It contained the word "vagina," and my explicit mission was to leave none of them behind.

But the vibe had shifted. I should not—ever—bring in writing *like that* with *that word*, the editor said to me in front of the committee. He frowned then, and his frown said, *The seat I added for you at the table doesn't mean you can talk about vaginas from where you sit.*

I tried to use my sense of humor—"Remember: no vagina left behind?"—but I was in the double-standard double bind where women in the workplace are placed in time-out for joking.[6]

The editor's scolding segued into a monologue about equality in publishing, about gender parity and how it existed. (This was years before Merriam-Webster threw "mansplaining"[7] into its pages in 2018, after the author Rebecca Solnit first published the essay "Men Explain Things to Me" in 2012.) Was he talking to himself? I made the resting dead face that appears on women when a certified male genius talks all over them.

---

6 A team of researchers conducted the study "Gender and the Evaluation of Humor at Work" and found "when men add humor to a business presentation, observers view them as having higher levels of status (that is, respect or prestige) within the organization, and give them higher performance ratings and leadership capability assessments.... However, when women add the same humor to the same presentation, people view them as having lower levels of status, rate their performance as lower, and consider them less capable as leaders." This team also found that humor can be perceived as "functional" (as a method to connect, unwind, and showcase one's intelligence) or as "disruptive," and that men's humor falls under functional and women's under disruptive. And culturally, for every *Ghostbusters: Women This Time*, there's a feature in the *New York Times* Sunday business section debating (again) whether in Hollywood or life women can be truly funny.

7 Loosely defined by me as *When an ignorant man explains something to a woman who is an expert; usually the explanation begins, "Well, actually . . ." and ends with a heterosexual woman questioning her sexuality.* Example: a man on Twitter explained how a "vulva" is different from a "vagina" to a female gynecologist, and then he mansplained "mansplaining" after being called out as a mansplainer.

Everything is as it should be, he seemed to say (a thought that allows those in power to stay in power). *We've come so far*, he seemed to agree with himself (a saying that relieves anyone of going a far way).[8]

"Really," I said to the editor.

The only practical response was none. I had the receipts, and it was, by then, my millionth rodeo with this same conversation. A man who wore his hair in a bun (and seemed like the type to wear his blond hair in dreadlocks) once told me that systemic inequality is *just people's feelings*, as in *certain people feel discriminated against*, which is *those certain people's problem*, and that *we all get to choose our own reality* in a breathtaking fusion of mansplaining, whitesplaining, psychoanalysis, shaman speak, and misogynistic bravado. But discrimination is not subjective, and in 2019 the *Washington Post* reported on a study substantiating that men seldom know, or only pretend to know, what they're talking about, like prophets with nothing to say who still say it and still define all meaning.

In my bedroom after work my mind stayed awake drafting what I wished I'd said to the editor. By morning I had an annotated Gloria Steinem anthem that would end sexism, and I'd memorized the dialogue that should have been, dialogue that wouldn't disappoint the

---

8 Many progressive people believe that everything is as it should be and that we've come so far; "the public's widely claimed support for gender equality is undermined by contrasting beliefs that gender equality has gone far enough," according to *The Missing Perspectives of Women in News*, a 2020 report "on women's under-representation in news media; on their continual marginalization in news coverage and on the under-reported issues of gender equality." There's "widespread gender blindness," and the "more accepting the public is of the status quo for women, the less driven people in power and journalists are to prioritize gender equality issues."

About medical research, a "more novel approach to addressing the problem of female under-representation...is simply to claim that there is no problem, and women are represented just fine," jokes Caroline Criado Perez in *Invisible Women* and gives as an example a paper "published in the *British Journal of Pharmacology* entitled 'Gender differences in clinical registration trials: is there a real problem?'" in which "the all-male-authored paper concluded that, no, the problem was not 'real.'"

suffragettes—something like *"In my experience, everyone..." is a slogan of institutional sexism and racism that sugarcoats and denies people's realities as well as empirical realities, until sexism and racism seem less like sexism and racism—*

but by the time I arrived to work, I'd returned to understanding where the editor was coming from.

There is no greater defender of a man than the woman he dismisses. In my boss's defense, since men leave the womb being listened to, they're set up to bomb at empathy (those who receive all of it have nothing to give). How can any male editor recognize that he, his body, and his voice are not the center of the universe when most everything affirms that they are and should be? If another's experience or perspective doesn't square with his own, or it lies beyond his or implicates him and his reality, or it grosses him out, then to uphold his own truth and innocence, he should reject the truth and innocence of others. He should banish the language and stories he doesn't understand. Even good men who want to change the world still imagine themselves in charge of it, determining who has an authentic point of view while invalidating those who don't.

Then the invalidated write the Next Great American Nothing because how do you write a book that's been burned before you've drafted it?

I started seeing my first psychiatrist, a Barbra Streisand doppelgänger who prescribed Prozac and Xanax for working for men in independent publishing. Once I shared a car to a donation-based meditation center and spent hours learning how to meditate and have compassion. (During the lunchtime Q & A, I asked, "How do I be compassionate toward compassionate people who are not compassionate to me?" I couldn't hear the answer over the audience laughter.) But the pills and meditation didn't make the job any easier.

The editor and I had an unspoken, unpaid agreement that I was "on call" for him. I felt safe from the phone and his criticism only when he slept. If he called and I didn't answer, or if FedEx closed earlier than when he thought it should close, then he would speak to me in the tone of a disappointed dad using the language of an abusive dad.

One weekend I wasn't working because it was the weekend, and I traveled to St. Louis for a George Clinton / Parliament-Funkadelic concert, and I went without telling him. He called when I was on the tram, but I couldn't pick up, or else he'd hear the automated tram announcer. He called when the plane was boarding, but I couldn't pick up, or else he'd hear my row being called. *You must call back, you idiot,* I heckled myself.

I called back, near-feral with fear—*How would he roast me?*—but he didn't pick up, so I left a message. Since he didn't know I was at the airport, and since every sound around me disclosed an airport, I had to lie, and I didn't plan to say it, didn't mean to, but—

I said I wasn't available, but it came out deranged and as this sentence: "I am flying to Denver to see my mother," someone who sounded like me said, someone in survival mode who would say whatever it took, "who has cancer." At the time of the voicemail she had been in remission for years.

I called my mom and told her everything. She asked for the editor's number. Then she called him and left a voicemail and left a voicemail explaining that she had breast cancer years ago and that her doctors thought it returned but it was a false alarm. (Some forms of disease are hereditary; empathy can be hereditary; lying may be hereditary.)

When he and I did speak, he didn't mention the cancer. As far as he knew my mom had cancer, and he didn't mention it? Somehow I was offended while knowing I'd created the opportunity for my own offense by lying about cancer.

Soon after, my psychiatrist gave me the words for what I had to do.

"May we speak privately?" I asked the editor late one Tuesday after a meeting.

He said we should speak in his car.

He drove without purpose as I spoke, reciting the lines I'd rehearsed in therapy. "This job is not a fit for me."

"Are you sure?" he asked.

I wasn't, but I said, "Yes."

He asked what was wrong with me, then suggested what it might be. "Are you having boyfriend or girlfriend problems?" Yes, always, but how was it relevant?

"This job just isn't a fit for me," I repeated as it was the only line I had prepared.

"Well, I was going to fire you anyway," he said.

The rest I remember like this: I remember that the car stopped, either at a red light or because he'd pulled over, and that he pounded the steering wheel. *I hate what an asshole you turn me into*, I remember he said. I remember he used the platitude "You're making the biggest mistake of your life," though I don't remember if he said "life" or "career." I remember he went on and on, about my life and his. About his life I remember thinking, *I read the book. My friend gave me an inscribed copy for my eighteenth birthday, and if ever I were sworn into office, I would've sworn my oath on that book.* He told me that I would regret this, that I wouldn't work in this town again, that no one else he'd employed had ever quit, and that he could and did do my job when he was my age with no difficulty and under more duress.

He said it, and it was true: I hated what an asshole I turned him into. I'd made the biggest mistake. What *was* wrong with me? I was always having problems. I did regret it. I didn't work in that town again (for a while). Like everyone else, I should not have quit. Like him, I should be more like him.

If men are right, and they are, automatically, right, then I shouldn't feel how I feel, and I should not have spoken up about how I feel, I said to myself with the ideas he and other men had put into my head that then I thought and repeated. So, after many unemployed months, I wrote the editor a handwritten letter of apology, of atonement. "It was my first job," I explained, as if that explained everything. I hand-delivered it, along with his favorite food, a loaf of Jewish rye bread.

He was in his office, which didn't have a door, and we sat facing each other. He asked what I'd been up to.

Taking benzodiazepines. Watching movies like Cannibal Holocaust. But I said, "Writing."

"About what, if you don't mind me asking?"

"A short story I started in college about a lesbian who drowns herself in a bathtub."

"Are you," he began, lowering his voice, "suicidal?"

Maybe when I said "short story," which is fiction, which he knows, he heard "personal essay." Or maybe he asked because his friend David Foster Wallace had recently died by suicide.

"It's hard to be out of a job, I guess. If that's what you're asking. I guess I am." I'd felt so obliged to tell him what I thought he wanted to hear that I agreed to be suicidal, to admit that I regretted leaving and wanted to die having left.

I was not suicidal, not then. My voice just said these things and had taken on a life of its own.

This was just the shit that happened, so no one put it in writing. I tried to put it in writing—tried to craft a piece of such wit, profundity, and butane that publishing as we knew it would go up in smoke, and all literate people everywhere would pass through the mind-heart-soul of an award-deserving woman writer who'd Found Her Voice to arrange the broken heart into prose that healed it—

But friends, colleagues, mentors, agents, and academic faculty reminded me:

1. I'd be defined by writing about it, and nothing else I said, ever again, would matter.
2. The writing would be gossip, not art.

3. I'd be working from behind my oppression. "Women must work from behind their oppression," says Dick in the adaptation of *I Love Dick* about why women's art isn't art. (But didn't everyone know that the oppressed can't think about anything other than their oppression and their oppressors?)

4. In "spite of a vast literature documenting the phenomena of psychological trauma, debate still centers on the basic question of whether these phenomena are credible and real," writes psychiatrist Judith Herman in *Trauma and Recovery*; enough said.

5. Whatever I wrote and however I wrote it, it would come off as vindictive, and I'd lose opportunities and income, and no one would network with me, and at events people would avoid *that crazy psycho bitch who's obsessed over this one thing and who will talk to someone* once then *#MeToo him on Twitter on his wedding day.*

6. My subject is a great man. A philanthropist. A thought-shaper. Renowned. "And who are you?" another male writer asked me in another conversation about not writing about it. We were in a San Francisco bar decorated in red velvet with hanging portraits of buxom women.

And who are you? "I am twenty-three years old," I answered, ten years later. What was the fortysomething man's excuse? That he is (rich enough to be) a philanthropist? By asking me who I was, did the other writer mean to say that no one would believe me, a woman in her twenties, one year out of college, who wasn't a philanthropist? Did male genius both eclipse and justify a young, selfish nobody's suffering and well-being? Was this a patriarchal word problem in which the good cancels the bad? Should I view men in the opposite way they viewed me and overlook their flaws to appreciate their intentions?

7. For a long time, up to and including now, I thought that what had happened, how he acted, was my fault.

8. The editor would say that what had happened had not happened. I remember he told me that no one had a better memory than his—okay, but a girl never forgets her first time looking up the definition of "gaslighting."

9. I'd expose him; did I really want to expose him? No. I wanted to please him, this adult man, and all men, and only then could I be happy.

10. Perhaps he was doing me a favor, making me great how horses are made great, as Mary Gaitskill describes in her novel *The Mare*: "You make a horse great by making it feel like shit. Because it knows it is not shit and it will turn itself inside out to prove it to you."

11. None of what he did, at least to me, was criminal, so there was no real story.

I kept working for men like the editor and for his friends, and rather than get better at standing up for myself, I got better at putting up with them. At acclimating. At expecting abuse and discrimination, and at tolerating it. At reflexively asking directions to the nearest stake where I may be immolated. Because enduring misogyny is like boiling a frog—if you put a woman in lukewarm water and bring it to a boil gradually, then the woman will cook to death without protest.

A year later, in January 2009, I emailed a local San Francisco author about his new online literary magazine. He replied asking if I wanted to volunteer. Four years later I was still volunteering for him when, at a mutual friend's book party in New York in 2013, he told me that I would, one day, "take him down." Five thoughts banged into my mind: *(1) He thinks the worst of me. (2) So he admits he's done things to me and to others worthy of a public takedown. (3) He knows I am so desperately hurt that I would betray him. (4) How much dirt does he think I have? (5) This is why I shouldn't go to parties.*

"I'll show you!" began the imaginary one-sided conversation I had with him later that night when I was alone in my apartment. "I'll never say anything to anyone! About anything!"

I didn't say anything to anyone about how he'd keep his hand in my back pocket at literary events or that he'd ask me to take naps with him or would yell at me in public or wear me down until I dropped whatever I was doing to spend time with him. And I didn't say anything about this:

The site started a monthly book club, and in its first year, to balance the gender ratio of authors, we needed a book by a woman for November. The online literary magazine founder couldn't find one that would be a fit. The senior literary editor and I wanted to show off how easy it was to find and to publish one since we found and published writing by women of every age, race, orientation, and style on the site daily. We put a book together in one month, and to publicize the anthology of women's writing, titled *Rumpus Women, Vol. 1*, the online literary magazine founder posted a blog post with photos of himself. He titled the post "How to Hold a Rumpus Woman," and in two photos he held the book with the front cover and the back, and the caption for the photo of the back cover said, "How to hold Rumpus women from behind." My co-editor and I complained. He redid the post with another photo of himself, now with the book in one hand and a sandwich in the other, and the title, "Rumpus Women or a Roast Beef Sandwich? Now You Don't Have to Choose."

"That's when I stopped wanting to tour or promote the book," my co-editor told me. "I'd worried *this*[9] was what I had to endure to make our book happen, and in fact it was."

---

9 By "this," she said that she meant the "unpredictable treatment: heaps of authentic appreciation could flip in an instant to blatant misogyny, disregard, even humiliation.

But I laughed it off because I was cooking to death without protest. And because it was a little too on the nose: a man's blog post promoted a book that gave women a voice, and in promoting it, he took away ours.

I gave up working for men in publishing in San Francisco to work for men in television in New York. For six years I worked as a writers' assistant for an award show that honors comedians and recognizes individuals for their cultural impact through satire and an "uncompromising perspective on social injustice and personal folly." Behind the scenes, everyone in production was white. Those in charge were white male senior citizens. One so-called challenge in booking the show—and this was before the #MeToo movement and Black Lives Matter—was finding one (1) famous female comedian and one (1) famous BIPOC comedian. The white male senior citizens joked about the burden of being woke, inclusive, diverse. The excuse was: it's just so hard to find them. But the formal dilemma was wanting to try, in TV and in publishing (where *women just don't write or publish the best*) and in medicine (where female bodies aren't included in medical research and in medical trials because they're *just too complex and unfathomable*), where women and BIPOC don't have a voice because of a choice, not because they don't exist or aren't funny or don't write or are unfathomable.

At this job I didn't say, "No vagina left behind." I didn't say anything, again and again.

"To date rape!" the executive producer of the award show toasted after the 2011 show, evincing that behind every uneven ratio was a man being creepy.[10]

You never knew if your contribution would result in praise or punishment. And that's saying something, because we were constantly contributing."

10 As one example, the *New York Review of Books*—whose former editor left after the *Review* published an essay by Jian Ghomeshi, who was accused by twenty people of

I'd met him at my first Passover Seder in New York. He was my friend's dad, and I told him I'd like to work for him for free, which was how I applied for jobs.[11]

"Where's that cunt with ears?" he'd ask regularly about a woman, as a joke, since he was a "comedian" who believed comedians can and should monologue with immunity and a laugh track (every time he said it, and he said it a lot, I was that laugh track). We also worked from his home, from his bedroom, just the two of us, and he'd pee with the bathroom door open. He was from a different generation, the Cuomo generation, and like former governor Andrew Cuomo, he kissed me to say hello and goodbye—and what in the world was there to say? *Don't celebrate by toasting to date rape. Don't kiss employees or call them cunts. Close and lock the bathroom door while you urinate.* Except saying that would make each situation uncomfortable, and even though I was uncomfortable, I'm much more comfortable with that.

---

sexual assault and was later acquitted of the four charges brought against him—"had the most pronounced gender disparity" in 2017 with "23.3 percent of published writers who are women," per VIDA: Women in Literary Arts' annual "VIDA Count."

11 How does a woman ask for money? She doesn't. I was a believer in the gender pay gap, in which a woman's work is unpaid or underpaid (women in 2010 earned 77 percent of what men earned, and the average working woman will lose more than $530,000 in her lifetime). Giving me work seemed to be a favor and a leap of faith, then subject to final review. The editor had verbally promised me certain fees for certain projects, to be paid after the fact, after I reminded him and checked in with him and hounded him, and I remember being paid less than we agreed, at least once, because supposedly I'd performed worse than he expected. A former colleague told me about her experience getting paid at the independent publishing house: "I had to argue, beg, cajole, irritate, and threaten leadership to get a check that they'd verbally committed to giving me months prior. Our office embodied a rampant repressive conceit (about the sanctity of an unpaid internship or underpaid position at a lauded institution that promotes privilege as it sidelines those less well-connected): if you can afford to work for free or for less than a living wage, then your payment is being a part of our name-brand; you're welcome."

*   *   *

"Let's have sex," another producer of the award show said to me at a colleague's open-bar karaoke birthday party.

"But," I began, "you have a wife and a child." The most polite defense I could manage to ward him off but not piss him off.

"It's okay," he said, "the kid's adopted."

He helped himself to a handful of my butt and said next, "You can have any writing job you want" on the other shows he produced. "Like," he proposed, "writing for Rachel Dratch."

Was he—a married coworker with an adopted kid—trying to seduce me with promises of writing for Rachel Dratch? I didn't ask, and we did not have sex, and I didn't follow up. I ended our conversation by fleeing into a cab instead of ordering an Uber or Lyft, since both were under investigation for thousands of reports of sexual assault.

In 2017, Rebecca Traister wrote that the #MeToo movement isn't (just) about sex; it's about work and gender inequality, which "explains why women are *vulnerable* to harassment before they are even harassed."

The funny man Oscar Wilde once said, "Everything in the world is about sex—except sex. Sex is about power." Laughter, I'd learn (from the award show; from the independent publishing house, which runs a popular humor site; from editing a humor column;[12] from doing improv[13]), is also about power; it's a sound of surprise, which is a sign

---

12 I started the column after I submitted humor writing, and I was rejected—I mean "it," the writing, was rejected—and then rejected again, and instead of taking it personally, I counted the female contributors at humor publications and found a 1:4 ratio of women to men, at best. I counted since I was in the tradition of collecting receipts that showed systemic sexism overriding personal failure.

13 In 2012 I graduated from the Upright Citizens Brigade Improvisational and Sketch Comedy Training Center—the only accredited improv and sketch comedy school in the country. Improv's core philosophy of "Yes, and" would be a utopian practice if only

of handing over control and status to whoever makes you laugh or laughs at you.

"I don't remember where I first heard this simple description of one dramatic contrast between the genders, but it is strikingly accurate: At their core, men are afraid women will laugh at them, while at core, women are afraid men will kill them," writes male author Gavin de Becker in *The Gift of Fear*, a number 1 national best seller. Maybe he first heard the simple description from Margaret Atwood—whom he summed up, popularized, and did not credit—who said it before he did in her collection of essays *Second Words: Selected Critical Prose*:

"Why do men feel threatened by women?" I asked a male friend of mine.... "They're afraid women will laugh at them," he said.... Then I asked some women students in a quickie poetry seminar I was giving, "Why do women feel threatened by men?" "They're afraid of being killed," they said.[14]

---

improv didn't attract so many assailants. UCBT, as the theater is known colloquially, churned out a handful of alleged creeps and was sued by one in August 2016. After multiple women accused Aaron Glaser of rape (which he denied), UCBT investigated and then banned him, and then he sued UCBT for gender discrimination (he sued the place he met his accusers for protecting his potential future accusers). Before this, comedian Jasmine Pierce called Glaser a rapist on social media, and he sued her for "defaming" him. (A former cop once gave me a tip: do not accuse anyone on social media because you can be sued for defamation; accuse assailants properly, which is, unfortunately, through a police report.) Glaser dropped his $38,000,000 suit against Pierce, and a federal district judge dismissed the case against UCBT. A few years later the training center and theater closed in New York.

14 The dichotomy has become an unofficial cultural catchphrase with various versions:

Women fear violation; men fear women will report violation and disregard men's good intentions.

Women fear men, and men fear women's "irrationality."

Women fear exploitation, and men fear humiliation.

Men fear being accused of sexual assault while women fear being sexually assaulted. (My unsolicited advice to men who do not want to be accused of sexual assault: don't sexually assault anyone.)

If men are afraid that women will laugh at them, then consciously or not, men are afraid of what women will express, if we find the voice to express it—as if a woman's expression is violent and should be met with violence if she uses her voice against a man. Maybe, like Samson from the Old Testament who had his strength in his hair, which his lover Delilah cut off, a woman's strength is in her laugh, her voice, and that's why men (as lovers, as employers) try to cut it off.

8

MUST-SEE DEAD-GIRL TV

One of my favorite childhood memories is watching Kelly Taylor in *Beverly Hills, 90210* confess in the "Slumber Party" episode that her first time was date rape. Behind my eyes, which had become spirals, ideas were seeding, like that women lose their virginity via date rape and that damsels must be distressed for their lives to have meaning and that a violated woman is an inevitability and assault is a girl's Bildungsroman, her birthright, her rite of passage, and her tragic flaw.[1]

How saps feel about love, I felt about the television. (And I felt about love how the unplugged must've felt about television, that it's a profound time-suck, energy waster, and indoctrinator.) *Will Joey Potter/ Felicity Porter lose her virginity to Dawson or Pacey/Ben or Noel?* was more important to me than anything, more than my own virginity or thinking of TV as a mass medium of pedagogical socialization or communal hypnosis.

Joan Didion famously admitted she didn't want to be a writer. "I wanted to be an actress. I didn't realize it's the same impulse. It's

---

1 Since I knew I'd be raped, I planned how I'd defend myself: either by lying that I had AIDS or by peeing on the rapist.

make-believe. It's performance. The only difference being that a writer can do it alone."

I was as thirsty for fame as any millennial and thought I might want to be an actress also.

Although my acting résumé was blank (minus *The Vagina Monologues* and the bedroom), I'd clocked more viewing hours than anybody I knew and was offered two roles based on my personality.

First I starred in *30 Rock*, in season 7, episode 8, "My Whole Life Is Thunder," when Liz Lemon, played by the show's creator Tina Fey, is being honored as one of "80 Under 80" in media, and I played "the Usher." I handed Lemon and her plus-one, Jenna Maroney, event programs as they walked in; then I stood in the back of the ballroom the whole time. In a deleted scene, as Jenna runs out of the room after a change in lighting reveals that she is old, I throw the programs in the air as I dive out of her way, improvisationally. The fifteen hours of filming were perfect; I had no notes and no lines, and earned $115 and two meals.

Next I was in the 2012 "metamodern film" *The Comedy*, starring male actor Tim Heidecker from *Tim and Eric* and costarring male actor Eric Wareheim from *Tim and Eric*. I played "Hipster Girl" and wore my own clothes and was in the movie's party scene, where the characters and the stars who played them were blitzed on alcohol and party drugs.

The experiences, like the sets, were antithetical. (The TV set was in Queens, inside a schmaltzy event arena that looked like a discotheque inside of a chandelier museum from the point of view of a Sears portrait studio. The film set was a warehouse party inside a real Brooklyn person's apartment loft.) In *The Comedy*, the male director told the hipster girls and hipster boys to dance even though there was no music (it's added in postproduction) and to appear as if we were talking. "Mime talking, mime listening, mime understanding," we were told as we swayed and twerked to the music in our minds and fake-laughed at each other's nonverbal jokes and spoke only body language.

"I want to dance with a girl!" was one of the male actor's lines. The background actors were to react and respond to whatever was going on around us, like life, so I sidled up to the male actor (I'm an amateur background dancer as well), who then yelled at me, "I SAID A GIRL," and danced off with someone else, a girl.

I was both fake and real offended. I added this to my character's personal history[2] and gave "Hipster Girl" a gender-identity complex and performance anxiety and repressed rage. I was paid $0.

The TV show was created by a woman, directed by a woman, cowritten by a woman, and starred women, and the film was directed by a man, cowritten by three men, and starred so many men. The latter is the usual. In TV, film, and digital programs, women have comprised less than one-third of creators, directors, writers, executive producers, editors, and cinematographers, while tons of shows have employed no women whatsoever. Of the top two hundred fifty grossing films in the past twenty-four years, less than a quarter of all directors, writers, producers, executive producers, editors, and cinematographers have been women. And although people from underrepresented groups make up 42.2 percent of the US population, they have been virtually nonexistent as creators, directors, writers, and executives.

Since cave art, men have been the primary legislators of narrative, the guardians of meaning, and the executors of what we see and hear.[3] As a teleholic I saw with male eyes, heard with male ears, felt through male touch, discerned through the male point of view, and I used male language—so most of what I understood about myself, my body,

---

2 In my mind "the Usher" was a Female Tech Entrepreneur Working Her Way Up in a Male-Dominated Industry but Stuck Moonlighting Handing People Paper. "Hipster Girl" was an Artist Who Was Creatively Blocked and Just Needed to Dance Because She Had Hit the Glass Ceiling in Her Day Job.
3 Well, actually, it was long part of archaeological dogma that men made cave paintings, but it turns out mostly women did. Archaeological evidence came out in 2013 that 75 percent of the oldest-known handprints were left by women's hands.

history, and the future came from a man's mind, and my own senses lost their authority.

Man created, directed, and edited woman in His own ideal image of her. Every day I switched on the television to keep me warm, and I watched men be heroes and women be—well, what? Depended on the men.

Women had a few dead-end roles: ingénue, object that appeared smaller than it was, sex doll with a heartbeat and a mouth that was just for show, and wife and mother (women perform the miracle of birth half a dozen times if they are any good at womanhood). Whatever her role, a woman served as a fun-size looking glass for a man that reflected him double his actual size (women also paraphrased Virginia Woolf).

If or when they talked, women had one conversation only: "Men, men men men men—men men men. Men? Men men: men men men men men ... men. Men men men men men men, men, men! (Men men men men men.) Men—"[4]

Judging from the screen, it seemed that white women accounted for less than 33 percent of the US population and that there were five or so Black women and women of color and LGBTQIA+ people on the planet. White men, ubiquitous, ran the world, and they objectified[5] women for sport.

---

4 A BBC analysis counted Academy Award Best Picture winners from 1929 to 2019, and more than half failed the Bechdel Test.

5 Philosopher Martha Nussbaum has broken down objectification's seven gory elements: Instrumentality (exploiting a human being for its usefulness). Denial of autonomy (divesting a human being of choice). Inertness (stripping a human being of the ability to act). Violability (rejecting a human being's boundaries). Fungibility (regarding a human being as replaceable and interchangeable with any other). Ownership (handling a human being like property to be claimed, bought, sold, given, taken, traded, and trafficked). Denial of subjectivity (neutralizing a human being's interior world until it's emptied of lived experience, sensitivities, wants, tastes, reason). Basically, objectification is a total depersonalization until a woman's physicality eclipses all else—like a spirit, well-being, artistry, and the power of thought and speech.

Unlike a man, a woman objectified herself, since appearance was her primary concern and purpose on earth.

If a woman onscreen was not a spouse or a sidepiece who had forgotten her own personality while volunteering to be a man's soul for him, then her single-lady days were meaningless and cursed, especially on national holidays. (If she said otherwise, she was lying.) A childless woman was purposeless and unhappy, and her choices sparked public debate over why in G-d's name she disrespected the American flag like that.

On any heroine's résumé her special skills were: passive, helpless, decorative, ethereal, receptive, and affected by uncontrolled extreme emotion. "Chores" filled "previous experience," since a heroine had servitude in her heart and couldn't handle a conversation or anything more than a broom, a baby, or men's every desire.

And as I saw on TV and on the set of *The Comedy*, the male gaze[6] and the male ear have a type. Women ranged from blindingly beautiful to secretly beautiful, from thin to skinny, from white to tan. Women stayed girls and sinned by growing up. Women were 8s or above out of 10, and any woman below an 8 should kindly drown herself. And women were freezing since they weren't allowed pants.

Even in my rotation of female-led, female-centered, female-focused shows, heroines were given voice, life, and low-cut tank tops by men who have never heard a woman's thoughts. Mondays were for Aaron Spelling's *Beverly Hills, 90210* and *Melrose Place*, and David E. Kelley's *Ally McBeal*. Tuesdays for Joss Whedon's *Buffy the Vampire Slayer* and Kevin Williamson's *Dawson's Creek* and J. J. Abrams's *Felicity*. (Later, Sundays were for J. J. Abrams's *Alias*.) Wednesdays were for rest.

---

6 The Male Gaze Theory is about perspective and presentation—how we see things and how we are seen. In media we see women from a heterosexual man's vantage point and as the object of his desire. The Male Gaze Theory is the reason why many women hate themselves.

Must-see TV was Thursdays with David Crane and Marta Kauffman's *Friends* and Larry David and Jerry Seinfeld's *Seinfeld* and Michael Crichton's *ER*. Saturday night was reserved for Lorne Michaels's *Saturday Night Live* and Sunday for Darren Star's *Sex and the City*. All the women—however strong, however leading—were hot, tiny, youthful, feminine, next to naked, and the badass ones were a lot like men in women's bodies.[7]

I took the screen as Truth. I was supposed to. I was supposed to according to cultivation theory, a societal and communications framework that says the more hours we spend/waste "living" in the television or screen world, the more likely TV calls dibs on our thoughts and shapes them, stretches them out; and the fine lines between life/art, corn syrup/blood, her/me become so fine to us we lose them.[8] As Rebecca Solnit phrases it, "the elephant in the room is the room itself."

This happened on TV became *this happened to me* based on Laura Mulvey's theory of "screen surrogacy"—I saw myself in the characters I fixated on, identified with, projected onto, and later imitated, deliberately or not. And since men devise and immortalize certain stories, they boss us into their version of how things go, so the narrowest and eeriest interpretations and imitations emerge. Watching anything, I'd look up at the screen and then look down. *Not a temple.* Even as I zoned out, my ego kicked in, and I'd see two things at once: the scene in front of me and myself in it. I'd make it about me. As if I was there and Angel

---

7 About being a "Strong Female Lead," actor and filmmaker Brit Marling writes in the *New York Times*, "I became aware of the narrow specificity of the [Strong Female Lead's] strengths—physical prowess, linear ambition, focused rationality. Masculine modalities of power." Because a woman can be seen if she acts like a man and heard if she talks like one.
8 Some evidence that what happens onscreen bleeds into the area around it: Crockpot's parent company's stock tanked after a malfunctioning and fictional Crockpot sparked a fire that killed a lead character in *This Is Us*. Peloton stock also dropped when the character Mr. Big in the *Sex and the City* reboot *And Just Like That…* died of a heart attack moments after a Peloton ride. More sinisterly, the immigration detention hotline featured in the final season of *Orange Is the New Black* was shut down in real life after the show.

kissing Buffy landed on my tongue. Or more as if I wanted to be Buffy, a vampire slayer who loses her virginity to a man who becomes a monster. Or even more as if I'd scan Buffy's body for imperfections where I had imperfections—upper arms, stomach, thighs, calves, ankles;[9] cellulite, stretch marks, pale skin, acne—and in this way, I believed, I'd know myself, by how I compared and judged myself.

This is the serrated edge of the feedback loop. My screen surrogates were sexy and perfect, and freaks in the sheets and ladies on the streets, so it was dire for me to be sexy-perfect-freak-lady. Because girls who grow up sprayed in the retinas by the male gaze become women created in its image. Because the reality of the white male gaze and ear is our reality.

At twelve years old I knew exactly who to be, and when America Online in the '90s asked me to create a screen name, noting that a "creative screen name is your tool for carving out a unique identity," I typed "VictSectAngl" (or some abbreviation of "Victoria's Secret Angel" until I secured a screen name that wasn't taken as legions of us wanted to abbreviate ourselves this way).

The sound of the modem dialing up and connecting activated my first menstrual cycle, and staring at the TV-size computer screen I saw real estate—to build a second life and inhabit another, better, sexier self, to collude with power dynamics and fulfill a fantasy self that was someone else's fantasy. I created two more screen names: KandiAppls and FemBot00, just counterfeiting myself in the mercenary process of choreographing an online presence and curating myself for love.

For the profiles I invented and edited and upgraded myself—asking myself *Which side of myself should I project, exaggerate, or hide, and will*

---

9 The reviews were in childhood, and they weren't good; I was the type of girl who would be a bet. My dad once called me "Elephant Legs," and one of my best friends in middle school once called me "Pizza Legs" (my skin is so pale that my freckles, moles, veins, bruises, and cuts stand out like toppings on mozzarella), and I haven't worn shorts or swimsuits since seventh grade because "once" was enough.

AOL respond, and to what exactly?—until I was born again. It was my version of a sport. "VictSectAngl" was spiffed up and accessorized: "she" was precocious yet mature, innocent and enlightened, independent but not lonely, strong plus soft, pure though flexible, never pushy or bitchy or bossy. "She" was layer upon layer of persona plopped onto a Build-a-Bear identity, someone who, at times, resembled me only in number of legs. I'd be wearing an acne mask, tweezing the hairs on my legs that I missed shaving, and typing like a woman who did not need to wear or do those things. The better, sexier me lived online, neighboring the betters of every other girl. (I'd even wished that I could audition other people to play me better than I could play myself.) I'm sorry, but should I have had to put together my own self out of what I had to work with? Out of nothing?

Later, in high school, I'd set my alarm for 4:20 a.m., three hours before the 7:20 a.m. bell, to make over myself into a sexy, perfect sixteen-year-old. My routine:

> shower and shave my body so I'd be slick as a seal
> shampoo, blow-dry, straighten, then curl my naturally curly long,
>   brown hair, and spray it until it congealed
> nap
> apply clown makeup
> stick in contacts incompatible with my dry eyes
> squeeze into a different outfit with different high heels every
>   single day.

(Now, in my thirties, I put on mascara before a self-defense class, which I think is full-blown patriarchy?)

All of this was in an act of worship and propitiation to male desire, to love myself in male terms.

Even the fourteenth Dalai Lama believes in male desire. He said his successor could be a woman because the "female biologically has more potential to show affection...and compassion," but he clarified that her "face must be very, very attractive." He added, "Otherwise not of much use." (Four years later he apologized for his comment while doubling down on it.)

I knew what the Dalai Lama knew, that my face must be very, very attractive, otherwise I would not be of much use. I knew it because state-sponsored objectification of girls and women is so prevalent that girls and women self-objectify—we perceive ourselves as bodies only, nothing if not desirable and desired. (The American Psychological Association calls self-objectification a "national epidemic," a disease tied to depression and lower cognitive functioning in girls, and to rock-bottom self-esteem, body-image psychosis, starvation, surgery,[10] and self-harm—a radical thinning of self and suicide of spirit that makes us critical of how we look and of our every action, word, and thought.)

"If [women] spent a tenth of the time thinking about [the world's problems] that they do thinking about their weight, I mean, I think we'd solve all the world's problems in a matter of months," says Susan Molinari, former member of the US House of Representatives in the 2011 documentary *Miss Representation*. I remember during Hillary Clinton's concession speech in 2016, before I cried, before I felt galvanized, before she said, "To all the little girls watching... never doubt that you are valuable and powerful and deserving of every chance and opportunity in the world," I thought, *This is by far her best look. The purple is so flattering.* Why hadn't that mindset died in me? The mindset where a woman's first thought about herself or another woman is weight and appearance and *Do I like what she's wearing? What's my opinion about it?* The mindset where the first words out of a woman's

---

10 Like the "Snapchat dysmorphia" and "Zoom dysmorphia" trends in which women, who would rather mutilate themselves than be themselves, get plastic surgery on their eyes (bigger) and lips (poutier) and labia (smaller), addressing both sets of lips before voice. (The labia—the nether outer lips—is the firework part of the vagina, and reducing it reduces a woman's pleasure, which is in short supply as it is.)

mouth to another woman is—nine times out of ten—about how she looks. What else might we talk about? Revolution?

The internet keeps the mindset alive by making self-objectification more convenient than ever. Now I can compare my face and weight to the attractive faces and weights of my friends and of my exes' new "friends" with limber-sounding names. *These women?* I'll think about the limber ones. *These women you love and not me?* (I decide my exes love/will marry other people by being photographed with them.) *These women who can pull off shorts? These women who are created of the same matter as the universe and as I am, the same light, and are also special, each one, but who are ruining my goddamn life by living theirs?*

"What is self-hatred?" the face-obsessed fourteenth Dalai Lama inquired when he was asked how he contends with "self-hatred." Any American woman could've whipped out blueprints, PowerPoints, and dioramas. I hated myself and other women as much as the world hated us, because when hatred is environmental, anyone can catch it, then perpetuate it, until women are misogynistic masochists with toxic masculinity. The patriarchy almost doesn't even need men. (I SAID ALMOST.)[11]

TV and I went on a break when I was in college and lived in San Francisco. But when I moved to New York to live alone, I subscribed to Netflix. I selected my plan: $7.99 per month for instant and endless TV and films and the neural approximate of anesthesia, of coffee and lullaby, of a good man's love, of ravaged women and dead girls, of what the Taoists call the "ten thousand things" distilled into pure bandwidth. I could cancel anytime, but I never, ever would.

---

11 Thank G-d my puberty predated Instagram, before publicizing one's image became monetizable and we started reducing ourselves to filtered selfies and captions in the shallowest version of "show, don't tell." Prepuberty I wouldn't have known that the "undesirable woman," along with the "crazy psycho bitch," is an invaluable economic fiction that asks everything of a woman and nothing of the men who look at, rate, and make money off her.

Newly available were all the series and movies I'd missed. I could return to my roots, to onscreen women being date-raped and more.

There was a lot to choose from. There was Charlotte King on the *Grey's Anatomy* spin-off *Private Practice*, who was raped by a mental patient, against whom she refuses to file charges. There was Joan Holloway on *Mad Men* who was raped by her fiancé. There was Julia Wicker on *The Magicians* who was raped by a god she summoned to cure her friend's cancer. There was Buffy the Vampire Slayer who was almost raped by a vampire without a soul. At the end of each, hundreds of men's names rolled in the credits (and later crammed award nominations), and I'd need to shower.

We've had millennia of male geniuses show us how to live through art, and what do we know? That we like to watch women chained to a wall.[12] That we enjoy montages of women turning themselves into better prey. That we want female characters' breasts and guts exposed, their bodies invaded, defiled, and butchered as they're stalked, abducted, molested, mutilated, starved, eviscerated, and axed in front of our faces on our screens, on every screen, big and small, in every house and TV-equipped treadmill. That we're fixated on a genre that neatly transmutes sex objects into adorned meat-sacks minus a voice that we can live without. That women relieved of humanity is entertainment. That one trauma isn't enough. That even dead chicks are bangable. That women are created just so we can see them bleed. That these women—the trauma woman, the dead girl, the crazy psycho bitch, the hysterical woman, the silent love interest—are the women of men's dreams.

It is "art" when mostly men—having not endured such experiences—write, direct, produce, and edit scenes of extreme violence against women in session after session of pain karaoke.[13] It is "entertainment"

---

12 "The No. 1 script motif I read is a woman chained to a wall. It's almost de rigueur now," said director Karyn Kusama in 2015.
13 The films *Black Swan*, *Requiem for a Dream*, and *mother!* all feature violence against women and are all directed by the "auteur" Darren Aronofsky.

when women's storied lives are made quiet or tragic as a narrative device. Gender-based violence often ignites plot and fuels dialogue, giving the male characters something to talk about that gets everyone to listen. Like Laura Palmer's rape and murder in *Twin Peaks* (created by Mark Frost and David Lynch, starring Kyle MacLachlan as dreamboat FBI Special Agent Dale Cooper).[14] Assault is also a character-building mechanism. For a male character, avenging an assaulted woman catalyzes the dark knight's metamorphosis into the white knight, and a woman's body spurs his hero's journey, like on *True Detective* (created by Nic Pizzolatto), season 1 and season 2. For a female character, assault initiates her transfiguration, and her pain is romanticized, her unwanted trauma thus neutralized. "You're higher and holier because of the suffering you have been put through," *Downton Abbey*'s (created by Julian Fellowes) Mr. Bates tells Anna once she admits she's been raped by a visiting valet. (I cried at his next line: "I've never been prouder nor loved you more than I love you now at this moment.") Assault also strengthens female characters and is the way a woman defines herself. Russian spy and assassin Elizabeth Jennings on *The Americans* (created by Joe Weisberg) was raped as a teenager by her Soviet trainer, and Claire Underwood on *House of Cards* (created by Beau Willimon) was raped in college and becomes president of the United States. And assault explains why a female character is a detective: Detective Robin Griffin on *Top of the Lake*, who solves a child-rape-ring case, was gang-raped as a teenager on prom night; Detective Olivia Benson on *Law & Order: SVU* was a child of rape; private detective Veronica Mars was raped and solves it herself; private investigator and superhero Jessica Jones was raped repeatedly as a prisoner under mind control.

---

14 This kicked off the "the Dead Girl Show" genre, a category of TV that author Alice Bolin named in her collection *Dead Girls: Essays on Surviving an American Obsession*, which continued with "*Veronica Mars, The Killing, Pretty Little Liars, Top of the Lake, True Detective, How to Get Away with Murder,* and *The Night Of*," half of which were created by women.

Someone, at some point, suggested that I not binge rape. Haha-hahaha. What else was on? The uncountable true crime podcasts and documentaries and docuseries about dead girls who can't tell you what happened to them?

Even content that previewed no ravaged women/dead girls/ abducted teens would end with one or the other or all three. I almost had to laugh. (I SAID ALMOST.) Forget the happy ending—America yearned for the murdered-slut beginning.

"One in eight movies commercially released in 1983 depicted violent acts against women," reported the *New York Times*, "a sharp increase from 1982 when the rate was one movie in 20." By 1989, jour-nalist Susan Faludi noted in *Backlash: The Undeclared War Against American Women* that every woman nominated for a Best Actress Academy Award portrayed a victim except one. By 2016, half of the eight Academy Award Best Picture nominees showed or referenced rape. In 2017 an alleged accused sexual harasser won an Academy Award for Best Actor.[15] In 2019 convicted child-rapist Roman Polanski received the Grand Jury Prize at the Venice International Film Festival for a film about persecuting a wrongfully convicted man.

"I don't really do films set in the modern day because the female characters nearly always get raped," Keira Knightley told *Variety* in an article on her that begins, "Keira Knightley speaks her mind."[16] An IMDb search for the keyword "rape" spits out 6,904 titles, from cult favorites to bad TV to the prestige award-winners that everyone can-not stop talking or thinking about. If I binged *Game of Thrones*, then I'd see fifty acts of rape, as per one statistical analysis. "I joke, mor-bidly," critic Sonia Saraiya wrote in *Salon* in 2015, "that my job title has changed from television critic to 'senior rape correspondent.'"

---

15 The lawsuits were settled out of court.
16 Knightley also admitted this is changing: "I'm suddenly being sent scripts with present-day women who aren't raped in the first five pages and aren't simply there to be the loving girlfriend or wife."

What happens when women's subjugation and suffering are what we like to binge? When we spend our life watching and quoting Quentin Tarantino and Woody Allen et al. in order to ingratiate ourselves with boys who let us watch them play *Mario Kart*?

When Brit Marling moved to L.A. to act, she writes in the *Times* that during the day she ran "from men with chain saws in audition rooms," and at night she ran "from the man I shared a bed with," and she links these scenes with femicide statistics and rape statistics ("One out of every four women in America has been the victim of a rape"). "Our narratives tell us that women are objects and objects are disposable, so we are always objectified and often disposed of."

As a woman objectified, the fine line became finest for me while sick. One night I slid off the toilet seat from sweating and shitting out everything my body had to offer, and was about to call 911 as the apartment ghosts began to emerge from the walls, but first I showered and shaved my legs and armpits and did my twelve-step skincare regimen while I was dying so that I'd die pretty.

I didn't wind up calling 911 or dying that night. But many nights I thought I would, and on those nights I wrote and sent emails to god@gmail.com and mentally outlined my obituary.

Elissa, age thirtysomething, semi-devoted daughter of parents, author of many cries for help, will be solemnly missed by Verizon, Netflix, Hulu, Amazon, YouTube, HBO GO, Seamless, and her offline friends, too few to mention.

And moving eulogies:

Rabbi Foster: "Let us remember Elissa Bassist [pronounced incorrectly] as a woman, an ex-girlfriend, a masochist, thin-souled and a 'pathetic and confused weirdo' who couldn't just say what she meant. But let's take a solemn moment to reflect that in trainwrecks like hers, what Eliza might've written herself, had she been proficient at [checks notes] doing anything, is: 'There's way more to the farce, assholes.'"

Mother: "In sickness and in health, till death do...[interrupted by crowd]...you sure? Not her wedding?"

Netflix: "I was all she had in the world."

And I rehearsed a speech from beyond the grave, to be played after some service:

I just—
I'm sorry—
If I—
... may offer one pull quote, let it be: *Remember me whenever someone mentions "rape culture" or you can't speak up for yourself.*
[Hits laugh track.]

It was so easy to imagine I'd die on nights like these because when you live in a culture obsessed with dead girls and in a society where women are expected to hurt and are not supposed to survive, I couldn't help but picture myself as one of them.

In my first session with a trauma therapist (not covered by insurance), she asked me if I thought I had "vicarious trauma."

"I have literal trauma, thankyouverymuch," I said.

"Yes, but you may have vicarious trauma as well from consuming so much trauma in film, TV, the news."

"Uhh . . ."

"You can be traumatized in ways that either make you repress or remember how you have been traumatized." As if trauma were infectious (it is) and broke the fourth wall (it does).

I'd thought the opposite?

"But at their wormy core, sexualization and sexual force as storytelling mechanisms and aesthetic choices are shortcuts to feeling, and by overusing them, we feel less and less," I said, to dazzle her with how well I knew myself and storytelling mechanisms and how they can give us a taste for violence against women, or at least help us lose our distaste for it, if we're being entertained by it.

This was therapy, and I had to be honest. Content that aestheticized men's power over women and that ritualized predator-prey relationships and that silenced women through violence—these gave me beer goggles. Ugly behaviors appeared attractive and sexism seemed sexy and representation rounded down to reality and to what I expected of and from myself and boys, so before it even happened, I was an accomplice in my own violation, in my own trauma plot.

What's worse is I could relate to men like Brett Kavanaugh. In his opening statement during the Senate hearings on allegations against him of sexual assault, he described his teenage viewing kinks, invoking *Animal House* (a film with a scene of an angel and a devil debating if the character Larry should rape a passed-out sixteen-year-old girl, who later reveals she's thirteen) as an example of and excuse for the "goofy" behavior he emulated at seventeen (indelible in the hippocampus are '80s movies) when he allegedly trapped fifteen-year-old Dr. Christine Blasey Ford in an alleged bedroom, allegedly pinning her down so she couldn't move, allegedly, and allegedly trying to allegedly undress her against (allegedly) her will as he allegedly pressed his alleged hand over her alleged mouth to allegedly smother her alleged cries.

And I could empathize with those in power who agreed that what Kavanaugh did was fine, or that he didn't do what Dr. Christine Blasey Ford said he did, or that he did but so what?

Because vicarious trauma is change through empathy, and it happens on a level deeper than deciding.

A playwright told me how theater, TV, and film are naturally coercive and set off mirror neurons (specialized nerve cells) that mimic the action onstage or onscreen; the movement, sound, and emotion attached to the stylized action rubs off, so watching ballet, we feel what we see, and our muscles may flex, trying to dance, too. Or watching trauma, we may receive an injury without a puncture.

The trauma therapist didn't need to say it. Media affects different people—like the target audience and the targets of that audience—differently. And done enough for shock value, violence becomes more value than shock. And what we dismiss as "superficial distraction" is also an ideological weapon of mass (self-)destruction.

This was all part of the disbelief I suspended as a viewer.

But not as a background actor. When the shoot for *The Comedy* was over and I had to let go of "Hipster Girl" and the fake offense and the fake rage at being objectified and disposed of, I couldn't. Because although it was fake, it wasn't fake. My feelings about it and my reaction were real, and out of everything, the fact that it was fake registered the least.

The documentary *Miss Representation* shows how far suspended disbelief (to "temporarily allow oneself to believe something that isn't true, especially in order to enjoy a work of fiction") extends in real life, particularly in the transmission of sexism and its impact on the number of women in political office. Who wants to vote into public office a shrill wife or voiceless Whore #7 or a welfare queen or a servant or a belly dancer or a terrorist? (But a man named Brett who has been accused of multiple sexual assaults, and was appointed by another man accused of multiple sexual assaults—and who sobbed-shrieked "I LIKE BEER" in front of our nation—may become a United States Supreme Court justice and adjudicate sexual assault for the country until he dies or retires because he has experience.)[17]

---

17 And his alleged victim must move four times and start a GoFundMe to afford physical protection and security for her and her family, whom she can't see because it endangers them. (Dr. Ford donated all remaining GoFundMe funds to organizations that support sexual assault survivors.)

Entertainment is an institution like any other, in a direct relationship with other institutions, such that what our doctors watch on the couch affects how they manage pain on the exam table, which is due, in part, to "controlling images"—professor Patricia Hill Collins's theory that stereotypes, specifically of Black women flattened into caricatures, reproduce systemic inequality. Controlling images control us; they operate like a politicized cultivation theory or an almost supernatural force that conspire in discrimination by standardizing social hierarchy through oversimplistic representation.[18] These simplified images, like objectification, make a person less than human without visual effects. A stereotype is a sight to be seen and not heard and is not worth anyone's empathy or vote or news story. A stereotype can't speak for herself because others do that for her. A stereotype is a cross between flesh and a free sample, an outlet for dick, a joke, unable to hurt or heal. And because a stereotype is a thing, not a person, she's easier to touch, easier to harm, easier to forget.

"What is art but an expression of how we all live and feel?" asks editor and author Jessa Crispin in her foreword to *How to Suppress Women's Writing*. Art "is not separate from life, it is not frivolous or decadent, it is an articulation of our souls. And if our souls are sick due to unexamined racism, misogyny, or homophobia, then looking at and criticizing art is another way of looking directly at and diagnosing our souls."

---

18 Controlling images also explain why a deviant becomes a mascot, like the serial killer known as "Buffalo Bill" in *Silence of the Lambs*. In the film, Buffalo Bill kills and skins fat women for his "woman suit," which will complete his "transformation" into one—a scenario that began a real-world anti-trans legacy. Trans activist and actor Jen Richards stars in the *Lambs* TV spinoff *Clarice* as an FBI informant, and she spoke about Bill's representation at a premiere event for *Clarice*: "Right prior to my coming out as trans, I started to delicately tell a few friends and colleagues I was thinking about transitioning... and one looked at me and said, 'Do you mean like Buffalo Bill?'" There was "no other image to counter" being trans than an "incredibly monstrous person who literally steals the female form and tries to embody it."

Art is an articulation of our souls, and our souls are sick and undiagnosed.

As Cher Horowitz explains in her original oral on the topic of "Violence in the Media" in *Clueless*: "So, okay. The attorney general says there's too much violence on TV, and that should stop. But even if you took out all the violent shows, you could still see the news. So until mankind is peaceful enough not to have violence on the news, there's no point in taking it out of shows that need it for entertainment value."

There is too much violence against women onscreen but nowhere near enough coverage on the news, and mankind is not peaceful enough. The news cycle may get hooked on one story every week of a white cis woman or girl disappearing or going missing or being kidnapped or being murdered—but it leaves out thousands more. Stories of sexual harassment, rape, and sexual assault comprise only 1 percent of news stories. Meanwhile, every seventy-three seconds an American is sexually assaulted, the majority of whom are women and under eighteen.[19] That humankind doesn't report violence against women on the news, yet shows and films need violence against women for entertainment value, is one prank of rape culture. It renders rape culture not as bad as we've seen it reproduced onscreen so that ignorance remains bliss and we can keep pretending that nothing is happening while being afraid that anything could. Real women are turning into tropes and are hurt every minute of every day for it—whether by the US president or someone else—and we're all asking each other, "What are we going to watch tonight?"

---

19 When I fact-checked this statistic one year after writing it, "every seventy-three seconds" had changed to every "every sixty-eight seconds."

9

STFU

I didn't always want to be a woman writer—

Okay, I did, but I wouldn't admit it because "writer" was not a profession to my dad or to any dad. There were three professions only: lawyer, sales associate, wife and mother. These didn't require explaining or defending, or involve embarrassing oneself and one's dad.

Nevertheless, I persisted in writing. I was a kindergartener memoirist and posted personal stories on classroom walls about my mom's marriages and divorces. My first professional gig was as editor and font stylist of an AOL newsletter about the brother boy band Hanson, and my hundreds of subscribers were other tween girls I met in Hanson chatrooms, and we were all going to marry Taylor or Zac or Isaac, but mostly Taylor. My college reputation was that I gave great email— I wrote beautiful books in emails to audiences of one, to seduce an out-of-my-league boy with grammatical acumen and sentence arias, and not superficial stuff like body or face.

Freshman year of college I was prelaw (thank you), but after thousands of emails, by senior year I thought, *If I type into a Word document instead of a message box, then I can earn college credit and one day money and superstardom.* For an assignment in Exposition I wrote my autobiography through the lens of grilled cheese. All art looks bad at first, but not mine; a favorite teacher (of another class, from another semester) told me she read "Grilled Cheese in Paradise"—it was going around the creative writing department, and not as a joke. I was famous! Before I could ask if she wanted me to autograph her copy, she said, "You should know that you're not an analytical writer." (I'd written analytical papers in her class, so she knew what she was talking about.)

From that moment on I navel-gazed in my own lane and demoted every "we" to "I" (and every "I" became "I, I, I") and relegated any cultural commentary to personal secret as I was mindful that my experience was not logical. (If I ever had any deep, universal, or cogent musings, then I'd stencil them on Post-its and either stick them on my bathroom mirror to cover up my reflection or chew them up and shit them out because women don't write about those things and have been hanged for doing so.)

I just didn't have it in me, didn't have that Y chromosome in me to be a writer professionally, which is why I decided to work for writers in San Francisco. Quit before I failed, etc.

But once I quit/failed working for writers, suddenly there was time to write. Now I had a lot of material. So I moved to New York to be an *artist*, someone who lived off her talent and charisma and attended graduate school for a master of fine arts in creative nonfiction writing. There I'd write a Me book about Myself (the only topic I knew well) with an unlikable protagonist and unreliable narrator.

I arrived in Brooklyn the summer Jay-Z's "Empire State of Mind" played on repeat, when social media and streaming went mainstream and no one could be bored, imperfect, or unknown, and I rented a one-bedroom and named my Wi-Fi network "Famous."

When would it all begin? I had to know. *The career, the salary, the social circle, the partner, the followers, the stardom, the name in lights?*

When it didn't begin after one month, my thoughts went wild. I'd sit down to write, and an internal voice said, *Can't.* My plans to write were interrupted by fantasies of lives unlived, of applying to law school or marrying the wrong person instead of write another word. *Welcome to my pity party!* Only I was invited. To behold the emptiness of the room become a metaphor and see missed boats expand crazily. *Welcome to my pity after-party!* When the self-gaslighting and the soul's dark night got cracking. *Since infancy things have not, ever, been okay.* I thought these thoughts-of-no-origin and thought about unthinking them but couldn't. The thoughts had their own thoughts, and they sounded like a medley of every man I've ever known and of trolls who can't beat a woman at her own game and of my inner critic's greatest hits, the paralyzing anthems and rumors I spread about myself.

I had nothing to write about, nothing to say. I had one story only, the one I liked to keep myself awake at night picturing alternate endings to, the story about my college boyfriend, which I hadn't yet put into words because writing is hard and also the reaction to talking about trauma is itself traumatic.[1]

But the writing program had extended a formal invitation . . .

Workshop was Tuesday and Thursday evenings, and around the workshop table sat the white male instructor, who was also the program director, and fifteen students all up their own assholes. Before workshop we'd email our pieces for written comments and compliments, which we'd discuss at length in class. The original title for my personal essay competed for most stupid: "How Not to Lose Your Virginity."

ALTERNATE ENDING 1

After my cervix-shattering romance, I graduate college and undergo a makeover-of-soul-forged-in-fire to pull off a vigilante revenge spectacular involving castration.

---

1 Many people have humbled me by wondering if maybe talking about trauma wasn't my trauma.

ALTERNATE ENDING 2

I pack my baggage (actual, figurative) and just move on, incredibly resilient, and ponder in voiceover narration, *Is it better to love and lose and lose and lose than to live artlessly?* at my ex-boyfriend's funeral before I fake my own death to live off the grid and study the tools of the patriarchy to dismantle the patriarchy.

ALTERNATE ENDING 3

My ex goes on a self-redemptive journey, and in a come-to-Jesus moment, he realizes that someone whom he said he loved had to live with his behavior while he did not. By the end he suffers some kind of consequence, any kind, literally any kind at all. (This ending is written, directed, edited, produced, designed, lit, scored, choreographed, and helmed by women. It stars multidimensional women reimagined as more than their bodies. It's shot through the female gaze, complicating the prevailing point of view with new perspective while showing what female consciousness can do. It's a critical darling, a box-office hit, and a soon-to-be franchise that radicalizes media, which radicalizes human perception and behavior.)

ALTERNATE ENDING 4

Instead of seeing my ex in court or eating his heart with a knife and fork, when it counts I say no, and he listens (empathy's pregame). He says, without irony, "That's fine." With special effects, we communicate.

ALTERNATE ENDING 5

In the sci-fi biopic version, my ex-boyfriend tries on my womanhood
and walks a mile in my vulva and lets whatever could happen,
happen. He feels everything as I felt it; he feels pain (existent,
political, unconnected to anyone's opinion of it) and hurts as only
a woman can be hurt by a man. He tears a cervix he doesn't have
while he cops to the fact that he cannot tear there (certain scenes
have to be faked when the camera lens melts). He lies down on
plastic tables in gowns of rough paper and spread-eagles his
shaved legs to be entered by unknown hands and steel devices for
the finale. He suffers in a way that's uneventful and negligible until a
man has to suffer in that way. And he carries it all, every day, always.
(But he stops participating when he's asked to come of age as a girl
and live as a woman day in, day out.)

ALTERNATE ENDING 6

There is no sixth alternate ending to a story that for me doesn't
end—because what's the point of fiction? A shredded cervix
is flesh; it is fact.

A male classmate titled his critique of my essay "How to Make a Guy
Cringe," and in one single-spaced page, he wrote that I should "invent a
new word" for my "situation." He pitched "Diet Rape" and "Rape II" and
"Caffeine-Free Rape, a rape substitute" and "I Can't Believe It's Not Rape."

He wrote, "Just trying to interject a little humor in here. Not sure
what to say. I hope your cervix is better."

The next semester I sat in the Student Health Services waiting room
filling out forms before my annual exam, and I reached a box asking if

I had ever been sexually assaulted. I could either check the box or not. For years I didn't think I had been "sexually assaulted." In the personal essay I didn't use the phrase "sexual assault" or any variation. But the box asked me to choose. There was no "Other; please explain, specify, and defend in 500 words (minimum)." I checked the box.

And just like that I had been sexually assaulted. I started to say, "I was sexually assaulted." Sometimes I'd say, "I was raped" or "I was sexually abused," trying on the phrases like short skirts. Labeling was tricky, and it's even trickier for women who aren't white; in the Black women's stories Tressie McMillan Cottom read and loved as a girl, she writes in *Thick*, "what did not qualify as rape was anything done to a black girl."

Talking about experience changes the experience—just as emotions are composed of how they're expressed, too—so which label was right for me? What had happened, and what could I say had happened?

If I were "abused," I wouldn't say I was "abused-abused." Which suggested that what isn't "abuse-abuse" is normal. Still, I couldn't say, "Being scared to death is abuse," or "Emotional carnage is abuse," or "Pain is abuse," or "Physical damage is abuse"; I couldn't widen the definition of abuse until people were solely kind to each other.

Anyway, no term felt like mine.

There was a lot of that going around. The two gynecologists I saw in college for "a broken vagina," both of whom peered into me and said nothing was wrong, did not say that what I called "painful sex" might have been called "violence," or that the problem wasn't with my body but with my boyfriend's behavior. So when the third gynecologist said my cervix was shredded, I almost burst into flames with relief. To quote an embroidered pillow I read once: *When you name something, it loosens its hold on you.* The pain was no longer "naiveté" or "theatrics" or "hysterics." I had not imagined it. Now I could say something had happened, when something had, in fact, happened. Acknowledgment imposed proof of force, and proof was somehow necessary. In part because half of pain is its wordlessness, and without words there's no recovery.

After I checked the box in Student Health Services, a nurse in the exam room reviewed my forms and asked about the checkmark. "Are you in any current danger?" she asked. I wasn't. Should I not have checked the box?

The classmate who brainstormed the phrase "Diet Rape" wrote a note in black ink in the margin of his critique, "'Rape' hints @ a criminal act. Was this criminal?"

There wasn't a box to check for that!

Once I told a friend about my college boyfriend, and I added the caveat: "I mean, it wasn't back-alley rape." Her response: "Yeah, I was not-back-alley raped, too."

We were both not-back-alley raped while we were watching our backs for "real rape" and "criminal rape," avoiding spring break booze cruises and walking alone while scantily clad at sinister times of night in foreign neighborhoods' back alleys so that we wouldn't have to check a box later.

On the Student Health Services exam table with my feet in stirrups, I thought, *How did I end up like this?* A box checker. I thought also of a conversation at a bar with grad school friends, about what we lost when we lost our virginities. The three women in the group didn't share moments of awkwardness or cringe or tenderness but violence. After a few drinks, the male friend was frustrated. He just didn't understand why women remain in situations where no obvious force is forcibly being forced at them, at us.

He asked, "Didn't you know? How'd you let it happen? Why didn't you leave?"

Ah. Why didn't I say no, no, no.

I cannot count the times I've been asked these questions and cannot fathom why they're asked, nor why the responses to a woman's story are so predictable. On repeat I've heard:

"That's not true."

"Not all men."

"I don't do that."

"No offense, but I don't believe anything you're saying."

"You're too cynical."

"But do you think you brought it on yourself?"

Sometimes I hear this stuff while my thigh gets caressed.

"Aren't you over it yet?" a man to whom I'm related asked me while at dinner with my dad. Then he demanded, "Get over it already." Then he laughed. Then he decided, "You're over it by now." He was telling me about my not-back-alley rape. (My dad continued eating without a word.)

A man at a best friend's wedding pondered aloud to me why his ex-wife who had been assaulted couldn't move on from the assault in which he wasn't assaulted.

These men were angry, more angry at me and at their exes and at women than about what happens to people who aren't them.

Some women—not me—would have told these men to shut up. (Some women can speak up for themselves without breaking a sweat.) But "shut up" could not make it out of my mouth. I didn't want to humiliate the men with a conversation or an expectation of empathy.

For my family and the ex-husbands and the guy friends, to not laugh off violence, to not move on from it, and to understand it was asking them to think about it, to go through their own histories, to accept statistics, to see that the classroom is not far from the back alley, to realize that a woman's problem is a man's problem, too. I guess they didn't want to do that, and I wasn't going to force them.[2]

I reported "Diet Rape" to our instructor, the program director. He took immediate action by softly suggesting I talk to the male classmate myself, alone, because the classmate was a very nice guy who'd listen, really.

Instead I published a piece online about workshopping sexual violence titled "My 'Diet Caffeine-Free Rape'"—

---

2 That would be thought-rape.

And made more men angry. Commenters asked me to die in a fire; they called me a sperm dumpster, an idiot, someone who deserved everything she got. Trolls debated if I was, in fact, assaulted and if I should be and why and how and with what. They said my writing belonged in a tween zine. (A girl always remembers her first comments section.[3])

After reading the comments I sat for hours in my dry bathtub listening to "Rainbow Connection" on repeat and wondering, *What moves a stranger to request the death of a woman who went public with her pain?*[4]

There wasn't a good answer—there was only example after example begging the question, example after example of what an "outspoken" woman says being flipped and directed against her just because she spoke. Like when US senator Kirsten Gillibrand called out Al Franken's sexual misconduct, and the public reviled her for speaking up about it and defended Franken for doing it. Or when Hillary Clinton "lost"—lost because of her husband (because a woman is her husband); lost because of her emails (because of her text); lost because she had too much experience (because she had experience); lost because we just don't like her (because she's unlikeable); lost because she's strident and monotone and loud and annoying and abrasive (because of

---

3 Advancements in technology have facilitated hate to travel farther and faster: in 2021, I received emails about another essay on sexual violence from servers created for men to harass women anonymously and with ease and convenience.

4 And what moved hordes of strangers to request the death of a woman named Anita Sarkeesian who held workshops on feminism in games journalism, or another named Zoë Quinn who made a video game called *Depression Quest*, about living with depression, which received one positive review, even though it supposedly "sucked," and Quinn "must have sucked dick for it"? This was Gamergate, in 2014, when hundreds of thousands of men from the gamer population launched hate campaigns from Reddit, 4chan, and 8chan against Sarkeesian, Quinn, and game developer Brianna Wu. The attacks ranged from disseminating revenge porn and rape threats, to vandalizing Wiki pages with pornographic images, to doxxing—a popular attack because it exposes someone's personal details to enable their mass harassment.

her voice, because of her voice, because of her voice, because of her voice, because of her voice); lost because her flaws are more society's than hers.

"I received an interview request from CNN today but I had to decline because last time I spoke on their platform I received death threats both personally & at work. Next time you think media is skewed, consider why people with first hand knowledge are declining being interviewed," tweeted @nursekelsey, a trauma ICU nurse in December 2021 during the coronavirus pandemic.

And Black women and women of color receive the biggest counterblasts for using their voice, like Congresswoman Ilhan Omar, who referred to 9/11 as an event "some people did," and countless people took the clip out of context and reframed her comment as a brush-off of the terrorist attacks and in turn terrorized her. Serena Williams was penalized at the 2018 US Open final for "verbal abuse," for disagreeing with the umpire and acting a little like men do all the time without penalty. Gabrielle Union's contract with *America's Got Talent* wasn't renewed after she reported Jay Leno's racist joke, and a "show insider" said Union was labeled "difficult" following her whistleblowing. (It's not possible to include or keep track of every example.)

In the dry bathtub I grasped, really grasped, beyond learning by example, that when women speak, the facts are automatically in dispute, as is the speaker, and the speaker's license to speak, with or without a smile or pleasant tone, and that if we react to shitty treatment—or stay quiet about it—then we asked for it.

Since I'm hysterical, crazy, insane, hormonal, and emotional, I published a few versions of the personal essay from my MFA program, trying to get it right but making myself a myth in the process: the broken-record woman doomed to tell her same story until she figures out how to tell it (she won't), and with every iteration there's someone or a mob who tells her that despite how much she tried or how well she did or how articulate she was, she still said it all wrong.

The latest version appeared in an anthology that was vetted and edited by the publisher's lawyer to avoid liability and protect the contributors from being sued. (Before publication I had to line up witnesses who would corroborate my story in court if it came to that.) Regarding edits, the lawyer suggested I delete "he hurt me" and replace it with "I hurt." ("He" should be deleted in what hurt. But with "him" gone, what "he" did became what "I" did.) Next the lawyer suggested I delete "get hurt" and replace it with "feel hurt." (I was allowed to hurt and to feel hurt, but not to allege anyone had hurt me or that I had gotten hurt by someone, somehow.) This made me rethink, *What if it wasn't as bad as I'd worded it?* Rather than "He hurt me," I could say *I was inexperienced and dramatic.* Or *I was violently in love and made love to violently.* Or *I was fucked; I was nailed, banged, destroyed, torn into, messed up six ways from Sunday; my V-Card was punched, my pussy crushed, my poon slayed.* Or *I was [something]— [something] because what is the name that contains everything I felt and still feel?* The issue, perhaps, was in the wording.

My personal myth lengthened: as long as I told my story, someone would question it, me, and my wording.

I wrote about the lawyer's edits in another essay, and when the publication fact-checked my writing, the male fact-checker fact-checked me and my language. About scenes from my first job, the male fact-checker asked for a source. I explained I was the source for my experience, and there was no reporter on the scene or evidence of my observations. I said I did see what I said I saw, but if saying so were a potential legal issue (the editor could say I was lying and sue me for libel), then I'd cut the sentences to be safe. (How much is cut from women's stories "to be safe"?) Only two of us were there, but only one gets to be believed, and it seems that women cannot be sources,[5] especially not when what happened may have happened only to her.

---

5 "I didn't assault her," he says; "Who's your source?" no one asks him.

Yet again, I was a trope, now a Cassandra—the prophetess to whom Apollo gave and took back the gift of prophecy with a catch. The classicist Mary Beard characterizes Cassandra's lot in life as "always to prophesy the truth but never to be believed," a "twist on the idea that women's speech is never authoritative: even when it really is true, it doesn't seem so to listeners." Which drove Cassandra crazy. Cassandra's curse appears elsewhere; in *Cassandra Speaks: When Women Are the Storytellers, the Human Story Changes*, author Elizabeth Lesser mentions the Mishnah, "a sacred Jewish compendium of laws," that indexes the nine curses that G-d gifted women, including not being "believed as a witness."

"That's the root of #BelieveWomen," writes Jennifer Wright in *Harper's Bazaar*. "We need a world where women can actually talk about what's happening to them and be believed to the same extent men would be believed or listened to."

Speaking the truth is one thing; being believed and listened to another. The voice needs an audience other than itself.

(If that's not asking too much.)

Oppression can entail violence, perspective, speech, and listening: who can talk about what, whose stories count, who says so, who speaks with authority and on anything, who gets the benefit of the doubt, who can change minds (their own and others), who's edited and how much, who is heard without prejudice, and who is discredited, belittled, besmirched, castigated, denigrated, and persecuted for speaking up.

My male classmate's comments—and the program director's comments and the lawyer's comments and the fact-checker's comments and the ex-husband's comments and the comments section—are part of a bigger mechanism of silencing, in which those who undermine the social order are subject to the ancient annihilating force that upholds it. I call it "the language machine," a metaphorical apparatus of linguistic smoke and mirrors. A woman's story goes in the language machine one way and comes out another. "He hurt me" goes in and comes out "I got hurt somehow? I don't know; I'm a girl and can't math."

"Sex that is out of a woman's control" goes into the language machine and comes out "bad sex" or "disappointing sex" or "regrettable sex."

"Why didn't he stop?" comes out "Why didn't you stop him?" The language machine flips who did what to whom; "what he did to her" becomes "what was done to her" becomes "what she did."

The word "oppression" comes out "a difference of opinion" or "a misunderstanding." The word "assault" is "rough horseplay" or "Can't you take a joke?"

The language machine rebrands anything unwanted as a compliment or "misconstrued" or "a rape substitute," so that force supposedly yields "harmless fun" or a gaffe or a joke, not discomfort or damage. The language machine says that men define "fun" and "jokes," and that a woman's welfare jeopardizes "fun" and "jokes," and that "femaleness" designates sexual assault as fun and funny, and that women who forget to laugh are "buzzkill bitches on a witch hunt."

The language machine ensures a crime isn't illegal or so bad. It helps us mistake rough horseplay as the norm and crimes against women as romantic overtures with phrases that take on a myriad of meanings that pervert meaning, as games of violation that render the violation benign. The language machine works dynamically, as precursors to worse things and as insurance that worse things will seem typical or trivial, and it's common decency to go along with those.

The language machine downplays an assailant's actions and highlights the fault in his casualty's story, then makes the fault the story itself. "He was drunk" changes to "She was drunk" changes to "She deserved it" changes to "Is she lying?"

"He sexually assaulted her" changes to "She put herself in that position" changes to "Stanford swimmer is no longer an Olympic hopeful because one night a drunk girl wore certain clothes near him" changes to "Girls her age are drawn to self-victimization."

The language machine, like the US justice system, puts the burden on victims and survivors—they "seduced" and should protect the criminal who wants nothing to do with his crime.

A woman goes into the language machine and comes out a crazy psycho bitch who today says she was raped and tomorrow says, "I mean, I wasn't back-alley raped."

As with pretty much everything else, cis white men instituted the language machine and would claim credit even though I just invented the metaphor. Because the potential end of white male privilege is so terrifying that those who have it will say and do anything to keep it.

Because of the language machine, "calling out" is "whining." "Asking a question" is "nagging." "Reporting" is "complaining." "Expressing one's experience" is "crazy talk." Because of the language machine, such sugar-and-toxin-coated language has nine lives, outliving all other words until they're the only ones we have.

The language machine exists in our own minds. Women who think *no* may say yes. Women who think, *I do not care how you are* may say, "How are you?! Tell me everything!" Women who think "." type "!"

The language machine is binary; "woman" means "cis woman."

The language machine is racist; "woman" means "white woman," and "feminist" means "white cis feminist," and "patriarchy" means "patriarchy as experienced by a middle-class cis white feminist."

In big news stories, the language machine intervenes. In the same news cycle, Elizabeth Warren was labeled "angry" and "antagonistic" for running for president as white men who murdered trans women of color were labeled "misunderstood." Indeed, every time we find out that a white man mass-murdered women of color, or a wealthy white man sex-trafficked children, we don't hear it that way. We hear "Sad boy had bad day and acted out on withholding un-American whores who don't have names." We hear "Lolitas who appeared and acted like women, who impersonated women purposefully and deviously, took advantage of influential men with their girlhood." We hear "Isn't the real victim here the guilty man?" Since no one wants to associate "girls" with sex trafficking, girls won't be called "girls," although they are girls, and the girls were sex-trafficked, and the girls were sex-trafficked by adult men.

The language machine is international, like how the royal family formally investigated Meghan Markle's "rudeness" years before Prince Andrew's alleged pedophilia.

The language machine feels bad for "bad" men. Male reporters are more likely to use quotes about the impact on the alleged perpetrators than quotes about the impact on the alleged survivors, framing violence against women in ways that discredit survivors and shield perpetrators, and reifying a cultural ethos where men get away with murder and women are blamed for being murdered.[6] (The societal MO to empathize with men is so profound and on parade that Cornell philosophy professor Kate Manne invented the word "himpathy," in which we perceive men as de facto victims and can't feel for women assaulted or otherwise in pain.) Once I wrote about an alleged serial rapist, and the male fact-checker asked me to tweak the alleged serial rapist's description to "a comic who had been accused of serially sexually assaulting women," even though the alleged serial rapist is literally an alleged serial rapist and promoting "rapist" to "comic" waters down what he did (which is rape multiple women, allegedly) and further shields him since "a comic who has been accused of serially sexual assaulting women" is more flattering and open to interpretation than "alleged serial rapist."[7]

The language machine interferes with a woman's life stories and a woman writer's livelihood. Our essays begin as pitches like, "Something occurred that I didn't want, and I don't know what to call it." Editors know what to call it, know what gets clicks, know how to replace verbs with stronger verbs. A writer friend pitched an essay to a women's glossy magazine about her and a man, about aggression and memory gaps and blood, about "the gray area"; she did not present it as

---

6 This—blaming victims for dying and survivors for surviving—is the same everyday ethos where women are charged $300 for a haircut and are condemned for paying it.
7 In my own googling I saw that the alleged serial rapist is referred to as a "comic" or "comedian" in the news stories about him.

"I thought I was raped," but her editor did. Because word choice matters: "I'm a woman" (no one cares); "I'm a girl" (warmer, better); "I am a victim of sex trafficking" (fucking nailed it).

"The dominant mode by which a young, hungry writer could *enter the conversation* was by deciding which of her traumas she could monetize…be it anorexia, depression, casual racism, or perhaps a sadness like mine, which blended all three," author Larissa Pham writes in her essay collection *Pop Song,* about the testimony industry. Leveling up in my writing career involved contributing my assault to publications that profit from women's blood-sweat-tear-splattered words through hateful clicks that exploit writers and expose them to harassment, doxxing, and actual physical violence (somehow, even letting us talk about our pain is yet another form of silencing). For a follow-up feature article about the fallout of publishing "My 'Diet Caffeine-Free Rape,'" an editor sent me a list of twenty-six bullet points detailing what she and the publication and the public wanted me to address for a fee of $1,000, including:

8. Did you make excuses to avoid sex? And did this sadden you, as not the relationship you'd hoped for? . . .

19. Has it surprised you how many people have been negative? What have they said and who are they? . . .

24. Does it make you sad that so many women experience this "diet rape" and either don't realize it or just put up with it as "normal"?

Once I reached the end of the list, I emailed the editor my regrets about not being able to write the essay after all.

Of course, I should've been more grateful for the opportunity. For five years thereafter my pitches on rape culture were rejected: my experience wasn't bad enough, wasn't good enough, wasn't news.

For sure, stories like mine aren't news, and newsmakers have made sure of it. That is, until #MeToo, the hashtag that hung a Temporarily Out of Order sign on the language machine.

#MeToo, as a social media campaign, did more than imply that women are not believed or respected or safe as men are believed and respected and safe. It did more than insinuate that women are abused or assaulted or propositioned or targeted or coerced or groomed or subject to aggression (*or, or, or*) in broad daylight, persistently, in ways that start early and don't let up or seem bad or abnormal enough to report or even bring up. It was testimony in the millions. (The Pew Research Center found that "#MeToo" was tweeted more than nineteen million times within its first year, more than fifty-five thousand uses per day.) The hashtag measured the silence we live in in a historic display of misery loving company.

But I didn't tweet #MeToo in 2017. Or #WhyIStayed in 2014 or #WhyIDidntReport in 2018. Because on the same platforms that emboldened women to speak out, we were also asked to kill ourselves for speaking out, for crucifying ourselves a little bit to prove the basic points that women should be heard, that women should not be harassed or raped or murdered, that restricting reproductive freedom is restricting women's freedom.

Activist Tarana Burke created Me Too as a social movement in 2006, but she was ignored as a Black activist by the white public. And that's best-case scenario. Many "women of color, working-class women, immigrants, minorities, Indigenous women, trans women, shelter-dwellers...live feminist lives but rarely get to speak or write about them," writes Rafia Zakaria in *Against White Feminism*. This is because, as bell hooks explains in *Talking Back*, speaking up "is truly, on a deep level, a real race and class issue 'cause so many black folks have been raised to believe that there is just so much that you should not talk about, not in private and not in public."

Even though I could tweet with impunity, I wouldn't. I had learned my lesson. So I didn't tweet about my college boyfriend or about any of the shitty men in media.

Then, in no time, the #MeToo movement had gone too far. Women had put off people with their trigger warnings and had fatigued everyone with too many personal essays and had ruined enough lives and said enough.

(Though "ruined," really? For every Charlie Rose who was fired or every Matt Lauer who had a short apology tour before making a comeback, there was a Bill Cosby released on a technicality or a comedian like Louis C.K. who, after claiming he was canceled, went on a national stand-up tour and won a Grammy in 2022 for Comedy Album of the Year, about cancelation. Male recording Academy CEO Harvey Mason Jr. defended C.K.'s nomination as well as accused alleged serial sexual rapist and abuser Marilyn Manson's[8] nomination: "We won't look back at people's history, we won't look at their criminal record, we won't look at anything other than the legality within our rules.")

The #MeToo movement seemed to go too far once women cried, "Assault!" almost as often as assault occurs. That was too improbable, too unpalatable. After so many accusations, the accusations begin to sound false. Male minds could not comprehend. An accused male journalist wrote in *Harper's* magazine that, well, actually, #MeToo was a revision of reality, a "recalibration of millions of events" in which statistics were fictionalized and women faked accusations like orgasms.[9]

Fact-check: the "recalibration" is not of "millions of events" but of statistics and social awareness adjusting to the reality of victimization as a constant.

---

8 Manson denies the accusations.

9 The hysteria movement and #MeToo began and ended the same way: *Let women talk! But, wait, now that women are talking, we see that too many of them have been hurt by men, which isn't realistic, so this movement sucks, is fake, and is over now.* Nineteenth century doctors had believed women with hysteria and recognized that women's physical symptoms had psychological origins, often in sexual trauma, but then "hysteria" went into quotation marks and was just too common and "beyond credibility," Dr. Judith Herman writes in *Trauma and Recovery*. "Freud stopped listening to his female patients" and recanted "the traumatic theory of the origins of hysteria" because, as Caroline Criado Perez explains in *Invisible Women*, "it would have implicated too many men."

Fact-check: the revision is of those being called out and held accountable.

Fact-check: the fiction is male innocence.

Fact-check: to be traumatized is to be inarticulate. Sad songs can't explain trauma—the traumatized need red string push-pinned to maps and written statements from eyewitnesses who weren't there to adequately capture the trespass and duress of the body—so survivors may look like liars, may even lie, may appear to be hysterical, and may even become pathological.

But never mind all that because one false accusation jeopardizes the movement! If one woman speaks wrongly, then the entire movement is compromised. Women, it must be said, should speak perfectly or not at all.

I chose "not at all." I feared being that one woman, feared beating a raped horse, feared the credibility of my public accusations if I tweeted them, feared that the facts would not hold up in court since the facts made the circumstances look like my choices, and feared my own voice as I had since around the time I learned to talk.

Something that is everywhere can also be said to be nowhere, and #MeToo unveiled the unlegislated "gray area."

I picture rape culture as an iceberg, where at the peak is murder; below that is rape, sexual violence, and abuse; next is verbal attacks and threats; then emotional abuse; and then entrenched power imbalances and systemic dehumanization. At the bottom level is the gray area:

sexual pressure
transferring all emotional labor
evoking a woman's voice but leaving her out of the conversation
   or narrative
reiterating men's words solely while tuning out women's

acting on deep-seated conscious or subconscious animosity
    toward fucking bitches who need only be women to earn
    men's dislike and mistreatment

and routinely:

condescending to or steamrolling women
talking women out of their feelings
cutting off or shrugging off women
assuming authority over women
reminding women of their place and putting them in it

as well as regularly:

insulting women
assessing women
policing women[10]

and perhaps:

apologizing insincerely while expecting women to be
    appreciative—

and doing all of it with amnesty.

But none of this seems worth mentioning. Like nothing worth
mentioning happens to women, and nothing that happens to women

---

10 Some of the language above, which is really a dialect of patriarchy, is also known as
"DARVO"—"Deny, Attack, and Reverse Victim and Offender"—a rhetorical strategy
abusers use to defend themselves and to further gaslight those they abuse.

could be worth mentioning. It's just not worth it. It hijacks our days and our one wild and precious life, but it's just not worth it.

Yet the iceberg illustrates that abuse, whatever kind, is connected and is its own point, and that "minor" isn't synonymous with "acceptable" but with the term "death by a thousand cuts," a torture technique and psychology term that refers to a significant negative effect that occurs incrementally, imperceptibly, slowly, so that no one reacts to a cut or calls it an injury. Each cut, although part of the thousand that lead to death, appears normal and is normalized—it passes as conversation or constructive feedback or funny or flirting or heated debate or passionate defense—despite its violent implications. This is how millions of women die by a thousand cuts.

As I told Bill Murray, "rape" in "rape culture" is the violent terminus, the end point of silencing women and of convincing us (with or without our consent) to silence ourselves.

"Silencing" is a verb, an action. Right now, mostly white male senators across the US are voting yes on anti-abortion bills and on similar health-related legislation that will deny women the full use of their voice by legalizing oppression and criminalizing living in a woman's body.

Silence, a noun, is a place. In the silence where men have stranded me, I've kept their secrets for them, which were theirs and are mine now. In this silence I've internalized men's bad behavior, i.e., he ghosts/cheats/yells/abuses, and I suppose I provoked him.

"Silencing" is active, yet silence itself speaks and condones, and the noun becomes a verb when it enables as much violence as silencing inflicts, when it suppresses or disappears a group of people and their problems or choices, and when it tricks a woman into silencing herself.

10

SILENCE AND NOISE

On Facebook everyone was thrilled to share their unpopular opinion. On Instagram it was bikini weather. On Pinterest it was wedding season. On Reddit there was a war on women. On Twitter the revolution was being tweeted, and there were one thousand new #MeToo tweets and ten thousand replies from heterosexual white male supremacists telling women what they shouldn't be saying. And the internet begged me to donate myself. But my experiences across time and space had reinforced silence as my best option.

In October 2017, I'd been sick for nine months; Alyssa Milano tweeted, "If you've been sexually harassed or assaulted write 'me too'"; and the anonymous Google spreadsheet titled "Shitty Media Men" circulated for half a day among women in media to warn each other of men whose behavior was sexually unprofessional or abusive, unlawful and/or icky. The spreadsheet, a ladies' locker room organized virtually, expanded for the twelve hours it was live with alleged misconduct that ranged from inappropriate lunches to rape. The writer Moira Donegan later revealed she started the list.

No one sent me the link. If I'd had access then to the seventy plus names on the list—names I knew and had worked for and had been with alone—I would have added some more.

News of the list went public, then viral. Some men were actually fired because of it. A few media outlets reached out to me for comment because the online literary magazine founder was accused via the spreadsheet of sexual harassment, coercion, and rape.[1] I said I had no comment or didn't reply. The online literary magazine founder himself emailed me to talk and to apologize to me if I thought he had to. I didn't reply to him either.

What bad timing for me personally! I had put the shitty media men behind me.[2] What else was there to do but forget, never forgive, and repress?

"Always when people tell you you will have to face this sometime, when they hurry you matter-of-factly towards whatever pain or obscenity or unwelcome revelation is laid out for you, there is this edge of betrayal, this cold, masked, imperfectly hidden jubilation in their voices, something greedy for your hurt," writes Alice Munro in her novel *Lives of Girls and Women*, articulating my thinking about tweeting.

Silence is for the best, I'd thought when the pressure to speak out eclipsed the pressure to keep quiet.

Social media and I had a past. In the early days, whenever I posted something—*I'm thrilled! I'm humbled! I'm traumatized!*—underneath the characters pulsated "BEAR WITNESS, PLS." I prayed that my posts would reach someone/anyone/everyone anywhere/everywhere, and I'd await positive feedback or viral acknowledgment of my pain. There was nothing to it, just sit in front of a screen, open a vein, and wait to see how many times you're seen. *Maybe*, I'd thought, *the more I give away my pain and the more people pick it up, then the less of it I'll*

---

1 He denied the claims and published his defense and a vilification of the #MeToo movement on another site that, in my liberal opinion, publishes racist, transphobic, and misogynistic writing.
2 Name of my sex tape.

have, like a horror movie plot. This appeared to be the point of social media, vulnerability in exchange for visibility and chemical rushes. But my posts were—after I'd put myself out there—ignored, and in their place were these changelings, this viral photo meme of an unimpressed lizard.

Whatever my numbers were, they were too low. Even as I confirmed more friends and gained more followers, there weren't enough friends or "friends" or strangers online or on Earth who could fill my need or deaden my pain or take away my doubt or assuage my fear or meet my emotional quota.

Which only dared me. *What if there were enough? If only I were enough?*

The stillborn moments were information, that because insufficient people showed or showered me with love right that second, then no one would, ever. I'd want to go back in time—*I shouldn't have posted what I posted. I should delete it, delete my account, die.*

Still, I couldn't look away; it felt like I *had* to look at social media, and as much as I looked at social media, social media looked at me, so I was further obligated to be loud, to produce myself and to produce a certain self.

It was already tough to communicate and to grow a self. Then social media showed up, and *who I am*—the fact of being—hinged on what I said in text boxes with word limits and autocorrect and a publish button (and a quote button, an approval button, and a reply button). Inevitably, I cracked, too-much punched in the heart and undelivered. Posting wasn't salvation: I couldn't list "the internet" as my emergency contact.

Silence is sexy, I reminded myself as I scrolled through the hashtags and stories of abuse and abuse itself that was favorited and retweeted, or quoted and interpreted and criticized. Whenever I opened Twitter, a hashtag was trending that demanded, via subtext, women bleed for the masses, just as religions have demanded human sacrifices. Via subtext, the hashtags said:

the private should be public;
a woman should divulge what haunts her to an
     uncomprehending, forgetful nation;
we should signal-boost our trauma on platforms designed, run,
     and overrun by men and trolls who used to be men;
pain should be excavated on the terms of those greedy for a
     woman's hurt (or greedy to behold women hurting);
any woman is complicit if she doesn't do this, but she's a lot
     nastier than that if she does.

I agonized over contributing to the discourse. *The time is now? Now is the time? Right now?* I was smack in the middle of repressing, in doing what I was told.

And what if people "liked" or linked to my wounds? Or worse, didn't? Or even worse, salted them? Contributing to the discourse felt like relinquishing control of it. And how to keep my wounds to two hundred eighty characters when no characters are characters enough for trauma? Or for nuance?

And would I ever break free from discussing men? Before #MeToo, it seemed like women had two options to be heard publicly: (1) write/talk about men; (2) write/talk against men, to educate and explain men to themselves. Then there was a third option: talk about how men have hurt us. While we have been known for our marital status, now we're known for our trauma status. When will there be a Bechdel Test for trauma? (It's not even that men as a group oppress women, actively or passively, but that having to write about men and talk about men and listen to men and think about men and fear men as much as we do is oppressive.)

But is silence for the best? This was an embarrassing question, so I didn't ask it. *When is saying nothing required to survive the day, and when is it being selfish or apathetic or self-vanquishing?* I didn't know, so I kept scrolling and swiping—to keep my questions at bay, to hear any and every voice but my own, to keep monitoring the bottomless feeds until my thoughts teemed with everyone else's thoughts and I couldn't tell whose feelings I was feeling.

As Oprah asked the Duchess of Sussex, Meghan Markle, "Were you silent, or were you silenced?" Yes. To cope with being silenced in my twenties, I chose silence in my thirties. After consenting to sexual violence, and after all but complying to burn to ash for writing and talking about it, I was sick of saying the wrong thing and the right thing, sick of speaking with male words, sick of speaking and of facing repudiation for speaking, sick of sending or posting or publishing and regretting it instantly, sick of one wrong or right word too many coming back to bite me.

To fear less and to regret less, I expressed less. Less on social media (what kind of self did I have to promote anyway?), less in Microsoft Word to promote later, less at events because I didn't go to events anymore.

Quitting writing was 11 out of 10, would recommend. Ever since writing workshops and comments sections, I had decided that I should write so well, so perfectly and unimpeachably that no one could deny my story or my right to speak or tell me to get raped. I'd tinker with one sentence for months, replacing a comma with a semicolon, then replacing that semicolon with a comma and so on a thousand times (just now I changed "a thousand" to "a hundred" to "fifty" back to "a hundred" back to "a thousand" then to "twenty" before considering "three thousand" and then settling on "a thousand"), until I was so overwhelmed that I'd delete the sentence.

It didn't matter anyway. However unimpeachable my writing or however many semicolons I used or didn't, I had to respect that there was "a time" and "a place" in which there was no time or place where I could publicize my opinion or experience and still feel safe and sane.

I couldn't make it as a freelance writer who wrote one sentence every three months, so some years after grad school, I applied for jobs that didn't require much of a voice. I was a barista who used the same thirteen words ("Hi, what may I get for you?" "What size?" "We're out of bagels.") I babysat two teen girls who did most of the talking and walked the dogs of celebrities and was a freelance editor who deleted other writers' wordiness.

It wasn't weird, at first, to talk less. Silence felt right, right in the way that it's standard to push down [every single thing], to relegate real communication to some sort of affliction, to leave a play or museum—newly aware that there was and is and can be more—then immediately check the phone, unable or unwilling to verbalize any of what we feel. It felt right to let the neocortex take over, the part of the brain that withholds, disguises, and lies to help primates survive and to meet exes for coffee and be breezy, dressed for business (not revenge), and act as if expired love is water under a burned bridge.

The more I courted silence, the more sense it made. After all, news media asks us to feast on the world's tragedies and have zero emotions about it in order to function. The internet asks us to rely on our hands to be intimate for us, to do the job of throats and genitals, while technology enables relationships that protect us from relationships. Streaming services ask that we get better at closing off and ignoring each other, at shunning the vulnerability we can't live without.

Also, silence seemed to be a side effect of growing up and growing out of feelings. Adults just don't talk about how we feel as much as we once did. Or we don't feel as much as we used to. Or we're simply out of feelings after blazing through them, like the love has run out and adults are cement inside, totally despaired, dead of heart. Or something like that. Whatever. My feelings were worst at fourteen (also nineteen, twenty-two, and twenty-six), when I had so many, too many, and after a breakup at twenty-six, I decided feelings were not for me and talked myself out of them. "Feelings" was how I became diagnosed with depression, and "feelings" made me undateable and unemployable, so yeah, no.

Leading up to getting sick, however, my silence got weird. I couldn't meet the people I should have met for coffee or drinks because I glimpsed only the end of the meeting, the disappointment between all persons, so I canceled (dramatically) or rain-checked (vaguely), then cried when I had no place to be. I wanted to want to have fun, but the idea of small talk or any size of talk made me wince. I'd put on makeup in the morning and wash it off before bed, having not gone outside. If I had to go to work, then I would, but I wouldn't go anywhere else, at any time, for any reason.

Brooklyn apartments impelled other silences. My downstairs neighbor complained that I walked loudly, so I walked quietly. My upstairs neighbor complained that I talked loudly on the phone, so I talked quieter and less. I could hear the neighbor across the hall use the bathroom, which implicated my bathroom, so I peed and pooped and everything in between under the cover of fans and running water (to maintain the charade that women's bodies have no sound or digestive system or biology at all).[3] And since I lived alone, days would go by when I spoke not at all.

Eventually, silence was just: life.

At last I'd become the ideal woman: not a perfect woman, but a silent woman.

Yeah, sex is cool, but have you ever been celibate? My second year of grad school I began experimenting with full-body silence. For a long time. "For a long time" isn't one month; it's many tens of

---

3 "Here's the problem: you're a woman, and women don't poop," writes author Bonnie Miller in her book *Women Don't Poop & Other Lies*. "If you're like the majority of women (71%), you'll search relentlessly for a solution to hide the fact that you do this normal human thing." We lie, go to Starbucks and other second locations, hold it, etc., while men brag openly. (And as with almost everything else, toilets were designed for the average man and are too tall for most women, according to this well-researched book on shitting.)

months, during which my Facebook friends' children were conceived, announced, revealed, born, and grew long hair and personalities. For a long time I had no intimacy, no skin-to-skin, no kissing or flirting or whispered whatevers. I'd take off my clothes, of course, if someone asked, if someone were a medical practitioner who asked.

Regarding sexual intercourse and women's speech, "it is an axiom of ancient Greek and Roman medical theory and anatomical discussion that a woman has two mouths," writes Anne Carson in "The Gender of Sound." She has a face mouth and a genital mouth "connected to the body by a neck" that "provide access to a hollow cavity [the throat and the cervix] which is guarded by the lips [face lips and labia]." Both also work best shut and have a direct relationship: "an excess or blockage of blood in the uterus will evidence itself as strangulation or loss of voice," or talking too much may stop a woman's period, or virginity loss may show itself in an engorged neck and a deeper voice. Changes in the lower mouth are changes in the upper mouth and vice versa. And trauma in the lower mouth may show up in the upper mouth and vice versa.

When my upper mouth closed, so did my lower. Or was it vice versa?

"I don't understand how that's possible," a jerk said to me about my celibacy in a tone that implied it's a public shame and biological phenomenon to have no sex. But heterosexual men like him made it possible. As did one in particular, a boy I met at summer day camp in the '90s.

In the '90s we were preteens and boyfriend-girlfriend, but rather than dry hump and fingerbang, we played one-on-one soccer, which meant we would die for one another. He was an older man and later my first kiss when I was fifteen and he was sixteen and played acoustic guitar for me. In our late twenties we reunited again, this time with alcohol, and we ended up in a parking lot on the trunk of my 2000 Honda Civic reenacting our first kiss. In our early thirties he planned to visit New York, and it was a given that we'd have sex. Why was it a given? It just was.

Except maybe it didn't have to be? This was a new thought. *I'm not going to get naked*, I told myself, empowered.

"I'm not going to get naked," I texted him before meeting up for drinks with his college friends.

But after last call, he didn't get in the cab with his college friends. He would stay at my place, he said, although I hadn't invited him.

I wasn't going to get naked, so I didn't do my routine, which was to excuse myself to the bathroom and very quickly brush my teeth, recover up my zits, shave everything, pluck whatever had to be plucked, rinse my armpits, rinse my vagina, blow my nose, and clean up my bathroom. Instead I excused myself to the bathroom to pee with the sink faucet running.

I returned to my bedroom to find that he had lit every candle I owned, *even the display candles.*

We made out in my bed, which was good for me.

But what was good for me wasn't good enough for him. Since he got one green light, he must have seen straight green lights ahead. He's a foot taller than I am, and under him, I was so small, so helpless, so defenseless, so powerless, so immobilized. I laughed as he pinned me down and did what he wanted to do, and I made jokes, actual jokes, to justify his laughter. But I wouldn't get naked, and I didn't.

In the morning, I wouldn't get naked again, and now he was mad. What I'd said last night, the thing about not getting naked, that did not and could not apply to the morning. Where was the sex? It wasn't there.

I'd been in this fight before, only not with him.

So he left.

That's all he did.

I was so grateful, so unharmed, so thrilled, so intact, so fine.

He was gone, and I thought: *I'd said what I didn't want . . .*

[APPLAUSE BREAK]

. . . and it changed exactly nothing.

I thought: *I don't want to be near beds with men anymore.* I thought: *I don't want to date men anymore.* And I didn't. For seven years or so I didn't.

A woman named Alana came up with the compound word "incel" in 1997, envisioning what she called the Involuntary Celibate Project as a supportive, inclusive community for the lonely and the hurt and the questioning and those who felt removed from the traditional plot of human sexuality. But then, Alana says, sex-starved and pissed-off men took "incel" for themselves as a "weapon of war."

I was an incel as Alana imagined it, kind of. My celibacy was involuntary and not. Incels would call me by many names, one of them might be a "volcel," a voluntary celibate. Voluntary because although I was lonesome, I wasn't searching. Involuntary because what real choice did I have in a patriarchal rape culture where loneliness is political, where women must balance desire and need for company and touch with systemic oppression and threat of violence, where dating and fucking can be dehumanizing, even deathly processes? My thinking might make me a "femcel," a part of a group that has borrowed Alana's concept. "Many femcels would say that sleeping with men who disrespect them or abuse them makes this 'choice' akin to choosing between starving and eating poisoned food," writes author and editor Nona Willis Aronowitz in the essay "The Femcel Revolution."

Doctors tried to diagnose my celibacy, from "sexual anorexia" to relationship PTSD to the *Lysistrata* approach.[4]

I self-diagnosed my celibacy: heterosexuality. Symptoms include bad sex, mediocre sex, uneventful sex, unwanted "sex" (which is assault), sex that I felt I couldn't decline, and sex where it seemed unsexy to advocate for my desire or security.

After I'd had it enough, heterosexual sex was…sexist? And heterosexuality made no narrative sense. Consider: the orgasm gap and

---

4 *Lysistrata* is an ancient Greek antiwar rom-com about the title character's plan to end the Peloponnesian War by persuading all women to withhold sex from men until fighting stops.

the pink tax[5]; waxing and yeast infections and urinary tract infections and hospitalizations for UTIs that become kidney infections; HPV that may become cervical cancer and cervical biopsies; birth control side effects[6] and pregnancy scares and pregnancy and birth and miscarriages and abortion and restricted access to abortion and to birth control; the mess and the expense and assuming responsibility for the mess and the expense; the pressure to give and the pressure to not receive; the body shame and bodily vulnerability (submitting to penetration) and cultural orthodoxy (succumbing to sex on men's terms with men who exercise power through sex); chancing dissatisfaction, pain, harm; the expectation to want any kind of sex (bad/mediocre/uneventful/unwanted "sex"/assault/unsafe sex); and all the primping and the performance and the self-abandonment that heterosexual women do for the success of the male orgasm.

So it wasn't that I'd run out of feelings but that I felt too much. (Again.) (Always.) As Susan Sontag wrote in *Regarding the Pain of Others*, "The states described as apathy, moral or emotional anesthesia, are full of feelings; the feelings are rage and frustration." My feelings of rage and frustration matched other mostly heterosexual women's feelings of rage and frustration. On Facebook in late 2016 I was invited to the event "Women: Stop Having Sex with Men in America"—a *Lysistrata* posted on social media and the first of many dick-sabbatical calls I've seen since, including those to cancel heterosexuality and divorce Republicans. Full-body silence seems like a reasonable reaction to the last decade; sex is even more ridiculous and dangerous with hard-won

5 The price discrepancy/discrimination wherein "pink" products—products marketed to women, like women's deodorant—are more expensive (and often less effective). The average American woman—who earns less than the average American man—will pay over $1,300 per year in "pink tax."

6 Pill side effects: headaches, nausea, sore breasts, depression, spotting, discharge. IUD side effects: blacking out from pain upon insertion, cramping, complications that lead to hysterectomy. Diaphragm side effect: in *Sex and the City* Carrie's diaphragm gets stuck up in her body, and Samantha must pull it out for her.

reproductive and civil liberties in peril, with politicians wistful for marital rape, and with women's bodies up for literal and legislative grabs whenever the mood strikes (and the mood strikes constantly). Many of us feel we owe it to ourselves to not.

By the time I was sick I'd lost my voice. Early on in my medical drama, my headache branched out into my neck and shoulders, so I booked a pricey Biodynamic Craniosacral Therapy (BCST) massage therapy appointment with my mom's credit card. The website said BCST influences the central nervous system as well as "the fluid that bathes" the brain and spinal column, to "affect the whole body, mind, and spirit." Dope.

For ninety minutes a woman circled my body on a table and hovered her hands over me. She touched me here and there, lightly, as if not at all. Her work went on above me, with whatever my central nervous system emitted.

For ninety minutes I waited for the massage to begin. I could have surrendered to the energy medicine, but the pain in my neck and shoulders wouldn't let me. For ninety minutes I battled myself inside my head. *Say something.* I needed to tell the massage therapist what I wanted. *Say something!* I wanted a regular massage. I didn't even want the massage therapist to understand or resolve what was wrong inside me. *SAY SOMETHING.* All I had to do was open my mouth and ask, "May I have a normal massage, please?"

I got as far as opening my mouth.

"And that's our time together," she said after ninety minutes. Then she left the room, and I lay on the table in rage pose, and five minutes later I tipped 20 percent.

It happened again but gross. An ophthalmologist placed his hand on my upper thigh during an exam. *He's just being friendly*, I assured myself. And furthermore, there was nowhere else to put his hand *except* my thigh, I convinced myself. *Anyway,* I bargained with myself, *the exam is almost over.*

What former president [BLEEP] said is true: we let them do it. I had let so many people do it.

My inability to speak up became so extreme that my psychopharmacologist referred me to an obsessive-compulsive disorder specialist. It was a left-field referral since I didn't wash my hands a weird amount or touch light switches more than once, which was my total understanding of OCD from TV.

At our intake session the psychopharmacologist had asked hundreds of diagnostic questions, including, "Do you need things to be 'just so'?"

"Not at all," I told her without a second thought. "Except after every text or conversation I mentally replay it seven or eight times and come at it from every angle, close-up and extrasolar, to parse it out—"

"And do you—" the psychopharmacologist interrupted, but I wasn't done.

"—and home in on the most mortifying parts, then judge my sentences on a scale of 1 to 10, forecast the damage, adjudicate if I should or could be forgiven, and consider what the other person must think of me—*She didn't laugh when I said*—. *Does she not like me? Did I offend her? Did I say something offensive?*—then I play out substitute dialogue and meditate on the feasibility of a redo, all while standing stock-still five hundred feet from the original conversation and staring into middle distance, trying to stop thinking amid the impossibility of stopping because if I stop, then bad shit will and does happen. So I try to limit my everyday conversation to the current season of *The Bachelorette* and never text.

"I can't even journal—*communicate with myself.*

"Also, I wash recyclables to perfection before I'm physically able to recycle them."

The psychopharmacologist diagnosed me with OCD.

I was a perfectionist, and a Virgo, and once I handwrote fifty or so drafts of a love letter because whenever I made a mistake I'd pull out a fresh sheet of college-ruled notebook paper until I wrote the letter without one paper-based typo, at which point I crossed out a few words on every page to make it look like I was okay with making mistakes and moving on—but OCD? No, thank you.

"Silence can be a symptom of OCD," she explained, "in that you stay quiet, compulsively, because you fear, obsessively, that you won't say things as they 'should' be said."

I didn't schedule an appointment with an OCD specialist for another year, even though my silence was snowballing and had gone beyond habit, beyond writer's block and spirit-stuckness, beyond self-consciousness and wishing that I didn't say what I'd said or that I'd said exactly what I wanted, beyond love and traditional gender roles, beyond being a Jew instinctively hesitant to disclose it, beyond perfectionism and regret and coping—

My silence *was* obsessive, compulsive, clinical—

I'm afraid I'm not saying it well. Which was, I'd find out, part of why I was sick.

11

HYSTERIA REBOOT

In the spring of 2018, the fourteen-year-old girl I babysat—my charge and protégé since she was nine, who was more little sister than job (I imagined she'd attend to me in hospice when I got there, and in exchange I'd radicalize her)—jumped out her fifteenth-floor window five days before her fifteenth birthday and landed on scaffolding, and how can I say this? She died.

Kate Spade killed herself a few months later, then Anthony Bourdain, and I couldn't type, text, scroll, sleep, or function without splints. The pain was back and more mysterious than ever.

The orthopedic hand surgeon diagnosed the pain as bilateral carpal tunnel syndrome/wrist flexor tendonitis, and I took the F train to occupational therapy twice a week. Every day I did a series of wrist stretches and smeared my body in CBD oil and magnesium spray, and I wore ice packs and heating pads, bought ergonomic everything, and borrowed a transcutaneous electrical nerve stimulation (TENS) machine from the celebrity couple whose dogs I walked. In my apartment, I'd hold out my forearms in a gesture of receiving and stick electrodes from my wrists to my elbow, and once I selected the lowest setting, electrical impulses pumped into my arms and flooded my nervous system so that pain signals couldn't reach my brain. But I didn't feel better, only much, much worse, and throughout the summer my arms maintained their form but had no function.

One day in late August Louis C.K. "returned to stand-up" at the Comedy Cellar in New York, after admitting to sexual misconduct allegations, and as I reached for cheese in the fridge, an electric jolt tore through my back and sent me to the floor, where I stayed and then swam on my stomach from room to room. The pain in my arms vanished. Or rather, the pain left my arms and moved into my lumbar spine.

During the fall—and the Brett Kavanaugh SCOTUS confirmation and the online literary magazine founder's federal lawsuit against Moira Donegan and thirty Jane Does for defamation and $1.5 million in damages for the "Shitty Media Men" list[1]—my lower back spasmed three more times. Urgent care prescribed oral steroids for a "pinched nerve"; the rehab spine specialist rediagnosed it as a herniated disc and wrote a prescription for physical therapy. The physical therapist, whom I saw twice weekly until I ran out of sessions covered by insurance, gave me back-bending and pelvic-thrust exercises to do daily, and I wondered if I'd made sickness a habit I could not break.

"Your pain is following the news cycle," a friend's boyfriend said to me. He was right. One month after Donald [BLEEP]'s inauguration, I had a headache, which was ten years after the sexual trauma I'd begged for. Then, when men everywhere were accused of sexual assault and harassment, my throat and stomach went into a panic. Then the suicides, the SCOTUS confirmation, the lawsuit, and my nervous system crash hit in succession.

When I was in pain, the only conversation I had was about the pain. I called a woo-woo friend to tell her about my pain, and she told me about woo-woo friends of hers who were in unending pain and

---

1 One of his lawyers is infamous for defending Paul Nungesser, a college student who claimed that Columbia University should have stopped student Emma Sulkowicz from carrying around her mattress on campus in protest of Nungesser allegedly raping her. (Nungesser's complaint was dismissed.)

then weren't after reading *The Mindbody Prescription: Healing the Body, Healing the Pain* by male doctor and professor John E. Sarno, MD, a book about people with "mindbody syndrome" and physical symptoms but no known disease or medical condition. "Psychogenic," or as Dr. Sarno calls it, tension myositis syndrome (TMS). A harrowed psychic state translates physically: emotions—rage in particular—pile up in the unconscious, going unarticulated until they hit max capacity and trigger the brain to create symptoms of chronic conditions that seem to come out of nowhere, which can't be explained by medical tests. That is, some types of physical pain are repressed emotional pain finding expression.[2]

Feminist interlude: "Since the 1950s, psychosomatic diagnoses have validated the very real ways that the mind can express itself through the body," writes Dr. Elinor Cleghorn in *Unwell Women*. But when a woman's mind expresses itself through a woman's body, then "recognized classifications...become entangled" with sexism, "with misconceptions about women's tendencies to exaggerate and feign their symptoms," and with doctors who don't listen to women and with research that isn't done on women's bodies and with claims that women's bodies confound science.

For years Western physicians as well as journalists have gossiped about the mindbody connection and how the body carries emotions,

---

2 None of which is cosigned by science. In the *New York Times* op-ed "A 30-Year-Old Best-Selling Book Might Hold the Key to Curing Chronic Pain," science writer Juno DeMelo reviews *Healing Back Pain: The Mind-Body Connection*, Dr. John Sarno's 1991 best seller before *The Mindbody Prescription* (published in 1998). DeMelo fact-checks Dr. Sarno's claims, and while some are dubious, she says Dr. Sarno "was right about" the "link between emotional and physical pain," and she points out that "scientists now look to the nervous system to understand chronic pain that isn't caused by nerve or tissue damage" but by "brain circuitry malfunction[ing], prolonging, amplifying and possibly even creating pain."

specifically regarding loneliness—a psychological state that scrambles hormone signals and gene molecules, and that can be fatal because it aggravates heart disease, diabetes, and neurodegenerative illnesses like Alzheimer's. Doctors now treat loneliness with pain-relief drugs (anti-inflammatories like Tylenol and blood pressure medication like beta blockers). But loneliness, Dr. Sarno says, is "conscious." We know when we're lonely and can (maybe) medicate it. Trauma, however, is fundamentally unknowable and unspeakable—it's too filled with static to narrate and too chaotic for a narrative since a narrative needs a beginning, a middle, and an end. The unspeakable becomes silence, and silence becomes fate because it's what we don't talk about, or refuse to think about, that sends electricity and flame to nerve fibers.

Audre Lorde's daughter knew this. When advising her poet-activist mother what to say in the speech titled "The Transformation of Silence into Language and Action," Elizabeth Lorde said, "Tell [the audience] about how you're never really a whole person if you remain silent, because there's always that one little piece inside you that wants to be spoken out, and if you keep ignoring it, it gets madder and madder and hotter and hotter, and if you don't speak out one day it will just up and punch you in the mouth from the inside."

One day the mad-hot piece inside me that wanted to be spoken out did.

"This'll be the challenge of your career," I told a Babeland erotic toy store employee after she asked if she may help me find something.

Another gynecologist had told me during another annual exam that my shredded cervix no longer looked like I'd given birth when I hadn't, and I thought I could go back to normal, too.

"I want to lose my celibacy and reintroduce my vagina to a penis, but not a human penis, or even a human-size penis," I told her, because I was ready for some things but not for others. "I have a sex opportunity on the horizon."

The deal was this: I couldn't tell the Opportunity about my celibacy, or I'd weird him out. I was scared that he'd be scared—of me, of my reality, of my feelings. Especially my feelings, which were unacceptable (and really one feeling: shame, the main feeling of trauma, which was speaking for me since silence is the main preoccupation when traumatized). I had weirded out and scared away other Opportunities by sharing this too-much-information, so losing my celibacy was an art that was hard to master. I had to resolve my body privately, with inorganic parts, and until then I didn't wish myself on anyone.

I spent money I didn't have on a rechargeable curved pink thinger, and that night I queued the *Magic Mike* soundtrack and story-driven erotica—

But upon contact with the curved pink thinger, my body remembered what my mind wouldn't (the body is an elephant that never forgets), and it clenched itself into a fist, squeezing sand into glass.

But I'd lit candles! I'd read Anaïs Nin.

My body didn't care about candles. My body understood something that my mind ("I") did not. My body had a mind, memory, and voice of its own.

I thought I could become normal by deciding, but thoughts are not facts; the body is facts. And if you silence the body, well, you can't.

Trauma "can be reactivated" at any time according to male psychiatrist Bessel van der Kolk in *The Body Keeps the Score: Brain, Mind, and Body in the Healing of Trauma,* a paperback that resurfaced on the *New York Times* best-seller list in 2020, 2021, and 2022, eight years after its publication in 2014 (when trauma was only on the tip of the nation's tongue). Trauma leaves corporeal footprints and can "mobilize disturbed brain circuits and secrete massive amounts of stress hormones" when set off.

"An experience becomes a trauma," male podcaster Ezra Klein summarizes in his interview with van der Kolk, "when it disconnects us"—from each other or mind from body. My mind, somewhere and at some time (college?), had tuned out my body. (It's just very hard to listen to someone you hate; hard also if you listen only to other people and forget that you're a person to listen to, too.)

"The devastating argument," says Klein, "is not that the body keeps the score, it's that the mind hides the score from us." The mind tells a lie that the "body doesn't believe," like *I'm fine now. I'm fine now* was a lie I told but couldn't live.

The failure of Anaïs Nin and silicone went down seven months into my illness. Coincidence or hysteria or trauma or all three?

In *The Lady's Handbook for Her Mysterious Illness* author Sarah Ramey connects archetypal storytelling that begins with a woman's rape or a woman's death or a woman's illness to "the story of all [literal] trauma." The prelude to most mysterious illnesses is trauma, "a marked separation from, or injury to, the soul—a break that can be initiated by one's own actions, but is more often initiated by external factors." Which is so ubiquitous it's almost standard. "Trauma" in storytelling "has become synonymous with backstory," writes critic Parul Sehgal in "The Case Against the Trauma Plot," and "like any successful convention, [trauma] has a way of skirting our notice."

Freud would have agreed. As would his inspiration, male neurologist Jean-Martin Charcot, who "focused on the symptoms of hysteria that resembled neurological damage: motor paralyses, sensory losses, convulsions, and amnesias," writes Dr. Herman in *Trauma and Recovery*. By 1880, Charcot "had demonstrated that [hysterical] symptoms were psychological," as in they arose in the mind. But because Freud later recanted, and hysteria got a bad rap, it would take centuries for research to circle back and hypothesize that trauma can and will return as something else in the body and that, as Dr. Herman writes, "the story of the traumatic event surfaces not as a verbal narrative but as a symptom," in a surge of cells.

Mindbody syndrome (and its many other names) may be a physiological response to trauma—and it may be that in lieu of a verbal narrative, the story of my traumatic event(s) surfaced as symptoms, by punching me in the mouth from the inside.

Hysteria was not my first choice of disorders. *It's psychological* had been thrown at me before, to hide my own sexual abuse from me. (But of course that was psychological; culture had schooled me as a girl that women should consent to be taken violently, and patriarchy's idea of love and of sex left me exactly as it said and I believed it would.)

Some of my unexplained symptoms had eventual explanations. Vision loss and the headache were side effects of the first mood stabilizer I was prescribed. The second mood stabilizer, which treated my vision and headache, ate away at my blood sodium until I had hyponatremia. The breast lump—well, my mother was a three-time breast cancer survivor.

Fear, stress, anxiety, depression, neurosis, and sugar likely exacerbated my physical symptoms in a "psychological overlay."[3] And "chances are," writes author and activist Soraya Chemaly in *Rage Becomes Her: The Power of Women's Anger*, "unexpressed or inadequately expressed anger plays a part in…discomfort, pain, or distress." She adds, "Ruminating and catastrophizing," which are "more cultivated and common in women, intensify feelings of pain."

My other issues, like treatment-resistant nerve pain in my arms and back, were literally medically unexplainable. "In my experience," writes Dr. Sarno in *The Mindbody Prescription*, "backache, stomachache and headache are almost always psychologically induced." And "upper respiratory infections are heavily influenced by emotional factors," because of their effect on the immune system (emotional factors reduce the immune system's function and efficacy, and so can be the source of infection). My sore throat straddled the middle—it may have come from emotional factors or too much Advil and subsequent acid reflux (which apple cider vinegar, sauerkraut juice, and the herbalists' teas and tinctures, once calibrated correctly, relieved). Acid reflux can damage vocal cords, but so can overusing them, or underusing them until they weaken, shrink, and waste away.

And honestly? Being hysterical didn't seem so crazy after my body had rejected me for two years. Hysteria—or a mindbody

---

3 Dr. Sarno disciple Juno DeMelo writes in the *Times*, "Stressors can promote inflammation in the spinal cord and brain, which is linked to greater pain sensations."

crisis—may be a realistic reaction to living gaslit in the Upside Down of Pantsuit Nation. Those like me who voted for Hillary Clinton were sucker-punched in the spirit (*I'll name my rape baby Roe Wade* is how far my fear-thoughts went), and for years afterward bad news stalked us, refreshing trauma and cortisol and hourly plot twists. There was (and is) always *more, another, again, always*—of accusations, hearings, hashtags, death tolls, rights on the line. No wound has time to close, and more are opening and reopening all the time. Events, thoughts, and seconds should scorch less over time in the space reserved for time to heal all wounds, but not in this economy. My own phone feels like a trauma site, a mobile stove that burns.

Women, who turn to the mothering grip of media the most, must experience perma-trauma compounded with perennial retraumatization. Silicon Valley obviously invented stressful methods to unwind to keep us (women especially, me specifically) loving what we hate, craving what tyrannizes us, appreciating whatever undoes our ability to think straight, and obsessing over reiterated realities that portray women as second-class citizens without a voice—such that we may never turn off the noise and may never find peace, may never remember what we were about to say and may never get furious enough to do anything but consume the content that takes up our day and our life, and that is an exit to it—an exit that's also an entrance. Relaxing this way reminds me of the last scene in the horror movie *Jigsaw* (directed by two men and written by two men), when the final woman, in a face-off with a man, shoots a trick gun and the bullet backfires into her own skull instead of saving her.

"I believe a kind of rage/soothe ratio may play a role in determining when physical symptoms will occur," writes Dr. Sarno.

If a rage/soothe ratio does play a role, then it's a question of who gets to rage and who must repress until ill from repressing. In *Rage Becomes Her*, Chemaly cites study after study that associates women, rage, repression, and illness: "Women who repress their anger are twice as likely to die from heart-related disease," and "certain cancers, particularly breast cancer, and particularly in black women, have been linked to what researchers describe as 'extreme suppression of anger.' " Heart-related disease and cancer are "socially acceptable" conversions of distress, but emotions, like rage, are not acceptable, because stifling rage—and trauma—is just good manners.

Trauma survivors are also uniquely vulnerable to future pain because of repression, because the "ordinary response to atrocities is to banish them from consciousness," Dr. Herman writes in *Trauma and Recovery*. If we think too hard or talk about it...no. We don't want to twist the knife. And what's nicer than feeling not one thing, than thinking no thought, than not talking about it at all? It's a survival tactic: forget or die. So we suck it up—every day, all day—and don't let it get to us and don't let it get to us and don't let it get to us, for so long, for so extremely long, that our bodies churn it back up, not in thoughts or in tears but in herniated discs.

"Forget and die" is truer. Unarticulated trauma remains in the body and in the body politic—it can be passed through generations and culturally transmitted, as in epigenetic inheritance, the theory that an environment of trauma affects the genes and memories of Holocaust survivors' and enslaved people's children and grandchildren and great grandchildren, ad infinitum. And to add injury to insult, research shows that the traumatized contract more diseases and die sooner.

Epigenetic inheritance isn't so dissimilar from medical mass hysteria. This phenomenon occurs when a group of people has the same or comparable symptoms that short-circuit the nervous system for no physical pathological reason (the reason may be psychological). Wikipedia—which, again, is edited by mostly men—lists recorded episodes of mass hysteria that have befallen mostly girls and women:

In rural North Carolina in 2002, ten high school girls had seizures for five months. In Mexico City between 2006 and 2007, more than five hundred female students at a Catholic boarding school experienced an outbreak of "unusual symptoms." Starting around 2009 in Afghanistan, it seemed that girls at various schools who were dizzy, fainting, and vomiting had been poisoned; the United Nations and the World Health Organization investigated—for years—but produced zero evidence of poisoning and concluded the girls had "mass psychogenic illness" (mass hysteria). In Malaysia in 2019, schoolgirls began screaming, which medical sociologists speculated was because of the school's adherence to strict Islamic laws—but the administration believed otherwise and felled surrounding trees that might have housed bad spirits. At the Starehe Girls' Centre in Kenya also in 2019, sixty-eight students came down with cough, fever, and sneezing; the administration closed the school, but only two students tested positive for the virus that causes the common cold, so all the students underwent psychological assessments, and specialists deemed the event mass hysteria.

At the memorial for the forever-fourteen-year-old, there was a table strewn with paper and pens to write her a note and put it in a box for her parents to keep. I waited until the end, until the other attendees, half of whom were kids, wrote and left, then I knelt down to write in a flower-patterned dress that I gave away after the service—

but there were too many words to choose from for ultimate heartbreak. I wrote draft after draft of not tribute nor requiem but "Fuck you"; then "I love you."

"Fuck you" because I had to be mad at her since I couldn't be the other thing. Being mad at her was the lie I had to tell myself to endure my grief. And anger was also the truth inasmuch as—

Have you ever said something you wished you'd never said?

"I want to jump out the window for what I've boiled down to is one reason: I can't write a book," I wrote to the famous online advice columnist Sugar (née Cheryl Strayed) in August 2010. And in April 2018, the forever-fourteen-year-old jumped out the window for a reason no one will ever know.

The forever-fourteen-year-old and I had spilled our guts to each other—but because no one knows how to talk to teenagers or about suffering, she didn't tell me how much pain she was in. (Her suffering is a question I'll ask forever, and mine is the silence and the impulse to ask the question even with the certainty that the answer won't come.)

My suffering had always divided me from "them." Suffering didn't tell "them" anything while it told me:

1. Everyone suffering suffers alone.
2. No one understands how to suffer.
3. Each suffering is a snowflake.
4. Suffering shows up in ways that do not resemble suffering.
5. When suffering, there is no "before" suffering, and there is no "after" suffering; all there is is floor and bed.

I'd sought out the Feeling in my ward-protégé-sister as she hit her teens and her emotions kicked in and turned sappy lyric-like, and because she and I had a lot in common. But her suffering was a snowflake, which she would suffer alone, without my commiseration or advice.

I wrote to Sugar for advice my first summer in New York, when I was hunched and spazzed and spiraling. In the letter I'd talked about myself: "I am a pathetic and confused young woman," a millennial who had to write publicly about being unable to write and who was "sick with panic." Why? "I write like a girl," I'd begun, and explained that I wrote about "my lady life experiences" in ways that came out as "unfiltered emotion, unrequited love, and eventual discussion of vagina as metaphor," and so on that reduced me to my body and my psychological state, which would be mocked and disregarded. But I couldn't help it—all my words came out stupid and female, unbearable and wrong—and I'd point and laugh at my sentences and mark them: *not good enough, not good enough, not good enough.* My writing was girly, and girlness was insufficient, and my insufficiency did not make me poetic, it made me want to self-defenestrate. Because not only was I not a household name, but also I didn't know how to do or be anything, not an artist or a heroine or a wife or an intern or an insect.

Sugar's advice to my cry for help was, among other things, "write, Elissa Bassist. Not like a girl. Not like a boy. Write like a motherfucker." Her advice was a talking cure that went viral. It ended up on coffee mugs that ended up on TV shows and on T-shirts and baby onesies. I was secondhand famous in niche literary circles for a phrase I didn't write (I didn't write, "Write like a motherfucker") and for my suffering that inspired it (I wrote, "I want to jump out the window"). For years I received well-meaning emails from people who hoped I had Written That Book and was Writing Like a Motherfucker.

I hadn't, and I wasn't. I was sleeping like a motherfucker. I was Netflixing like a motherfucker. I was sexting the emotionally unavailable like a motherfucker. I was recommending books written by male authors to guys I liked because they "didn't really read women" like a motherfucker. I was teaching other writers to write like motherfuckers. And after the suicide, the only book I could write like a motherfucker was *The forever-fourteen-year-old jumped out the fifteenth-floor window and splatted on scaffolding.*

Her suicide cracked open something in me huge and starless, and despite how much I felt, I would feel more. There was room inside this feeling for everyone, everywhere. But not room enough in my mind, so perhaps it shot to my wrists and converted into "carpal tunnel syndrome."

At the time I wouldn't say (soberly) that unvoiced rage had anything to do with my arms or central nervous system. Instead, I returned my massive iPhone and used my teeth as fingers and cried indiscriminately, like whenever friends joked about wanting to kill themselves or a dead girl showed up onscreen. But when my spinal disc slipped, and the pain in my forearms was just...gone, as *The Mindbody Prescription* predicted, I believed what I had read—that pain like mine skips around to other locations or organs, finding substitutes to express what the sick person won't. I had also read that the mind creates symptoms as a defense, to sidetrack the sick from emotional ruin; psychic pain is the true threat, and the protective gift of physical pain is its distraction.

"Your pain is a gift," a massage therapist told me. (For a fleeting, fleeting moment, I visualized smacking her in the tit.) As if the wound was the place where the light would enter me, as male mystic Rumi wrote. As if the pain would not go away if I kept banishing then refreshing it. As if it would not leave me alone until it taught me what I needed to know about my voice. "There are nothing but gifts on this poor, poor Earth," wrote male poet Czesław Miłosz.

12

SPEAK AGAIN

Rest, sex, vibrators, prayer, exorcism, asylums, torture, execution, hypnosis, hysterectomies, constant pregnancy. These have been some remedies for hysterical women with unexplained symptoms, along with Sticking It Out, Getting Over It, Not Talking About It, Not Worrying About It, and Not Thinking About It.

Rest, sex, vibrators, and prayer didn't help me, nor did Sticking It Out or Getting Over It. I did install meditation apps and actually meditated, and one summer afternoon, to celebrate being sick for eighteen months, I listened to the "Miraculous Relationships" edition of *Oprah and Deepak's 21-Day Meditation Experience* and experienced one of those moments of sudden revelation. Before male guru Deepak Chopra (once sued for sexual harassment, but the suit was dismissed before going to trial) led me in meditation, he described the throat chakra. In yogic tradition, the human body has seven chakras or energy centers. The throat chakra—"the expression center"—is the fifth, and it governs communication skills and the party trick of speaking one's mind. If it's out of whack, then it incites havoc in the body. A clogged throat chakra can become a sinus infection or a sore throat, or can imply being tongue-tied or lost for words—

In the middle of his dharma talk, I opened my eyes and looked down and:

My body . . .
was connected . . .
to my head . . .
by my throat.

What if my throat, which joins the body and the head—aka my fifth chakra, which unites the upper and lower chakras—is what I must address? What if my fifth chakra is clogged?

Others had talked to me about my throat chakra. A massage therapist who worked on my headache emailed me about using flower essences. "Yucca kept coming up for me with you," she wrote, because "it releases the head" and "is for seeing things in perspective, etc." And she mentioned grape hyacinth, "which is for the throat and self-expression."

Another massage therapist who worked on my back advised me to "change my relationship to pain" and to feel it in order to move through it, and to "hydrate, breathe, and vocalize" when feeling it.

"Vocalize?" I double-checked.

"Yes. Or else pain gets trapped."

To unclog my fifth chakra I called a renowned obsessive-compulsive disorder therapy center in Manhattan, finally, and asked for the cheapest therapist, and was placed on their wait list. There's nothing like Oprah, Deepak Chopra, and a child's suicide to inspire change, and also I was out of treatment options.

Before my first session in September 2018, I scanned the clinicians' bios and headshots, and saw that my soon-to-be clinician was pretty. Her hair was obsidian and long—too long, like a mermaid's. And she looked young, younger than I was, too young, which conveyed that she'd only studied problems and did not experience them. Still, I showed up and sat on a contemporary couch across from the master's-level clinician, and I just wanted to brush her hair with a fork.

During our early sessions I tried to convince her that I didn't have OCD as she convinced me that I did.

My patient handout "Obsessive-Compulsive Disorder: Some Facts" said that about six million Americans have obsessive-compulsive disorder, excluding the millions more who throw around the term because they're very clean. OCD comes in every variety, from fear of surfaces to fear of pickles. Maybe we're born with it; maybe the onset is gradual, and we develop it in response to stressors; maybe it metastasizes from prolonged Internetting and trying to win over avatars that simulate warmth but are cold (as may be my case, when I met Fucktaco and began living in my head and obsessing full-time).

OCD is two parts: obsessions that evoke distress and interfere with living life, and compulsions, or rituals, intended to quell the obsessions and reduce anxiety (but do the reverse, making everything worse in furious attempts to make one thing better, like popping a zit or extinguishing fire with gasoline). The clinician pinpointed my obsession as "fear of saying the wrong thing"[1] and "fear of retaliation for speaking," and my compulsion is to edit and silence myself, and

---

1 There are many ways to interpret "fear of saying the wrong thing." 1. Phobia. Americans' number 1 phobia is fear of public speaking (death is number 5, and loneliness is 7, so people are more afraid to talk out loud, in the open, than to die or die alone). As a debater, performer, and lecturer, I got off on public speaking, so fear of public speaking, or glossophobia, is not among my issues.

2. "White silence," which can come from fear of saying the wrong thing about race and racism or being racist. While I feared offending anyone—and feared saying something ignorant and perpetuating hate—I wasn't afraid of saying the wrong thing while *trying* to say the right thing and being corrected and then speaking better (after being defensive and apologizing).

3. "Cancel culture." I was not afraid of being canceled (or rather, being held accountable). As I write this, many are tweeting about a "free speech crisis"—but a crisis for whom? For peaceful protesters who are assaulted and killed? Or for Karens* who have no problem using their voice to be racist and to decry getting called out?

*"Karen" is a name reserved for "white women with a specific haircut who ask to speak with the manager," which was narrowed to "white women being racist and entitled" and now extends to "white women acting problematic in any way." The label is one more way to silence women (there will always be one more way to silence women), but also: fuck anyone who defends her right to talk all over those who don't have a voice that our culture registers.

give myself the third degree, as though led by some high-pitch frequency, as though every sentence tempts apocalypse or being hurt.

The OCD literature says that the fear system is primitive and evolved before language, so fear is learned and developed via behavior and experience. Every time I compulsively revise and perfect one text message for weeks, my brain clocks it and categorizes "saying the wrong thing" as "life or death" since I invest my whole being trying to elude it (to elude rejection), which supports my fear that my words could bury me, which further sensitizes me to any possibility of wrongness, so that the next time I'm about to type or open my mouth to speak, I don't. Although mine is a mental compulsion, it hurts—it physically, really hurts, like treading water, like there is no stopping, like the ancient Greek woman Timyche who set herself apart from other women by chewing off her own tongue instead of saying something wrong.[2]

Exposure and Response Prevention (ERP) is "the" treatment for OCD. It's a behavioral therapy in which the obsessed puts herself, deliberately, in tormenting situations that prompt her obsessions and the attendant distress (exposure). At the same time and with Sisyphean strength, the compulsive must stifle the irresistible urge to alleviate distress via routines that make life hard by doing what feels easy (response prevention).

I had to do all this with a pretty person, but OCD treatment clarified to me why I needed it. Understanding my fear didn't stop me from being afraid. Regardless of how much I knew as a literate feminist with ten thousand hours of therapy, the body and its systems would always know more. Fear ensured I could know better and not do better. (It's one of the minor human tragedies: to know better *and still*. To think no, no, no but still say "Yes!")

---

2 Her rationale: love. She talked about—what else?—*him*. Also, marrying him. She wanted to tell everyone about him and to talk to no one else but him. When she heard her echo—*What if he heard that he's all I talk about?*—her tongue had to go.

"Exposure is willingly doing what some inner voice says you should not, under any circumstance, do," the clinician said.

In my case, this was expressing myself. It was saying what I believed others didn't want me to say. It was writing something unreadable that may inspire the vitriol and reprisal of shitty men. It was saying no. It was asking questions. It was coming off badly. It was opening myself to being misunderstood or ghosted or judged and criticized, to being disliked or disrespected, to being regarded as not nice, curt, aggravating, abnormal, loony. It was speaking awfully but speaking anyway, again and again.

"Nothing will come of nothing," says the dad King Lear to his youngest daughter, Cordelia, in words written by male playwright William Shakespeare. "Speak again," he tells her.[3]

How, exactly, to speak again? How to do what women have been conditioned not to do? How to go against every instinct and societal directive in a world that prefers a woman's death to her opinion?

Author bell hooks had to change her name. "One of the many reasons I chose to write using the pseudonym bell hooks," she writes in *Talking Back*, "was to construct a writer-identity that would challenge and subdue all impulses leading me away from speech into silence."

Throughout time, there have been public and private methods to pull words out of women. Ancient cultures had ceremonial katharsis and coordinated ritual funeral lament for women, in which "laws were passed specifying the location, time, duration, personnel, choreography, musical content and verbal content of the women's [expression of grief or sorrow]," writes Anne Carson in "The Gender of Sound." Some women's festivals also set aside time for women to shout "abusive remarks or obscenities or dirty jokes at one another," and their stories suggested "a backlog of sexual anger." There were "leakproof ritual container[s]" for women to spew "unpleasant tendencies

---

3 Unfortunately, Cordelia's dad meant "Speak again" as *Give lengthy speeches about me and about how much you love me as quid pro quo.*

and raw emotion," and these occasions were for the good of the woman but more for the good of the city, to cleanse it of unlikeable female sound.[4]

In the late nineteenth century, catharsis was a therapeutic and psychoanalytical technique for women with backlogs of sexual anger. Dr. Freud and his male collaborator Joseph Breuer helped hysterical patients (women with acid memories and hideous feelings that tainted the soul) through hypnosis and by inducing them to talk about what they couldn't, with the hope that the mind and mouth, this time, were up to it. The male doctors then put the unnamable into a narrative and the symptoms into a critical interpretation—supposedly, ghostwriting and analyzing the women's stories rid them of their symptoms. Breuer's famous patient "Anna O.," whose real name was Bertha Pappenheim, called this the "talking cure." Freud found it "necessary to talk," and as Dr. Herman writes in *Trauma and Recovery*, for "a brief decade men of science listened to women with a devotion and a respect unparalleled before or since."

I'd fucked with giving the unspeakable a plot before. During one of my breakups with Fucktaco, I saw a Buddhist-type therapist in San Francisco who listened to me with devotion and respect, then tried an experimental psychotherapy procedure on me called EMDR (Eye Movement Desensitization and Reprocessing) that he used on 9/11 survivors to guide them through worst-case scenarios to the other side of their fear and to help them with post-traumatic stress disorder (not covered by insurance).

I'd thought, *How dramatic to use this on me, just another heartbroken girl.* Just another emotionally throttled girl. But I was game for any available exorcism. (Also, Bessel van der Kolk pointed out that events like 9/11 are "less likely to cause trauma because they were shared by the community," whereas breakups are not.)

---

4 It's too bad we left festivals like these in the past and now don't have templates or conventions for lamenting or screaming obscenities or venting sexual anger.

I sat on a soft couch across from a painting of mountains and coyotes, and in each hand I held cream-colored paddles and closed my eyes.

EMDR works based on the mindbody connection and the mindbody likeness—i.e., just as repeated physical injury doesn't heal, repeated mental injury won't either, and trauma is an injury to the psyche that "behaves like an open wound," as Freud said about the complex of melancholia.

Typically in EMDR a therapist asks a patient to recall a traumatic event while the therapist directs the patient's eye movements or taps their hands—and the varied sensory input helps neutralize a traumatic memory or unfreeze it to leave it behind. ("Memory" isn't even the right word because trauma isn't "remembered from the past"—it's a reaction, relived without end, like a grotesque cul-de-sac or chronic déjà vu where the traumatized confuses tenses and feels as if the past is the present and that there is no tomorrow. The traumatic moment must be made into memory; mind and body must move it from "now" to "then.")

How I injured my psyche, which behaved like an open wound: Gchat saves online conversations, and since most of my conversations with Fucktaco were via Gchat or Gmail or text, about 90 percent of our interactions were transcribed and stored, and the 24/7 access to our history suspended it and "us" and me. I wasn't with Fucktaco anymore, but I experienced time as if I were because I could return to the archive and fire up the relationship at will. (At the funeral for a relationship, if you mourn it enough, it resurrects, or, rather, a zombified version of what it was comes back.) Maybe I'd revisit a conversation from three years ago, an argument or a chat about what we'd name our daughter, an exchange that I was starting to forget, that I didn't want to forget, and by rereading I swapped "what is" with "what was" and "what should be," so it seemed plausible, even as I sat alone on my phone, that we would always end up together.

"Similar to a distinct catastrophe," the therapist said, "this overloads your brain until it can't integrate memory normally, and your memories resemble traumatic ones, unedited and locked."

He relayed my mental state and memory-processing system in an extended metaphor: A man in the dark gropes a wall to find a way out of his cell. He contemplates climbing over, tunneling through, dismantling it, unearthing a secret passage, and so on. Surrounding him are people giving instruction and counsel. These people love him. They say, *Turn around*. He says, *First I have to get around this wall*. They say, *Turn around*. He insists, *Not until I find a way out*. They chant, *Turn around, turn around*, and he's oblivious to them. He closes his eyes (to exacerbate his dilemma) and pats the stones and mortar, searching, frantic, snapping off his nails to the chorus *Just turn around*. The man is fondling a pillar. The wall is *in his mind*.

I heard the far-away swoosh of Ocean Beach as the therapist turned on the paddles, and instead of asking me to recall a distressing event, my therapist asked me to describe a fantasy nightmare I didn't want to see. (This is like another form of OCD treatment: imaginary practice, or imaginal exposure.) All I had to do was grip as he asked me to imagine my never-to-be-husband's wedding with someone who wasn't me.

"What does he look like walking down the aisle?"

I squeezed my eyelids trying to envision him in an aisle in a ceremony in a wedding costume. "He looks happy," I said as the therapist controlled the paddles, which vibrated rhythmically left to right ("bilateral stimulation").

"What are you doing while he is getting married?" he asked, then reminded me to breathe.

"I'm writing a novel," I said ambitiously.

"What's the novel about?"

"It is about a lost man," I said, because I didn't know what to say. I'd wanted to write an updated myth of Orpheus and Eurydice, about a man who looks back when he isn't supposed to and loses his love. In the flawless film *Portrait of a Lady on Fire* (written and directed by filmmaker Céline Sciamma), the character Héloïse reads the myth aloud, and the character Marianne suggests why he turns: "He chose the memory of her," she says. "He doesn't make the lover's choice, but the poet's." The poet's choice may be the healthier one. Love as consolation, having the memory and not love by your side, may be healthier.

Something was shaking loose. Other images and other ideas and other possibilities and other plans. Had they been available all this time, waiting, theoretical?

That felt like enough work for one day.

But the therapist wanted to know more. He trauma-splained that trauma amputates our imagination and arrests the stories we tell ourselves in order to live; we can't imagine anything could be different, and change is unthinkable. By asking me about events that hadn't transpired, the therapist was really asking me to write a new story and inhabit a new reality and experience an alternate ending and reroute my heart.

"Where is the wedding?"

"In a shul in Denver."

"What is the bride wearing?"

"An off-white gown. She's carrying a bouquet because that's what brides do. Roses, maybe." I couldn't think of other kinds of flowers. "She's on the arm of her aging father. Their flower girl is his niece, dressed in lace, throwing red rose petals with browning edges . . ."

"What do you feel in your body?"

I felt that for a wedding present I'd give Fucktaco the gift of me not being his wife.

The therapist asked about their life together, enmeshed, married. "What do you see? What do you hear?"

I saw Southeast Asia and skiing in Loveland, Colorado, for winter break, bundled in conjugal old age, arms wrapped around each other and around their two small skiers in black plastic goggles with perfect teeth, and I heard giggling while they posed for their annual Hanukkah e-card that they'd spam their family and thousands of friends.

The left paddle surged, then the right, messing with my sensory perception and neural networks. "Healing trauma may be a matter of repairing disconnected neural networks," the therapist had said when he introduced me to EMDR.

I wandered off mentally and went through my past plans about my future with Fucktaco to undo them, to rewrite what I'd written in my mind in stone.

We won't have a big wedding, nor a small one; our wedding won't be medium-size. Our wedding, which we had planned via Gchat, won't. No kids with vocabulary cards either. His fluids and mine won't merge into DNA that won't show itself in grandchildren, in generations to come. Unrattled rattles and vacant elasticized maternity wear will lay folded in other couples' shopping carts. Is there a nickname for this? A daughter or son's? Whatever, because we won't call our unmade nonkids anything, nothing honoring my grandmother or his, and the argument about which one won't take place, and I won't pretend to like a name just because he likes it.

We will not waste a lifetime together. Death will not do us part. Events powered by expectation will be Photoshopped out from the never-to-be-taken, never-to-be-family photo, untagged and unposted on Instagram. And we'll—no. Not even that. We won't even settle for each other.

The therapist turned off the vibrating paddles, and the old religion was over.

I cried until I lost muscle, until I was done crying over the lost man whom I had lost.

The therapist asked me if I was okay.

I was. I was okay in a different future and not disintegrated or dead at all the way I thought I'd be.

I may have been cured of that man but I was not cured. Years later, for my headache, the acupuncturist who had diagnosed my rage pre-scribed her own talking cure: confront and purge the other shitty men from my life, to get out of my mind what had manifested in my body by using my voice. As if that would fix anything and everything.

Her recommendation was a version of "expressive writing," male psychologist James Pennebaker's psychological remedy for pain and his theory that writing one's wounds helps close them. "The first systematic test of the power of language to relieve trauma was done in 1986," writes van der Kolk in *The Body Keeps the Score*. Pennebaker asked his introductory psychology students to think about the darkest shit that had ever happened to them, and then he divided them into three groups and instructed them to sit alone for fifteen minutes four days in a row and open a vein to write (like a personal essay class but for science). One group wrote about current life events (minimum emotional voltage), another group detailed their very bad memory (medium emotional voltage), and group three recounted the dark shit *and* how they felt about it *and* the lifelong impact (maximum emotional voltage).

Prior to the experiment the students were asked about their medical histories, and they disclosed "major and minor health problems: cancer, high blood pressure, ulcers, flu, headaches, and earaches"; in Pennebaker's results, students who wrote with maximum emotional voltage experienced "a 50 percent drop in doctor visits."

In repeated studies based on the same protocol, the results were the same: "improved health" *from writing* "correlated with improved immune function."

"In most studies of emotional-awareness and expression therapy," writes science journalist Eleanor Cummins in "Is the Pain All in My Head?," sick people "reported a significant reduction in their pain," around "20 percent," which is "on par with just about every pain-management tool including opioids, antidepressant and anti-seizure medications, meditation and mindfulness therapies, massage and physical therapy, and more."

Dr. Sarno also observed in his patients "a desire for conscious unification of thought and feeling," and once achieved, their physical pain faded. After "exorcising a diary's worth of negative feelings over four months," Juno DeMelo writes in her *Times* op-ed about Dr. Sarno's method, "I was—in spite of my incredulousness—cured" of chronic pain in her left piriformis. DeMelo admits, "Dr. Sarno almost certainly oversimplified and overemphasized the psychological origins of pain. But he also helped me see that both the mind and the body are responsible for our physical suffering. And that we're not powerless to change it."

For angry women in particular, Soraya Chemaly found studies showing that "even remembering an angry experience results in a decline in antibodies, the first line of defense in fending off disease," and "the survival rate for women with breast cancer who expressed their anger was twice that of women who kept their anger to themselves."

Though not documented, expressive writing must work miracles for women in general, who historically had to disguise their anger and their writing in private journals or letters, or as postscripts or parodies or fiction or ghost stories, because their language was too twisted and depressing, and it was misconstrued as madness; so, for women, writing is a refusal to disappear. It's a means to—how do I put this?—give birth to oneself. To be the subject for once.

To complete my acupuncturist's expression assignment, I emailed my dad.

I had written and sent hundreds of thousands of emails in my life, at least half of them emotional, but this email was my Everest. I stared into space and waited for thirty-five years of unsaid conversations to materialize in Gmail, and I thought and thought—

I was thinking too hard. Which is what my former psychologist would say. Every session she'd ask me how I was feeling, and I'd say, "I think I feel—"

"No," she'd interrupt, and ask me to begin with "I feel . . ."

But ever since I'd turned off my feelings like the vampires in *The Vampire Diaries* who "turn off their humanity," I could only think feeling, not feel it.

Because of the psychologist I bought a Wheel of Emotions art print and mousepad on sale, and I imagined her asking, *How does your dad make you feel?* My dad, whom I'd nicknamed "The Emotional Abyss."

I referenced the print with six primary emotions in the middle: "anger, fear, disgust, sad, happy, surprise." Each fans out into variations of the primary emotion. I traced "anger," and it fanned out to "hurt, threatened, hateful, mad, aggressive, frustrated, distant, critical." I traced "hurt," which fanned out to a third tier, "embarrassed, devastated." I traced "mad" that fanned out to "furious, enraged." "Sad" fanned out into "guilty, abandoned, despair, depressed, lonely, bored." I traced "abandoned" to "ignored, victimized." I traced "despair" to "powerless, vulnerable." I traced "guilt" to "remorseful, ashamed."

"Dad," I began the email. So far, so good.

In the email's prologue I updated him about the acupuncturist and the assignment.

Then I began with one "I feel" statement ("I feel angry that when we talk, it seems like you barely listen, like you're barely there"), and after I got going, it was all flow, all unsaid "I feel" statements ("I've felt mad for days, for months, years"), typing "I feel this" ("I feel frustrated that our communication is through my mom and that she has fought my battles with you"), and "I feel that" ("I feel devastated that you haven't been there for me and that I haven't been there for you"), as if I were playing jazz piano ("A few years ago we talked about our relationship through [my stepmom] as your mouthpiece and as our moderator. We promised each other change. I feel sad that nothing has changed"), as if my feelings were passing through my fingers and reaching my father and all fathers everywhere ("I feel pissed that you claim innocence and correctness by virtue of absence"; "I feel I need more from a father. Maybe you feel you need more from a daughter— I don't know because we don't communicate beyond the movies we've seen or haven't seen yet, which makes me feel unhappy").

The *whoosh* sound of the "send" button signaled my headache to go away, and it did, briefly.

Expressing myself and my every emotion would end our relationship, I was certain, since expressing myself had ended my other relationships with other men. But my dad replied, and with paragraphs. And he was kind. And open to change, and not defensive or expectant that I change.

Still, I had to change.

If only because my silence wasn't mine alone, and it didn't hurt only me.

I'd do formal expression exercises in OCD therapy with the young mermaid clinician who personalized Exposure and Response Preventions (ERP) to help me resuscitate my voice.

"Type a message," the clinician said in session, indicating I should pick up my phone. "I'll set a timer for five minutes," she said, "to preclude limitless rumination."

With my armpits dampening from the screen's glow, I composed a text, just a text, just a short text to recalibrate fear that was decades in the making.

"Now," she said, "send it as it is, with typos and no corrections or apologies, to be 'wrong' without defense or explanation or too much effort."

ERP was ridiculous, and I hated it: to feel bad temporarily in order to feel better at some point. Correcting myself had been my "me" time—although that time was short and was my undoing since my sole feeling was anxiety. I didn't think I'd die by text, but that whoever received my text would unlove / unwant / unfriend / unfollow / unhire or verbally attack me—and the regret over what I'd said to make them would be my three a.m. thought spiral for the rest of time. My every text and email and conversation were auditions for love, and I'd gotten used to speaking in ways that elicited or circumvented particular reactions, and to basing what I said on the anticipation of how it would be received, and so one typo risked it all.

I thought, *I cannot do this* as I was doing it, leaving a typo and not crying.

The clinician and I talked about how outcome, like approval, is irrelevant to treatment—I wasn't saying the wrong thing on purpose to win or lose someone but to restore my fear system, through different behavior, to its proper balance.

We also talked about how I didn't need the happy outcome I thought I needed, the fiction every girl is sold that she resells to herself in which a woman's final words are "I do." What I needed was to be less afraid of my voice and its flaws. I needed the meme wisdom of "Before you say I'm too much, ask yourself if you are even enough." I needed French feminist writer Hélène Cixous's lines: "Women must write her self: must write about women and bring women to writing, from which they have been driven away as violently as from their bodies—for the same reasons, by the same law, with the same fatal goal. Woman must put herself into the text—as into the world and into history—by her own movement." I needed to put myself into *a* text, to put myself back into the world (and maybe into history) by saying what I wanted without fear of disaster or error, and without a frantic, overwhelmed lurching, and aside from whatever would happen, or wouldn't.

"The real torture," the clinician said, "is denying so much of yourself just to avoid one misstep that you have less and less to offer each time you open your mouth. Also? Holding back and biting your tongue until it bleeds—that's not love. That's a Victorian novel."

Or was it patriarchy? OCD is known as the "doubting disease" because the OCD brain grabs on to doubt and fear, and it compulsively does whatever it can to gauge what is "correct." But as a woman, doubting and fearing were my cardio and my whole day because the female brain contains two thoughts: *Am I right? Am I good?* A sentence is scarcely out of a woman's mouth before her inner voice interferes. *Will I sound bonkers? Look bad? Make him mad? Am I being considerate? Fair? Sweet?* A woman can't simultaneously disagree and be safe. A woman can't say no and be right. A woman can't rebel as she warps her voice to garner validation. A woman can't. Even women who went to the Women's March are nervous to default on vows of silence we never took.

Personally, I had to distinguish between what was obsessive-compulsive disorder and what was patriarchy, a different disorder. My fear of speaking could be understood as a personal dysfunction, or it could be understood as a generalized response to women being censured for speaking, such that a woman's fear system perceives any and every act as a fight waiting to happen and to prevent. Homicide and rape statistics show that a woman *should* fear her voice—there's even the term "rejection violence" for the specific phenomenon of abusing, stabbing, shooting, raping, gang-raping, murdering, and mass-murdering women for saying no. And the unrecorded statistics of violence against BIWOC and LGBTQIA+ imply that marginalized groups should be even more afraid of their voice and, as Tressie McMillan Cottom writes in *Thick*, be more obliged to "screen our jokes, our laughter, our emotions, and our baggage" and "constantly manage complex social interactions so we are not fired, isolated, misunderstood, miscast, or murdered."

I asked the clinician, "Is there therapy for women with Patriarchy? I'm asking for every friend I have."

I was asking also for myself, a woman who has dedicated entire therapy sessions to workshopping one sentence to say aloud to the handyman so he'll listen without calling me "princess."

And I was asking my creative writing students, who, if they're women and they do speak up in class, it's to disclaim their writing and lived experience, as though their free speech and their license to live and to comment on living is in perpetual question, as though their writing is our millstone and their perspective is beside the point in a class they paid to participate in, a class where sometimes I beg women to ask questions because I'd have to be begged if I weren't the instructor.

There isn't therapy for patriarchy, so far. There's no Exposure and Response Prevention for patriarchy, either. Whenever the clinician and I came to these conclusions, we'd look blankly at each other and shake our heads until our time together was up.

Flashback: My first priority in late 2016 was to find the next available hand-to-hand combat preparedness class; I would not walk around in the Upside Down of Pantsuit Nation without training for it. Scared minds think alike because in a private Facebook comedy group, a stand-up posted about a gratis self-defense seminar led by a former cop who now works in television and film as a stuntman.

Westside Rifle & Pistol Range in Manhattan donated the space. Female comics in athleisure met in a basement classroom, but rather than hit the mat and disable a foam-outfitted samurai prone to psychopathy, the former cop lectured for two hours from a thorough outline that informed and terrified, and we took notes on how to avert victimhood and how to use our body parts as weapons and how to survive. *On the subway platform, the safest place to stand is behind an emergency call box. On the street, know where you are, and walk in familiar territory, on major streets. If you believe someone is following you, then trust your instincts, call 911, and at full volume give your location and describe the person behind you as best you can, homing in on distinctive, obscure details because we are our own best witnesses. Predators scout easy targets (the distracted, the headphoned, the sleepy, the lost), so look up and be aware and alert, to convey "I am not afraid." If attacked, then be loud: draw attention and first fight your instinct to whisper gently into your attacker's ear about how you may assist his attack. Attackers are most physically vulnerable in their eyes, jugular notch (the soft spot between the neck and the collarbone), solar plexus (the pit of the stomach), hair, and ears. And if there is a knife or a gun*—we all held our breath for the ex-cop's foolproof plan of attack or escape—*then pray to God that at least you get out with your life.*

Amid practice shots fired outside the room, I jotted it down, useful for public transportation and sidewalks.

In my notes was a hole, so I raised my hand, which was *so brave*.

"What if you're on a date with a man," I began, "and you're making out with him, but you don't want to make out with him, nor did you hint at wanting to, but you make out anyway, because," I justified, "it'd be so inconsiderate not to?"

The ex-cop searched his notes.

"This happened to me last week," the woman to my left volunteered. Her male friend—"overcome with passion," well-intentioned, lovesick, drunk—had overpowered her, and she kissed him consensually so that he wouldn't have sex with her nonconsensually. What if she protested and provoked him? So she gave a little to avoid a lot. She chose the position of least resistance, as one would steer a difficult conversation to the innocuous.

General self-defense was too advanced for us. I'd thought, *If only there were the prerequisite, self-defense communication to undo lifetimes of socialization and trauma-response conditioning.*

OCD treatment turned out to be my self-defense communication training.

The OCD clinician answered what the ex-cop couldn't: silence is a trauma response, a form of fight, flight, freeze, fawn, and other strategies for protection and control that are trap doors. These are instincts we develop to survive—not live, but survive.

As a girl I was unpracticed at "no," and this precipitated trauma, then as a woman the word "no" was entwined with traumatic experience. Some OCD experts suggest that OCD is characterized by "thinking mistakes" about harm. With men, I'm afraid that saying the wrong thing—"no"—will hurt them, and then they will hurt me (with silence or shouting or cervix-shredding). So, I lost "no," or I couldn't remember it. And I lost feminist theory and lost the fact that I'd been traumatized as well as the fact that it was a fact and not "my interpretation."

I had nonmedical aphasia, like Freud's patient "Dora" who lost her words.

Without "no," I was frozen in fawn, in people-pleasing, in gaining approval, in "no problem," in "whatever you want," in "yes."

What I couldn't explain to the ex-cop was that I wanted-needed-hungered to answer yes, regardless of the question. That I would say whatever whoever wanted me to and more, or less, a lot less, if what I said could be what he wanted to hear. That getting naked was easier than speaking. That between the lines of every word out of my mouth is *Please don't hurt me, thank you, and I'm sorry.* That trauma changed the locks on the brain, the body, and the throat, and I changed because of trauma, to evade it, to endure it. That YES! was my prepared response whenever I felt threatened and that I felt threatened all the time and that trauma responses had replaced my everyday ones.

Dr. Sarno posits that the unconscious perceives rage itself as threatening, "hence the dramatic overreaction in the form of pain and other physical symptoms."

Every therapy session I was in pain and brought an inflatable back pillow for sitting with a herniated disc. I'd been showing up to weekly sessions for two months, between physical therapy appointments, and my symptoms, disorders, tragedies, gender, and voice kept inter-secting as more was revealed about what being voiceless entailed and annihilated.

The exposures and response prevention only got more madden-ing because they were so basic and so undoable. For example, to kill my OCD and trauma responses with one stone, the clinician had me practice "no," first by messaging "no" on dating apps—to get used to it and get in the habit, to drop the carefulness that looks like agreement when I do not agree, and to not give in to the inclination (the pressure, the imperative, the survival mandate) to indulge a man just because he's a man; to hear "no" in my mind and see "no" before me so I could verbalize "no" aloud and then expand my range. *Please don't speak to*

me like that. I'm not comfortable with that. That doesn't work for me. I
don't want to. Nope. No way. Absolutely not. Under no circumstances.
Never. Not on your life. No.[5]

My embarrassment was so strong it had a pulse.

"ARE YOU FUCKING KIDDING ME that I cannot pronounce a
TWO-LETTER word?" I yelled in general in session.

I felt that feeling I'd heard so much about, rage. My mouth caught
on fire with it, and I couldn't stop, wouldn't stop.

"And because, IN THE PAST, I had asked for what I didn't want,
now and FOREVER I must live with the repercussions of giving men
what they wanted?

"And IT KILLS ME that (1) women are violated; (2) we expect
women to PUT UP WITH violation; (3) we are reminded CON-
STANTLY of women's violation via entertainment, news, social
media, and policy; and (4) we're supposed to KEEP CALM, not complain, and CARRY ON with our lives as if we're NOT at WAR?

"DO NOT EVEN GET ME STARTED that violence against
women is baked into the biographies of MEN who control our FACTS,
our STORIES, and our LAWS; and while these elected MISOGY-
NISTS vote on legislation to control women—as per establishments
that don't perceive women as human beings with a right to life, or life
without pain—we as constituents must SIT QUIETLY and CONTAIN
our rage, which only AGGRAVATES it, which is BAD FOR OUR
HEALTH and WEAKENS our immune system because SURVIVAL
steals so much focus.

"AND HOW DARE anyone, much less EVERYONE, presume
that women fail to live up to certain standards—to be quote-unquote
GOOD, to be quote-unquote RIGHT—standards WE invent, along
with our FAILURE?

"And THROUGHOUT IT ALL we are gaslit into believing that
none of this is happening or has happened or will continue to happen?!

---

5 "'No' is a full sentence," said Elizabeth Olsen about her sisters' best advice.

And then, AND THEN! we are told that to be happy we must have romantic, nurturing, lifelong relationships with men and learn to give them better blow jobs?[6] And. And. And. Actual girls are dying while we watch fictional girls dying, but we can't talk about that or them or mental health because 'life begins at conception' and who cares when it ends.

"ANYWAY."

"Hey Elissa, keeping busy?" a man on Bumble (or Tinder or BeLinked or Fuck, Marry, Kill or one of a thousand other dating apps) messaged. I thought, *No*, but feared being rude, and because of the potential for rejection violence, I feared rude's attendant outsize fear of being murdered.

"Lean into your fear," the clinician prompted me. She wasn't talking about Sheryl Sandberg's mission in her "feminist manifesto" *Lean In* about how to sit at a table during a business meeting with businessmen. She meant that whenever I questioned my words and was second-guessing and forgiving myself nothing but nothing, I should reiterate "lean-in statements"—to practice having a noncompulsive response and to agree to my fear and doubt instead of fight or flee or freeze or fawn.

I reread "Hey Elissa, keeping busy?" and typed, "No," then hesitated.

"You must be willing to feel some discomfort," the clinician said in a ruthless manner about going against my nature.

---

6 ... and MARRY them because our culture—which can go FUCK ITSELF—took something that, until the last century, was a nonoptional oppressive institution wherein a woman has NO legal or financial jurisdiction, and repackaged it to women as "ROMANCE" and "PURPOSE"—because if women aspire to *romance* and *purpose*, then we will (1) let men have sex all over us; and (2) wed men so we can serve them via childbearing, child care, housework, sex work, and emotional labor, while also working regular jobs that actually pay to support our grocery habit. And in exchange we get... companionship? Security? I AM ASKING HONESTLY: WHAT? WHY?

I leaned in. *Maybe I am rude. Maybe I will be murdered for being rude.*

Then I tapped the paper-airplane icon and my "No" appeared on the screen.

The next thirty seconds I was in turmoil sitting with uncertainty— *I said the wrong thing, didn't I? DIDN'T I? Did I?*—and trying not to bail by coping mechanism. Because that's what I had to do, what I did do and would do infinite times, like a redwood tree that must burn to grow.

"Hey! are you into films? Have you seen the new joker movie?"
"No."

"Elissa! Hello! Tell me, would you rather be a master of all
    instruments or be able to speak any language fluently?"
"What? No."

"20 questions! You have to give honest answers and you can't
    repeat any questions the other person asked. Deal?"
"20 answers! No. No. No. No. No. No. No. No. No. No. No. No.
    No. No. No. No. No. No. No. No."

"can we please get this relationship over with already."
"No thank you!"
"haha oh well"

"We should meet up tonight"
"I'm not ready to meet up yet"
"Merci Elissa, okay I understand when do you think you will
    be ready?"

From Tim, on March 5, 2020: "How many fingers would you
    be willing to sacrifice to be able to control the weather?"

From Tim again, on March 29, 2020: "Hey remember when
    the weather was our biggest problem?"
me: "No"

Each time I said no, it was the end of the world, until it wasn't. With every no, my anxiety and rage dissipated, and my physical pain, too, and I could almost feel distress purify through repetition.

"No" is still slippery. But when it's accessible—and it's more and more accessible—I feel as if I can do anything, like trust myself.

Also, saying no when I think no frees up a lot of time and attention that I had reserved to self-persecute.

Speaking again is not easy, but it's simple. "It's risk," the clinician says.

Risk "no." Risk the double-text. Risk being unlikeable and being perceived as unreasonable, and risk being called a fucking bitch. Risk "being a bitch." Risk "bad" words.[7] Risk mistakes and risk being corrected and risk losing those who won't forgive. Risk refusal. Risk acknowledgment. Risk trouble. Risk the question. Risk demanding care. Risk a voice that doesn't demure, a voice that is difficult, unaesthetic, charged, forthright, sappy. Risk it, or risk living a half-a-person life.

"The point isn't to be unafraid," the clinician also says. We may always be afraid. The point is to be afraid and risk anyway.

---

7 "Profanity is an essential tool in disrupting patriarchy and its rules. It is the verbal equivalent of civil disobedience. There is nothing polite about patriarchy. There is nothing civil about racism or misogyny," tweeted author of *The Seven Necessary Sins for Women and Girls* Mona Eltahawy, with the hashtag #WhyISayFuck.

13

RECLAIMING WOMEN'S VOICES

A plot hole, for sure, or a deus ex machina, but after three months of OCD treatment, I was pain-free. The pain ended as the pain narrative predicted.

If, on a podcast, someone were to ask: *Elissa, critically acclaimed author of many double-texts, can you pinpoint a symbolic moment that has stuck with you ever since, when you—pardon my language—turned a corner?*

I'd say:

Thank you so much for asking that great question. For my herniated disc a physical therapist recommended Pilates, the exercise for ballerinas and the injured. In class I'd watch the person in front of me or beside me to see what I was doing—because everyone else knew what to do, and I didn't, and also I was in a one-sided competition to be the best. *Fuck it,* I thought during one class after months of ERP, and I experimented with watching no one and moving without example. And it wasn't so bad to be wrong or to be the worst. It was alien and unbearable, but there were no consequences whatsoever, not physical or psychological. It was actually quite safe to be wrong. I could be wrong and still be so okay.

The very thought of "wrong" was suddenly stupid, vacant, a unit of measurement that miniaturized me. Who defined "wrong"? I didn't, and if most of my problems hadn't been defined by me, then were they really *my problems*? As writer Suzanne Juhasz says, "a poem works if it lives up to itself." What if "wrong" didn't mean what everyone pretended and threatened it meant?

Once I saw this word for what it was, everything changed.

Except the fear didn't change. Or the doubt. And I still get headaches. But they are less urgent, and there are new feelings, new thoughts, even new hopes, and more of these happen in between.

I didn't count on realizations at Club Pilates or change or the brain's plasticity or help that helped or myself or my pain being a gift.

My pain was a gift! A gift that could be a Fiona Apple album title like *A Day Without a Headache Is a Good Day—Nothing Else Has to Happen; Every Moment Pain-Free Is a Bonus and Can Host an Assembly of Insignificant Miracles and the Opportunity of a Lifetime: to Lose and Resurrect in Each Heartbeat That Tricky Flicker, an Appreciation: to Have a Pulse, Hulu, a Million Things and Counting Going Right.*

Or a gift like a compass with a magnetized needle that points away from what stings (social media, shitty men, email) and has special technology to indicate that I cannot go where I have always gone.

Or a gift like a remote that skips the following:

media that condemns powerless, inarticulate skanks who are
     sexualized, victimized, hated, or invisible;
content in which the male voice is omnipotent and most other
     voices are turned off;
casts of all men in tactical gear and one white woman in shorts
     with CGI cleavage who can't think but is an object of
     contemplation;

scripts without words for what hurts but with endless scenes of
    women hurting;

movie magic where yet another super-antihero that shoots sperm
    saves the world from itself;

everything I watched yesterday and the day before, and the day
    before that.

I needed pain's merch because on my to-do list below "speak again" was "fall in love with the female voice." Because it turns out I wasn't sick of my voice so much as I was sick of the male voice that told me to be sick of the female voice.

My dissimilar experiences as a background actor were proof enough to me that "reality" (whatever that is) is up for grabs, and that we have a choice—maybe not in terms of reproductive health but in reality, in what moves us through time and through other bodies, and I had to choose better: what to make meaning from, whose version of reality will move me through mine, and is there a dance crew that battles another dance crew?

"In the absence of water, people drink sand," Shonda Rhimes said about media that fails women. I drank so much sand. I couldn't drink sand anymore. And men will keep serving sand if we keep drinking it.

"Everyone who is born holds dual citizenship in the kingdom of the well and the kingdom of the sick," wrote Susan Sontag. "Sooner or later each of us is obliged, at least for a spell, to identify ourselves as citizens of that other place." When I was out of the other place and back in the kingdom of the well (for now), I moved into another Brooklyn apartment without mold, and on my new couch where there've been no unwanted sexual advances, I watch shows and films directed by women and written by women, and as often as possible edited, produced, choreographed, and reviewed by women, in which the lens continues to widen and the perspective is radical (meaning "another's"). I watch whatever stars multitudinous women who have more than one history (fetishized trauma) and are more than the love inter-est or the scorned woman or dead or Brunette #2 with no lines or a man's projection or a resolution to male melodrama. And I stream what subverts rather than reproduces cliché and recasts the marginal as central and doesn't resemble what anyone is used to. Basically, I watch *The L Word* and *Grey's Anatomy* over and over. As well as other shows and films—beautiful shows! beautiful films!—headlined and helmed by women and trans women and trans men and nonbinary people—and I could list them all, but that's the catch. Can you list all the cismale showrunners and male filmmakers, all the features about men, starring men, every male genius and kingmaker and landlocked god everywhere? There are too many; no one could.

Now I'm never not asking—in what I watch, in what I do and buy—*Are there people of other genders, and are those people numerous, centered, and in power?* I turn off news reported exclusively by men.[1] Most books I read are by nonmen, books in which women star and put into words all that's been unspoken in my life, books with truth that no male novelist could guess at, books that let me in on the joke and that narrate experience in ways that make me feel less alone in mine and that may change the world by changing the conversations we have with each other. As a teacher, I teach writers who have lived as women or live as a woman, and I don't point it out because it should be so common that it goes without saying. As a dog mom, I adopted from an animal rescue run by women. As a consumer, I buy kitchen sponges, toilet paper, granola, and dog treats made by women, and I buy weed from female growers. After all, doing the reverse is the norm.

In "Female Artists Are (Finally) Getting Their Turn," journal-ist Hilarie M. Sheets writes in the *New York Times* about galleries and museums "playing catch-up after centuries of women's margin-ality and invisibility," to "counterpoint the looked-overness," and to

---

1 News outlets are addressing this as well: the BBC instituted 50:50 The Equality Project; ABC did the same, and other media organizations have launched similar initiatives.

readdress the age-old shushing and subtraction of more than half the population's subjectivity. "I wanted to encourage the young women—they seem to get fearfully depressed," Virginia Woolf wrote to justify writing *A Room of One's Own*, about those who have a voice but can't prove it. In playing catch-up and in encouraging young woman there is, in Adrienne Rich's words, "the extraordinary sense of shedding... someone else's baggage, of ceasing to translate. It is not that thinking becomes easy, but that the difficulties are intrinsic to the work itself, rather than to the environment."

To reiterate King Lear, "Speak again." Speak again as if your life depends on it, because it does, and because mine does.[2] Speak again and again until our voices are undeniable, and because our voices are voices, too. Speak again like me since I have a voice now and use it impeccably.

Just kidding.

I still struggle because of course I do.

In a perfect world—not a man's world or a woman's world—I'd speak again easily and often, without overthinking or having to hype myself up in the mirror beforehand. My every word would be true, and I'd convey my feelings in ways that would be both believed and revered. (Because mental health would be the most popular, celebrated topic of conversation.)

I'd be free from the need to talk about men, men, men. I'd say no with abandon, and nothing more would happen. Or I'd say yes, and it would be because I want to. I wouldn't sanitize my wants, and I would want more. If an unwanted hand rested on my thigh, then I'd say, "Remove that hand from my thigh," on the spot and without internal deliberation. "Ow," I'd say during sex if sex hurt or during a medical appointment if what hurt was hurting. And since I allow myself to be interrup—

I wouldn't anymore.

---

2 "Without models, it's hard to work; without a context, difficult to evaluate; without peers, nearly impossible to speak," writes Joanna Russ in *How to Suppress Women's Writing*.

In a perfect world there would be no canon (or gender) and a woman's whine would win "Song of the Year" and I wouldn't worry about speaking too loudly to Alexa in case my male neighbor heard me. And in that world, we'd talk about menstrual cycles and everyone would just get used to it. There would also be venting festivals and days off to vent; venting would be a genre.

I'd be so emotional, as emotional as I am. And we'd use a new thesaurus for women with feelings. And I'd stop apologizing when I wasn't sorry, and I wouldn't be sorry for existing.

Systemic forces and biased establishments would topple as they should, and a woman's value would no longer be predicated on agreeability, likability, pliability, sexuality, or silence.

Men would respect my every word—or at least they'd listen (listen deep into the night and wake up listening; listen standing up and listen in public),[3] because in a perfect world everyone would be horny to change.

In a perfect world I'd leave and not return to any doctor who didn't listen to me, didn't hang on my every word.

I'd never feel too afraid to voice a scream in my head or feel too confined by conditioning to ask a question so as not to make a scene. My years of therapy would be accessible in every scenario. And speaking up would always be survival and not ever a death sentence.

But it's not a perfect world, not yet, not even close.

"In antiquity, it is true... almost without exception," writes Mary Beard, "you only hear a woman speak when she is about to die."

In my letter to Sugar in 2010 I alleged that "the unifying theme" of women writers was that their careers ended in suicide, that

---

3 And purchase listening tutorials for inventive ways to listen and pick up manuals to heat up their listening and take pills to help them start listening and more pills to prolong their listening; they'd google Eastern listening techniques and ask lesbians and spiritualists how to listen to women; they'd go to the listening store for listening toys, to listen in hundreds of positions; they'd commit to listening and wouldn't stop listening even if their hand hurt.

self-murder was baked into their panned biographies and was their final pronouncements of private and universal despair. Women were dead people, the signs said and kept saying. In 2010 I saw myself among these women who felt funerals in their brains, with at least one asterisk. What I meant by *I want to die because I can't write* was that being inarticulate—being incomprehensible, being unspoken, having a subpar voice—was a life not worth living, and I felt, in some sense, dead already, or that having a voice but not using it would be the death of me.

Before I got sick, and six months before the forever-fourteen-year-old jumped out of the window, we sat together eating candy on the couch where I would sit shiva with her parents in their fifteenth-floor Manhattan apartment, and we decided to rent a movie. Negotiations ensued. With a cartoon ghost PEZ dispenser in her hand, she argued for a film based on a novel written by my first boss. I flung my witch PEZ dispenser at her. I could not—*no matter what*—watch that. But we watched it, because she wanted to.

Holy shit, we agreed the "techno-thriller film" was the best worst movie we had ever seen. All weekend we'd say, "This Blow Pop is good," and then in unison, "but it's not as good as that movie."

Months later, the movie was available to stream on Amazon Prime Video, and I kept meaning to text her about it. Every time I signed into my account, there was the movie poster icon, and I'd cackle and remember that I had to text her, but I didn't, not ever again.

At her memorial I cried as quietly as I could and wished for things, like her undeath and that I'd texted her when I'd thought of her (about the movie and bisexuality and everything, just everything). I wished also, in general, to hold back less and to stay open more and to say something, however little or however much or however imperfect, rather than so much nothing.

I had learned, as every girl learns, to not risk and to prioritize fear—of vulnerability, of criticism, of ridicule, of rejection, of suffering, of violence—over authentic self-expression. What good had it done? Besides allow me to function in a society that can't stand women and doesn't listen to them? My silence had given me nothing, shown me nothing, introduced me to no one, and taken me nowhere.

To say nothing to not say too much, or to say nothing to not say anything wrong—what a waste.

Besides, the powers-that-be will delete women who speak or don't.

I had been criticized, ridiculed, and rejected in silence. I had *suffered*. Untold women have suffered and died in silence. I almost died! Thea Rosenfeld-Jones, age fourteen, did die.

"I tell you I could speak again: whatever / returns from oblivion returns / to find a voice," writes Louise Glück in her poem "The Wild Iris." I had also returned from oblivion and returned to find a voice, and I returned to say: it wasn't my voice that would obliterate me. It was my silence.

ACKNOWLEDGMENTS

Thank you to the editors and publications where some of these pages first appeared in a different form: "On Silence (or, Speak Again)" on Longreads, edited by Sari Botton; "The Never-to-Be Bride" in the Modern Love column of the *New York Times*, edited by Dan Jones; "My Diet, Caffeine-Free Rape" on the Cut, edited by Maureen O'Connor; "Why I Didn't Say No" in *Not That Bad: Dispatches from Rape Culture*, edited by Roxane Gay.

Thank you to:

Mollie Glick, my agent, for knowing what this book was and for helping me turn it into one.

The team at Hachette who liked me and my book just the way we are, and especially to my editor Lauren Marino, production editor Amber Morris, copyeditor Beth Wright, publicist Lauren Rosenthal, marketing manager Julianne Lewis, Niyati Patel, Carolyn Levin, and Mollie Weisenfeld.

Tammy Schulman, for being the first to tell me I would write this. Tracy Clark-Flory, for writing about masturbating to your dad's porn and kicking off the most important connection of my adult life (I couldn't write a better friendship than ours). Marion Rosenfeld, founding member of Club 19, for being my first reader and my winner mentor.

Cheryl Strayed, for giving me advice. Sari Botton (again), for soliciting and editing the essay that became this book. Roxane Gay (again), for accepting, editing, and publishing my essay in *Not That Bad*, for emailing with me about *The Human Centipede*, and for blurbing me (platonically). Julie Greicius, for being my editorial wife, a great kisser, an even better editor, and the best-ever collaborator. Marisa Siegel, Lyz Lenz, and Lisa Dusenbery—for my first matriarchy and forever sisterhood.

Sarah Madges—even though this book isn't dedicated to you, I wrote it to you and wrote it only with your help. Riane Konc—you could write my "thank you" to you better than me, and this book would not exist in its current form or at all if you hadn't emailed me that one time. Caitlin Kunkel—this book is its best self because of you.

Mary Dain, for the salad on the day I swore I would finish this book (five years before I did finish it). Dominique Johnson, for the years of commiserating and cheerleading, and for knowing when to do which. Julie Rossman and Amanda Reddington, for your stories and your rage.

Casey Scieszka and Spruceton Inn, for the room and bar of my own. Writing Between the Vines and Marcy Gordon, for the winery of my own.

Samantha Strauss, for *Dance Academy* and for disproving that one should never meet her heroines. Beth Montgomery, Kathleen Finneran, Janie Ellen Ibur, for teaching me how to write and think and feel.

Every single former and future student, for showing up.

Everyone who read parts of this book or supported me while writing: Braden Marks, Liza Birkenmeier, Michelle Orange, Lydia Conklin, Leigh Stein, Scott Cohen, Lora N. Barnes, Kristina Kearns, Maura McGee, Mira Ptacin, Yosh Han, Janine Brito, Mer Groves, Pushkar Sharma, Nikki Campo, Hannah Wood, Samantha Shea, Sara Levine, Allison Tatarsky, Claire Caplan, Lauren Zenner, Brenden Beck, Carolina Reiter, Miles Strucker, Mike Kelton, Will Hines, and Aaron Rabinowitz.

The four white-knight heroines of my story: the acupuncturist at the Brooklyn Acupuncture Project; my psychologist Danielle Rawda;

Dr. Gabriela Centurion, my psychopharmacologist, for believing me right away, for diagnosing me accurately, and for saving my life a few times; my clinician at the Reeds Center, for curing me and saving me from myself.

Dr. Kim Rottier for fact-checking.

Sarah Garfinkel and Jennie Egerdie, assistant editors of "Funny Women," who sent me a cake and an edible arrangement (respectively) when I sold this book.

My dad and stepmonster, for the material and for forgiving me in advance for using it and for loving me anyway.

My mom and Mr. Jay, my patrons of the arts and best friends, for your emotional and financial support all my life. My mom (again), for reminding me, "You don't have time to feel shitty about your writing." And my mom (once more with feeling), not only for giving me life but for giving me the life I wanted. And Benny Theodore Bassist, for being a very good boy.

UNACKNOWLEDGMENTS

No thank you to my ex-boyfriends and former bosses.

NOTES

INTRODUCTION

"female-shaped 'absent presence'": Caroline Criado Perez, *Invisible Women: Exposing Data Bias in a World Designed for Men* (New York: Abrams, 2019), 1.

In El Salvador, which bans abortion: Caitlin Cruz, "A Salvadorian Women Convicted of Homicide After Miscarriage Is Released From Jail," Jezebel, February 11, 2022.

NASA called off its first-ever all-female spacewalk: Jacey Fortin and Karen Zraick, "First All-Female Spacewalk Canceled Because NASA Doesn't Have Two Suits That Fit," *New York Times*, March 25, 2019.

Dogs are elected mayors: Natalie Colarossi, Kelly McLaughlin, and James Pasley, "Meet the Dog Mayors of America," Insider, July 7, 2020, www.insider.com/dog-mayors-of-america-2019-7.

a quarter of human mayors in 2021 were women: "Women Mayors in U.S. Cities 2021," Center for American Women and Politics, Eagleton Institute of Politics, Rutgers University–New Brunswick, May 2021, cawp.rutgers.edu/facts/levels-office/local/women-mayors-us-cities-2021.

women are "at least twice as likely to have chronic pain": Maya Dusenbery, *Doing Harm: The Truth About How Bad Medicine and Lazy Science Leave Women Dismissed, Misdiagnosed, and Sick* (New York; HarperOne, 2018), 3.

"medically unexplained symptoms": Dusenbery, *Doing Harm*, 79.

Endometriosis: Perez, *Invisible Women*, 220.

"I want you to understand this": Alyson J. McGregor, *Sex Matters: How Male-Centric Medicine Endangers Women's Health and What We Can Do About It* (New York: Hachette Go, 2020), 26.

Depression is 70 percent more prevalent: Paul R. Albert, "Why Is

Depression More Prevalent in Women?," *Journal of Psychiatry and Neuroscience* 40, no. 4 (July 2015): 219–221.

"About one in five women": Dusenbery, *Doing Harm*, 91.

adult women report a suicide attempt 1.6 times: "Suicide Data: United States," American Foundation for Suicide Prevention, January 2021, afsp.org/state-fact-sheets.

suicide rates among girls: "QuickStats: Suicide Rates for Teens Aged 15–19 Years, by Sex—United States, 1975–2015," Centers for Disease Control and Prevention, August 4, 2017, www.cdc.gov/mmwr/volumes/66/wr/mm6630a6.htm.

teenagers gorged on nine hours of media: "Landmark Report: U.S. Teens Use an Average of Nine Hours of Media Per Day, Tweens Use Six Hours," Common Sense Media, November 3, 2015, www.commonsensemedia.org/press-releases/landmark-report-us-teens-use-an-average-of-nine-hours-of-media-per-day-tweens-use-six-hours.

Men also report most of the news: "The Gender Gap in Coverage of Reproductive Issues," Women's Media Center (WMC) Media Watch, 2016, wmc.3cdn.net/3d96e35840d10fafd1_7wm6v3gy2.pdf.

In relationships women are more likely than men: Karina Schumann and Michael Ross, "Why Women Apologize More Than Men: Gender Differences in Thresholds for Perceiving Offensive Behavior," *Psychological Science* 21, no. 11 (2010): 1649–1655; Katharine Ridgway O'Brien, "Just Saying 'No': An Examination of Gender Differences in the Ability to Decline Requests in the Workplace," PhD diss., Rice University, 2014.

lowering women's cognitive functioning (fn): Olga Khazan, "Frigid Offices Might Be Killing Women's Productivity," *Atlantic*, May 22, 2019.

"The single best predictor of rape": Dr. Julia T. Wood, "Gendered Media: The Influence of Media on Views of Gender," in Natalie Fixmer-Oraiz and Julia T. Wood, *Gendered Lives: Communication, Gender, and Culture* (Belmont, CA: Wadsworth, 1994), 231–244.

Miller called then senator Kamala Harris "hysterical": Lily Herman, "Former Trump Aide Calls Senator Kamala Harris 'Hysterical' for Doing Her Job," *Allure*, June 14, 2017.

1. MEDICAL HISTORY

Casey Affleck: Eliana Dockterman, "Casey Affleck Just Addressed #MeToo and the Harassment Allegations Against Him. Here's What to Know About the Controversy," *Time*, January 25, 2017.

First, it was a migraine, classed as a "primary headache": International Classification of Headache Disorders, third edition (ICHD-3), ichd-3 .org/1-migraine.

forty-seven million Americans experience migraine: Stephanie Sy, "15 Percent of Americans Have Migraine Disease. Why Aren't There Better Treatment Options?" *PBS News Hour*, February 26, 2020.

hurting women are seen as "anxious," not "hurting": Diane E. Hoffmann and Anita J. Tarzian, "The Girl Who Cried Pain: A Bias Against Women in the Treatment of Pain," *Journal of Law, Medicine & Ethics* 29 (2001): 13–27.

medicine rarely acknowledges sex differences: Caroline Criado Perez, *Invisible Women: Exposing Data Bias in a World Designed for Men* (New York: Abrams, 2019), 196–197: "Researchers have found sex differences in every tissue and organ system in the human body, as well as in the 'prevalence, course and severity' of the majority of common human diseases." "Sex differences appear even in our cells," like "in immune cells used to convey pain signals." A study "found a significant sex difference in the 'expression of a gene found to be important for drug metabolism.'" One review found "the integration of sex- and gender-based medicine in US med schools remained 'minimal' and 'haphazard', with gaps particularly identified in the approach to the treatment of disease and use of drugs."

"most medical schools and residency programs don't teach": Jennifer Wolff, "What Doctors Don't Know About Menopause," AARP, August/September 2018, www .aarp.org/health/conditions-treatments/info-2018/menopause-symptoms -doctors-relief-treatment.html: "A recent survey reveals that just 20 percent of ob-gyn residency programs provide any kind of menopause training. Mostly, the courses are elective. And nearly 80 percent of medical residents admit that they feel 'barely comfortable' discussing or treating menopause."

"Female bodies": Perez, *Invisible Women*, 199.

Women report less pain than they bear: Alyson J. McGregor, *Sex Matters: How Male-Centric Medicine Endangers Women's Health and What We Can Do About It* (New York: Hachette Go, 2020), 24: "Women have both a lower threshold for pain and a lower pain tolerance," so women "are more likely to perceive and report a lower level of discomfort as 'pain' than men despite an equal degree of [pain]."

Eula Biss rates her pain a three: Eula Biss, "The Pain Scale," *Creative Nonfiction*, no. 32 (2007), 65–84.

rated her chronic pain lower than it felt: Sonya Huber, *Pain Woman Takes Your Keys, and Other Essays from a Nervous System* (Lincoln: University of Nebraska Press, 2017), 39.

A Yale study revealed that young boys' pain (fn): Brian D. Earp, Joshua T. Monrad, Marianne LaFrance, et al., "Gender Bias in Pediatric Pain Assessment," *Journal of Pediatric Psychology* 44, no. 4 (May 2019): 403–414.

"The more vocal women become about their pain" (fn): McGregor, *Sex Matters*, 25.

most medications aren't tested on women: Paula A. Johnson, MD, MPH, Therese Fitzgerald, PhD, MSW, Alina Salganicoff, PhD, et al., *Sex-Specific Medical Research: Why Women's Health Can't Wait: A Report of the Mary Horrigan Connors Center for Women's Health & Gender Biology at Brigham and Women's Hospital*, Brigham and Women's Hospital, Boston, 2014, www.brighamandwomens.org/assets/bwh/womens-health/pdfs/connorsreportfinal.pdf.

Dr. Nafissa Thompson-Spires resisted a hysterectomy (fn): Dr. Nafissa Thompson-Spires, "On No Longer Being a Hysterical Woman," *Paris Review* blog, January 6, 2020, www.theparisreview.org/blog/2020/01/06/on-no-longer-being-a-hysterical-woman:

> I have resisted hysterectomy on two principles, my age and history. I have resisted because of the oversterilization of black women (who have the highest rates of unnecessary hysterectomies). I have resisted because modern gynecology was founded on the torture of my ancestors, used at the whims of a sadoracist who tore apart the bodies of enslaved black women and children like wishbones. His name, though it shouldn't matter, was James Marion Sims. He forced archaic devices into black women and loosened the skulls of black babies with fish tools, and the many statues and monuments to him have only moved around, eulogizing the source of grief rather than the aggrieved.

false premise that Black people don't feel pain (fn): Elinor Cleghorn, *Unwell Women: Misdiagnosis and Myth in a Man-Made World* (New York: Dutton, 2021), 4: "Racist discounting of Black women's physical and psychological pain means they are prescribed fewer pain medications and are more vulnerable to misdiagnosis or to having their diagnoses dangerously delayed. And these disparities are killing them."

most medications, if tested on women, aren't tested during: Perez, *Invisible Women*, 202: "So far, menstrual-cycle impacts have been found for antipsychotics, antihistamines and antibiotic treatments as well as heart medication. Some antidepressants have been found to affect women differently at different times of their cycle, meaning that dosage may be too high at some points and too low at others."

dosages for "adults" are based on a man-size person: McGregor, *Sex Matters*, 20, 25.

women are overmedicated: Irving Zucker and Brian J. Prendergast, "Sex Differences in Pharmacokinetics Predict Adverse Drug Reactions in Women," *Biology of Sex Differences* 11, no. 1 (2020).

A friend of mine was prescribed Ambien (fn): Lisa Stark and Daniel Clark, "FDA: Cut Ambien Dosage for Women," ABC News, January 10, 2013.

"Nearly twice as often as men" (fn): Yasmin Anwar, "Lack of Females in Drug Dose Trials Leads to Overmedicated Women," *ScienceDaily*, August 12, 2020, www.sciencedaily.com/releases/2020/08/200812161318.htm.

women who don't report their own heart attacks: Maanvi Singh, "Younger Women Hesitate to Say They're Having a Heart Attack," NPR, February 24, 2015, www.npr.org/sections/health-shots/2015/02/24/388787045/younger-women-hesitate-to-say-theyre-having-a-heart-attack.

2. HYSTERICAL WOMAN

endometriosis has a "long history of being pathologized": Elinor Cleghorn, *Unwell Women: Misdiagnosis and Myth in a Man-Made World* (New York: Dutton, 2021), 6.

As late as 1980 the American Psychological Association: Carol S. North, "The Classification of Hysteria and Related Disorders: Historical and Phenomenological Considerations," *Behavioral Sciences* 5, no. 4 (December 2015): 496–517.

"The startling fact was this": Joan Didion, "The White Album," *The White Album* (New York: Farrar, Straus and Giroux, 1979), 47.

pain is "psychosomatic" or "stress" or "hormonal": Alyson J. McGregor, *Sex Matters: How Male-Centric Medicine Endangers Women's Health and What We Can Do About It* (New York: Hachette Go, 2020), 28.

women are more likely given: McGregor, *Sex Matters*, 101: "In one study of patients with similar symptoms of irritable bowel syndrome (IBS), researchers found that men were more likely to be referred for X-rays, while women were offered antianxiety medication and lifestyle advice."

The National Institute of Mental Health says it takes: Philip S. Wang, Patricia A. Berglund, Mark Olfson, and Ronald C. Kessler, "Delays in Initial Treatment Contact After First Onset of a Mental Disorder," *Health Services Research* 39, no. 2 (April 2004): 393–416.

"estimated that four out of five prescriptions" (fn): Maya Dusenbery, *Doing Harm: The Truth About How Bad Medicine and Lazy Science Leave Women Dismissed, Misdiagnosed, and Sick* (New York; HarperOne, 2018), 91.

3. CRAZY PSYCHO BITCH

Expressive women were madwomen: Anne Carson, "The Gender of Sound," in *Glass, Irony, and God* (New York: New Directions, 1995), 119–137: "Madness and witchery as well as bestiality are conditions commonly associated with the use of the female voice in public, in ancient as well as modern contexts," Carson writes, citing classical Greek mythology, the Furies, the Sirens, Margaret Thatcher, and Gertrude Stein.

"the new (and obviously preferable) lobotomy": Caroline Criado Perez, *Invisible Women: Exposing Data Bias in a World Designed for Men* (New York: Abrams, 2019), 221.

Most opium users were women: Erick Trickey, "Inside the Story of America's 19th-Century Opiate Addiction," *Smithsonian*, January 4, 2018.

women two and a half times more likely: Peter Wehrwein, "Astounding Increase in Antidepressant Use by Americans," Harvard Health Blog, October 20, 2011, www.health.harvard.edu/blog/astounding-increase-in-antidepressant-use-by-americans-201110203624. Perez (*Invisible Women*, 221–222): A "2017 Swedish study…found that it was men who were more likely to report depression." The same study also "found that women who have not reported depression are twice as likely as men to be prescribed antidepressants."

During the nineteenth century I'd be certifiable: Rachel Vorona Cote, *Too Much: How Victorian Constraints Still Bind Women Today* (New York: Grand Central Publishing, 2020), 147.

his patient "Dora": Peter Gay, *Freud: A Life for Our Time* (New York: W. W. Norton, 1989), 246.

"hysteria" as an allegation would be back in fashion: Alison Espach, "What It Really Means When You Call a Woman 'Hysterical,' " *Vogue*, March 10, 2017, www.vogue.com/article/trump-women-hysteria-and-history.

crazy psycho bitch (CPB): Kennisha Archer, "How *Gone Girl*'s Amy Dunne Challenges the Psycho Bitch Trope," *Film Queue*, September 2, 2016, thefilmq.wordpress.com/2016/09/02/how-gone-girls-amy-dunne-challenges-the-psycho-bitch-trope.

"the label 'crazy' ": Cote, *Too Much*, 139.

"talkativeness of women has been gauged": Dale Spender, *Man Made Language* (London: Routledge and Kegan Paul, 1980), 41.

"How can it be that so many people's ex-girlfriends are crazy?": Cheryl Strayed, *Tiny Beautiful Things* (New York: Doubleday, 2012), 213.

"social invisibility of women's experience": Joanna Russ, *How to Suppress Women's Writing* (repr.; Austin: University of Texas Press, 2018), 57.

4. WHO GETS TO SPEAK AND WHY

"What becometh a woman best": Thomas Wilson, *Wilson's Arte of Rhetorique, 1560* (Oxford: Clarendon Press, 1909).

The "nominal problem is excess": Jordan Kisner, "Can a Woman's Voice Ever Be Right?," The Cut, July 19, 2016, www.thecut.com/2016/07/female -voice-anxiety-c-v-r.html.

"Late-nineteenth-century criminologists" (fn): Rebecca M. Herzig, *Plucked: A History of Hair Removal* (New York: New York University Press, 2015), 71.

"An analysis of prime-time TV in 1987": Susan Faludi, *Backlash: The Undeclared War Against American Women*, 15th anniversary edition (New York: Three Rivers, 2006), 156.

Recent analyses by Martha M. Lauzen: Dr. Martha M. Lauzen, *Boxed In: Women On Screen and Behind the Scenes on Broadcast and Streaming Television in 2020-21*, Center for Women in Television and Film, San Diego State University, 2021, deadline.com/wp-content/uploads/2021/09 /2020-21-Boxed-In-Report-WM.pdf.

Men even talk the most in rom-coms: Hannah Anderson and Matt Daniels, "Film Dialogue from 2,000 Screenplays, Broken Down by Gender and Age," The Pudding, April 2016, pudding.cool/2017/03/film-dialogue. The article is a compilation of "the number of words spoken by male and female characters across roughly 2,000 films, arguably the largest undertaking of script analysis, ever" in 2016.

And in 2016 the *Ghostbusters* reboot: Abigail Chandler, "Why Does the Internet Hate the New All-Female *Ghostbusters*?," *Metro*, July 11, 2016, metro.co.uk/2016/07/11/why-does-the-internet-hate-the-new-all-female -ghostbusters-5999889.

"percentage of top grossing films" (fn): Dr. Martha M. Lauzen, *It's a Man's (Celluloid) World: Portrayals of Female Characters in the Top Grossing Films of 2020*, Center for Women in Television and Film, San Diego State University, 2021, womenintvfilm.sdsu.edu/wp-content/uploads /2021/04/2020_Its_a_Mans_World_Report.pdf. Lauzen's report is an annual summary and analysis that tracks women's employment in film-making and "considers the representation of almost 22,000 characters appearing in approximately 1,000 films" dating back to 2002.

Then, like now, mostly men reported the news: Luba Kassova, *The Missing Perspectives of Women in News*, International Women's Media Foundation, November 2020, www.iwmf.org/wp-content/uploads/2020/11/2020.11.19-The-Missing-Perspectives-of-Women-in-News-FINAL-REPORT.pdf: "Globally, in 2015 19% of experts or commentators were women. The use of women as news sources overall had marginally decreased from 2010 (20% vs. 19%). Women's expertise was heavily skewed towards...the sphere of the private, emotional and subjective vs. the public, rational and objective"; Kassova notes that 21 percent of protagonists in news stories are women and that "women have been substantially under-represented in news media coverage in this century, at a ratio of 5:1." In 2015, "women were 15% of the people seen, heard, or read about in transnational digital outlets," an improvement from past years (*Who Makes the News?*, edited by Sarah Macharia, Global Media Monitoring Project, 2020, whomakesthenews.org/wp-content/uploads/2021/11/GMMP2020.ENG_.FINAL_.pdf).

In 2016 and 2020 election coverage: Alexander Frandsen and Aleszu Bajak, "Women on the 2020 Campaign Trail Are Being Treated More Negatively by the Media," Storybench, Northeastern University's School of Journalism, March 29, 2019, www.storybench.org/women-on-the-2020-campaign-trail-are-being-treated-more-negatively-by-the-media. Frandsen and Bajak analyzed a hundred thirty articles from the *Washington Post*, the *New York Times*, the Huffington Post, CNN, and Fox News.

Cuomo used his media sources (fn): Michael M. Grynbaum, John Koblin, and Jodi Kantor, "CNN Fires Chris Cuomo amid Inquiry into His Efforts to Aid His Brother," *New York Times*, December 4, 2021.

Legal analyst for CNN, lawyer (fn): Brian Stelter and Oliver Darcy, "Jeffrey Toobin Is Back at CNN Eight Months After Exposing Himself on Zoom," CNN Business, June 10, 2021.

The head of Amazon Studios, Roy Price (fn): Ellen Killoran, "'Good Girls Revolt' Creator: Amazon Studios Head Roy Price Didn't Like Cancelled Series," *Forbes*, December 6, 2016.

boys talk more than girls: Anderson and Daniels, "Film Dialogue from 2,000 Screenplays."

boys speak more than girls in the classroom: Janet Holmes, "Women Talk Too Much," chapter 6 in *Language Myths*, ed. Laurie Bauer and Peter Trudgill

(New York: Penguin, 1999): "In a wide range of communities, from kindergarten through primary, secondary and tertiary education, the same pattern recurs—males dominate classroom talk. So on this evidence we must conclude that the stereotype of the garrulous woman reflects sexist prejudice rather than objective reality."

men speak more than women in work meetings: Christopher F. Karpowitz, Tali Mendelberg, and Lee Shaker, "Gender Inequality in Deliberative Participation," *American Political Science Review* 106, no. 3 (August 2012): 533–547.

heterosexual cis men, who, per evidence ad infinitum, are actually "too much": Felice Maranz and Rebecca Greenfield, "Men Get the First, Last and Every Other Word on Earnings Calls," *Bloomberg*, September 13, 2018, www.bloomberg.com/news/articles/2018-09-13/men-get-the-first-last-and-every-other-word-on-earnings-calls. One 2017 study by the research company Prattle examined 155,000 business conference calls from the past nineteen years in which men spoke 92 percent of the time.

they take more credit and interrupt more: Katherine Hilton, "What Does an Interruption Sound Like?," PhD diss., Stanford University, August 2018.

"A trans woman friend of mine": Melissa Febos, *Girlhood* (New York: Bloomsbury, 2021), 249.

"men tend to contribute more information" (fn): Janet Holmes, "Women Talk Too Much."

Even today's automated speech recognition technology: Allison Koenecke, Andrew Nam, Emily Lake, et al., "Racial Disparities in Automated Speech Recognition," *National Academy of Sciences of the United States of America (PNAS)* 117, no. 14 (2020): 7684–7689. This was the report on a study in which automated speech recognition systems (developed "by Amazon, Apple, Google, IBM, and Microsoft") transcribed structured interviews with white speakers and Black speakers, and "all five ASR systems exhibited substantial racial disparities" in average word error rate.

About voice recognition in cars: Graeme McMillan, "It's Not You, It's It: Voice Recognition Doesn't Recognize Women," *Time*, June 1, 2011. *Harvard Business Review* also cites research published by the North American Chapter of the Association for Computational Linguistics (NAACL) that indicates "Google's speech recognition is 13% more accurate for men than it is for women."

the average woman today talks in a deeper voice than her mother and grandmother: David Robson, "The Reasons Why Women's Voices Are Deeper Today," BBC, June 12, 2018, www.bbc.com/worklife/article/20180612-the-reasons-why-womens-voices-are-deeper-today.

When asked about "the heroine's journey": Maureen Murdock, "The

Heroine's Journey," in *Encyclopedia of Psychology and Religion*, ed. David A. Leeming (New York: Springer, 2016), maureenmurdock.com/articles /articles-the-heroines-journey.

this higher voice coming out of a female body: David R. Feinberg, Lisa M. DeBruine, Benedict C. Jones, and David I. Perrett, "The Role of Femininity and Averageness of Voice Pitch in Aesthetic Judgments of Women's Voices," *Perception* 37, no. 4 (April 2008): 615–623; Sarah A. Collins and Caroline Missing, "Vocal and Visual Attractiveness Are Related in Women," *Animal Behaviour* 65, no. 5 (May 2003): 997–1004.

Siri and Alexa default to feminized voices: Chandra Steele, "The Real Reason Voice Assistants Are Female (and Why It Matters)," *PC Magazine*, January 4, 2018.

headline I read recently about "chatbot abuse": Ashley Bardhan, "Men Are Creating AI Girlfriends and Then Verbally Abusing Them," *Futurism*, January 18, 2022, futurism.com/chatbot-abuse.

Right now women are being interrupted: Leslie Shore, "Gal Interrupted: Why Men Interrupt Women and How to Avert This in the Workplace," *Forbes*, January 3, 2017.

pseudoscientific and likely based on the oft-quoted study: Dilraj S. Sokhi, Michael D. Hunter, Iain D. Wilkinson, and Peter W. R. Woodruff, "Male and Female Voices Activate Distinct Regions in the Male Brain," *Neuroimage* 27, no. 3 (September 2005): 572–578.

female hummingbirds that avoid harassment: Sabrina Imbler, "Female Hummingbirds Avoid Harassment by Looking Like Males," *New York Times*, August 26, 2021.

"been in a lesbian relationship" (fn): Torrey Peters, *Detransition, Baby* (New York: One World, 2021), 9.

"Black women in particular" (fn): Karen Attiah, "America Hates to Let Black Women Speak," *Washington Post*, October 8, 2020.

"the humor gap" (fn): Christie Nicholson, "The Humor Gap," *Scientific American*, October 1, 2012.

"have, in their skill set, the ability to pretend" (fn): Susan Orlean, "The Rabbit Outbreak," *New Yorker*, June 29, 2020.

5. GIRLS VERSUS BOYS IN CONVERSATION

my first pitch: Ellen Fein and Sherrie Schneider, *The Rules: Time-Tested Secrets for Capturing the Heart of Mr. Right* (New York: Warner Books, 1995).

Pete Walker coined the term "fawn response": Pete Walker, *Complex*

PTSD: From Surviving to Thriving: A Guide and Map for Recovering from Childhood Trauma (np: Azure Coyote Publishing, 2013), 45.

"We are as much made of words": Alexandra Schwartz, "Shifting Identities in Sanaz Toossi's 'English,'" *New Yorker*, February 28, 2022.

"need different sentences to contain": Mary Gordon, foreword to Virginia Woolf, *A Room of One's Own* (New York: Harcourt, 1981), x.

"between the girl who wrote poems": Joanna Russ, *How to Suppress Women's Writing* (repr.; Austin: University of Texas Press, 2018), 17.

"All I wanted was": Cited in Russ, *How to Suppress Women's Writing*, 17.

bell hooks was able to think back critically: bell hooks, *Talking Back: Thinking Feminist, Thinking Black* (New York: Routledge, 2014): 18.

6. WHY I DIDN'T SAY NO

"The clitoris has been contested" (fn): Elinor Cleghorn, *Unwell Women: Misdiagnosis and Myth in a Man-Made World* (New York: Dutton, 2021), 48; Helen E. O'Connell, Kalavampara V. Sanjeevan, and John M. Hutson, "Anatomy of the Clitoris," *Journal of Urology* 174 (October 2005): 1194; Georgina Rannard, "*The Vagina Bible* Adverts Blocked by Social Media," BBC News, September 2, 2019; Doha Madani, "Delta to Investigate After Olivia Wilde Slammed In-Flight Censorship of 'Booksmart,'" NBC News, October 31, 2019; Tresa Undem, "My 'Top 20' insights over the past year on views toward women and equality," Twitter, August 26, 2019, twitter.com/teemoneyusa/status/1166039791131119618.

"What woman understands by love": Friedrich Nietzsche, *The Gay Science*, translated by Thomas Common (Edinburgh: T. N. Foulis, 1910), 363.

"when a girl's love is not self-sacrificing": Søren Kierkegaard, *Repetition and Philosophical Crumbs* (Oxford, UK: Oxford University Press, 2009), 14.

the "heterosexual script": Janna L. Kim, C. Lynn Sorsoli, Katherine Collins, et al., "From Sex to Sexuality: Exposing the Heterosexual Script on Primetime Network Television," *Journal of Sex Research* 44, no. 2 (2007): 145–157.

"What counts is what the heroine provokes": Laura Mulvey, "Visual Pleasure and Narrative Cinema," *Screen* 16, no. 3 (1975): 6–18.

"The cult of love in the West": Susan Sontag, *Against Interpretation and Other Essays* (New York: Picador, 1961), 47–48.

Faking Orgasm Scale for Women (FOS): Erin B. Cooper, Allan Fenigstein, and Robert L. Fauber, "The Faking Orgasm Scale for Women: Psychometric Properties," *Archives of Sexual Behavior* 43, no. 3 (April 2014): 423–435.

"twice every waking hour" (fn): Chris Brooke, "Women Tell More Fibs Than Men…Honestly! Four in Five Say They Tell a Lie on a Daily Basis," *Daily Mail*, June 3, 2015. Around two thousand people were questioned for the poll commissioned by insurance company Privilege.

In "Trigger Warning: Breakfast": Anonymous, "Trigger Warning: Breakfast," The Nib, July 8, 2014, medium.com/the-nib/trigger-warning-breakfast-c6cdeec070e6.

"tend and befriend": Shelley E. Taylor, "Tend and Befriend Theory," University of California, Los Angeles, December 1, 2006, taylorlab.psych.ucla.edu/wp-content/uploads/sites/5/2014/11/2011_Tend-and-Befriend-Theory.pdf.

every day in America three women on average are murdered: National Organization of Women (NOW), "Violence Against Women in the United States: Statistics," now.org/resource/violence-against-women-in-the-united-states-statistic, accessed February 28, 2022.

one thousand wives, girlfriends, exes, and love interests: Caren Lissner, "Men Are Killing Thousands of Women a Year for Saying No," *Dame*, October 24, 2017.

Ninety-eight percent of mass shootings since 1966: Michel Martin and Emma Bowman, "Why Nearly All Mass Shooters Are Men," NPR, March 27, 2021.

Black girls never have "no": Tressie McMillan Cottom, *Thick: And Other Essays* (New York: New Press, 2019), 184.

"I had to get out because of the warm air'" (fn): Jeffrey Toobin, "The Celebrity Defense," *New Yorker*, December 6, 2009.

"Girls are cruelest to themselves": Anne Carson, "The Glass Essay," in *Glass, Irony, and God* (New York: New Directions, 1995).

7. EMPERORS WITHOUT CLOTHES

"feminine rebellion was visible": Ann Douglas, introduction to *Minor Characters* (New York: Penguin, 1999), xxv.

"Female writers" (fn): Maureen Dowd, "The Women of Hollywood Speak Out," *New York Times Magazine*, November 20, 2015.

"She wrote it but look what she wrote" (fn): Joanna Russ, *How to Suppress Women's Writing* (repr.; Austin: University of Texas Press, 2018), 57.

after the author Rebecca Solnit first published: Rebecca Solnit, "Men Explain Things to Me," *Guernica*, August 20, 2012, www.guernicamag.com/rebecca-solnit-men-explain-things-to-me.

"when men add humor to a business presentation" (fn): Jonathan Evans, Jerel Slaughter, Aleksander Ellis, and Jessi Rivin, "Making Jokes During a Presentation Helps Men But Hurts Women," *Harvard Business Review*, March 11, 2019.

in 2019 the *Washington Post* reported on a study: Nikki Shure, John Jerrim, and Phil Parker, "Bullshitters: Who Are They and What Do We Know about Their Lives?," IZA Institute of Labor Economics, April 2019, ftp.iza.org/dp12282.pdf.

Many of progressive people believe (fn): Luba Kassova, *The Missing Perspectives of Women in News*, International Women's Media Foundation, November 2020, www.iwmf.org/wp-content/uploads/2020/11/2020.11.19-The-Missing-Perspectives-of-Women-in-News-FINAL-REPORT.pdf; Caroline Criado Perez, *Invisible Women: Exposing Data Bias in a World Designed for Men* (New York: Abrams, 2019), 200.

"the phenomena of psychological trauma": Judith Herman, *Trauma and Recovery: The Aftermath of Violence—from Domestic Abuse to Political Terror* (New York: Basic Books, 2015), 8.

women in 2010 earned 77 percent (fn): Elise Gould, Jessica Schieder, and Kathleen Geier, "What Is the Gender Pay Gap and Is It Real?" Economic Policy Institute, October 20, 2016, www.epi.org/publication/what-is-the-gender-pay-gap-and-is-it-real.

Uber or Lyft, since both were under investigation: "Lyft Report Cites Higher Numbers of Sexual Assaults," NPR, October 22, 2021, www.npr.org/2021/10/22/1048607981/lyft-sexual-assaults-safety-report.

#MeToo movement isn't (just) about sex: Rebecca Traister, "This Moment Isn't (Just) About Sex. It's Really About Work," The Cut, December 10, 2017, www.thecut.com/2017/12/rebecca-traister-this-moment-isnt-just-about-sex.html.

8. MUST-SEE DEAD-GIRL TV

women have comprised less than one-third: Dr. Martha M. Lauzen, *Boxed In 2019-20: Women on Screen and Behind the Scenes in Television*, 2020, womenintvfilm.sdsu.edu/wp-content/uploads/2020/09/2019-2020_Boxed_In_Report.pdf; Lauzen, *It's a Man's (Celluloid) World: Portrayals of Female Characters in the Top Grossing Films of 2020*, Center for the Study of Women in Television & Film, 2021, womenintvfilm.sdsu.edu/wp-content/uploads/2021/04/2020_Its_a_Mans_World_Report.pdf.

Archaeological evidence came out in 2013 (fn): Virginia Hughes, "Were the First Artists Mostly Women?" *National Geographic*, October 9, 2013.

"I became aware of the narrow specificity" (fn): Brit Marling, "I Don't Want to Be the Strong Female Lead," *New York Times*, February, 7, 2020.

Even the fourteenth Dalai Lama believes: Ishaan Tharoor, "The Dalai Lama Thinks a Female Dalai Lama Would Have to Be 'Very, Very Attractive,'" *Washington Post*, September 23, 2015.

Four years later he apologized: Marie Lodi, "The Dalai Lama Says He Was Just Joking About His Successor Needing to Be Hot," The Cut, July 2, 2019, www.thecut.com/2019/07/dalai-lama-says-female-successor-should-be -attractive.html.

"What is self-hatred?": Tara Brach, *Radical Acceptance* (New York: Bantam, 2004), 11.

"One in eight movies commercially released in 1983": Daniel Goleman, "Violence Against Women in Films," *New York Times*, August 28, 1984.

every woman nominated for a Best Actress Academy Award: Susan Faludi, *Backlash: The Undeclared War Against American Women*, 15th anniversary edition (New York: Three Rivers, 2006), 218.

half of the eight Academy Award Best Picture nominees: Lena Wilson, "The Long, Problematic History of Rape Scenes in Film," *Playlist*, October 26, 2017, theplaylist.net/problematic-history-rape-scenes-film-20171026.

In 2019 convicted child-rapist Roman Polanski: Hadley Freeman, "What Does Hollywood's Reverence for Child Rapist Roman Polanski Tell Us?," *Guardian* (London), January 30, 2018.

"I don't really do films": Brent Lang, "Keira Knightley on 'Colette,' Pushing for Social Change, and If She'll Ever Direct," *Variety*, January 16, 2018.

I'd see fifty acts of rape: Charlie Jane Anders, "Someone Has Done a Statistical Analysis of Rape in *Game of Thrones*," *Gizmodo*, May, 26, 2015, gizmodo.com /someone-has-done-a-statistical-analysis-of-rape-in-game-1707037159.

"I joke, morbidly": Sonia Saraiya, "The Truth About TV's Rape Obsession: How We Struggle with the Broken Myths of Masculinity, On Screen and Off," *Salon*, June 25, 2015, www.salon.com/2015/06/25/the_truth_about _tvs_rape_obsession_how_we_struggle_with_the_broken_myths_of _masculinity_on_screen_and_off.

And his alleged victim must move (fn): Amanda Mitchell, "Christine Blasey Ford Is Donating Her GoFundMe Money to Sexual Assault Survivors," *Marie Claire*, November 27, 2018.

"controlling images": Patricia Hill Collins, *Black Feminist Thought: Knowledge, Consciousness, and the Politics of Empowerment* (New York: Routledge, 2008), 69.

"What is art but an expression": Jessa Crispin, foreword to Joanna Russ, *How to Suppress Women's Writing* (repr.; Austin: University of Texas Press, 2018), 14.

Stories of sexual harassment, rape, and sexual assault: *Who Makes the News?*, edited by Sarah Macharia, Global Media Monitoring Project, 2020, whomakesthenews.org/wp-content/uploads/2021/07/GMMP2020.ENG _.FINAL20210713.pdf. Girls and women are underrepresented as subjects and sources even in stories that concern them, which the Project designates as stories of "sexual harassment, rape, and sexual assault"; in newspapers, women are 35 percent of subjects and sources on these topics.

every seventy-three seconds an American is sexually assaulted: "Statistics," RAINN (Rape, Abuse & Incest National Network), 2022, www.rainn.org /statistics.

9. STFU

"what did not qualify as rape": Tressie McMillan Cottom, *Thick: And Other Essays* (New York: New Press, 2019), 193.

Like when US senator Kirsten Gillibrand: Jane Mayer, "The Case of Al Franken," *New Yorker*, July 22, 2019.

Gabrielle Union's contract: Megan C. Hills, "Why Was Gabrielle Union 'Fired' from AGT? The Bring It On Star's Claims About Jay Leno's 'Racist' Joke," *Evening Standard* (London), February 12, 2020.

"Cassandra's lot was always to prophesy": Mary Beard, "Did Women in Greece and Rome Speak?," British Museum blog, March 24, 2014, blog .britishmuseum.org/did-women-in-greece-and-rome-speak.

Cassandra's curse appears elsewhere: Elizabeth Lesser, *Cassandra Speaks: When Women Are the Storytellers, the Human Story Changes* (New York: Harper Wave, 2020), 7.

"That's the root of #BelieveWomen": Jennifer Wright, "Women Aren't Crazy," *Harper's Bazaar*, December, 28, 2017.

Elizabeth Warren was labeled "angry": Annie Linskey and Matt Viser, "Is Elizabeth Warren 'Angry' and Antagonistic? Or Are Rivals Dabbling in Gendered Criticism?," *Washington Post*, November 6, 2019.

the royal family formally investigated Meghan Markle's: Emily Alford, "While the Windsors Investigate Meghan Markle's Rudeness, Perhaps They Could Look into Prince Andrew's Alleged Pedophilia," Jezebel, March 3, 2021, jezebel.com/while-the-windsors-investigate-meghan-markles-rudeness -1846400129.

Male reporters are more likely to use quotes: Eliza Ennis and Lauren Wolfe, *#MeToo: The Women's Media Center Report*, Women's Media Center, 2018, www.womensmediacenter.com/assets/site/reports/media-and

-metoo-how-a-movement-affected-press-coverage-of-sexual-assault
/Media_and_MeToo_Womens_Media_Center_report.pdf.

Kate Manne invented the word "himpathy": Kate Manne, *Down Girl: The Logic of Misogyny* (New York: Oxford University Press, 2017), 46.

"The dominant mode by which": Larissa Pham, *Pop Song: Adventures in Art and Intimacy* (New York: Catapult, 2021), 57.

Activist Tarana Burke created Me Too: Sandra E. Garcia, "The Woman Who Created #MeToo Long Before Hashtags," *New York Times*, October, 20, 2017.

"women of color, working-class women, immigrants": Rafia Zakaria, *Against White Feminism: Notes on Disruption* (New York: W. W. Norton, 2021), 11.

"is truly, on a deep level, a real race and class issue": bell hooks, *Talking Back: Thinking Feminist, Thinking Black* (New York: Routledge, 2014), 19.

accused alleged serial sexual rapist and abuser Marilyn: Maria Sherman, "Marilyn Manson Faces Criminal Investigation for Sexual and Physical Abuse Allegations," Jezebel, February 19, 2021, jezebel.com/marilyn-manson-faces-criminal-investigation-for-sexual-1846305831.

"We won't look back at people's history": Kylie Cheung, "Supposedly Canceled Men All Pick Up Grammy Nominations," Jezebel, November 24, 2021, jezebel.com/supposedly-canceled-men-all-pick-up-grammy-nominations -1848117489.

"beyond credibility" (fn): Judith Herman, *Trauma and Recovery: The Aftermath of Violence—from Domestic Abuse to Political Terror* (New York: Basic Books, 2015), 14; Caroline Criado Perez, *Invisible Women: Exposing Data Bias in a World Designed for Men* (New York: Abrams, 2019), 221.

10. SILENCE AND NOISE

"Here's the problem" (fn): Bonnie Miller, *Women Don't Poop & Other Lies: Toilet Trivia, Gender Rolls, and the Sexist History of Pooping* (Berkeley: Ulysses Press, 2020), 5.

"Many femcels would say": Nona Willis Aronowitz, "The Femcel Revolution," *Elle*, September 1, 2021.

11. HYSTERIA REBOOT

Louis C.K. "returned to stand-up": "Louis CK Admits Sexual Misconduct Allegations Are True," BBC News, November 10, 2017.

federal lawsuit against Moira Donegan and thirty Jane Does: Brittany Martin, "Defamation Suit Against the 'Shitty Media Men' List Creator Can Move Forward, Judge Rules," *Los Angeles Magazine*, July 1, 2020.

tension myositis syndrome (TMS): John E. Sarno, *The Mindbody Prescription: Healing the Body, Healing the Pain* (New York: Grand Central Publishing, 2001), 7.

In the *New York Times* op-ed (fn): Juno DeMelo, "A 30-Year-Old Best-Selling Book Might Hold the Key to Curing Chronic Pain," *New York Times*, November 9, 2021.

"Since the 1950s, psychosomatic diagnoses": Elinor Cleghorn, *Unwell Women: Misdiagnosis and Myth in a Man-Made World* (New York: Dutton, 2021), 6.

that can be fatal because it aggravates heart disease: Judith Shulevitz, "The Lethality of Loneliness," *New Republic*, May 13, 2013.

"Tell [the audience] about how you're never really": Audre Lorde, *Sister Outsider: Essays and Speeches* (Berkeley: Crossing, 2012), 30.

Trauma "can be reactivated": Bessel van der Kolk, *The Body Keeps the Score: Brain, Mind, and Body in the Healing of Trauma* (New York: Penguin Books, 2014), 2.

"An experience becomes a trauma": Ezra Klein and Bessel van der Kolk, "This Conversation Will Change How You Think About Trauma," *New York Times*, August 24, 2021.

"the story of all [literal] trauma": Sarah Ramey, *The Lady's Handbook for Her Mysterious Illness: A Memoir* (New York: Anchor, 2020), 228.

"external factors": Parul Sehgal, "The Case Against the Trauma Plot," *New Yorker*, December 27, 2021.

"focused on the symptoms of hysteria that resembled": Judith Herman, *Trauma and Recovery: The Aftermath of Violence—from Domestic Abuse to Political Terror* (New York: Basic Books, 2015), 11.

"the story of the traumatic event": Herman, *Trauma and Recovery*, 1.

"unexpressed or inadequately expressed anger": Soraya Chemaly, *Rage Becomes Her: The Power of Women's Anger* (New York: Atria Books, 2018), 7.

"backache, stomachache and headache are almost always": Sarno, *The Mindbody Prescription*, 60.

Women, who turn to the mothering grip of media: Women watch more news than men (Al Tompkins, "New Pew Study Says Local TV News Viewing Dropping Fast," Poynter, January 5, 2018, www.poynter.org /ethics-trust/2018/new-pew-study-says-local-tv-news-viewing-dropping -fast-2); watch 232 more hours of Hulu annually than men (Dana Feldman, "Hulu: How America Watched Television in 2017," *Forbes*, December

18, 2017); are the majority of moviegoers (*Theatrical Market Statistics 2016*, Motion Picture Association of America, 2017, www.mpaa.org /wp-content/uploads/2017/03/MPAA-Theatrical-Market-Statistics-2016 _Final.pdf); spend about 150 minutes more on cell phones than men (texting, emailing, checking social media, in that order; "Social Media Fact Sheet," Pew Research Center, April 7, 2021, www.pewinternet.org /fact-sheet/social-media); and make up the majority of Facebook, Instagram, and Twitter users (Jeff Clabaugh, "Why Women Check Social Media More Than Men," WTOP News, October 22, 2018, wtop.com/business -finance/2018/10/why-women-check-social-media-more-than-men), double-checking every social site just…one…more…time. A 2017 study on addictive social media use associated it with being young, female, and single (Cecilie Schou Andreassen, Ståle Pallesen, and Mark D. Griffiths, "The Relationship Between Addictive Use of Social Media, Narcissism, and Self-Esteem: Findings from a Large National Survey," *Addictive Behaviors* 64 [2017]: 287–293). While young, single women are more online, we're also leaving the internet more because of online harassment. "Today, globally, there are two hundred million fewer girls and women online than men," Soraya Chemaly writes in *Rage Becomes Her*.

"I believe a kind of rage/soothe ratio": Sarno, *The Mindbody Prescription*, 41.

"Women who repress their anger are": Chemaly, *Rage Becomes Her*, 53.

"ordinary response to atrocities is to banish them": Herman, *Trauma and Recovery*, 1.

the traumatized contract more diseases: "Past Trauma May Haunt Your Future Health," Harvard Health Publishing, February, 12, 2021, www.health.harvard.edu/diseases-and-conditions/past-trauma-may -haunt-your-future-health; Carina Storrs, "Is Life Expectancy Reduced by a Traumatic Childhood?" *Scientific American*, October 7, 2009.

In rural North Carolina in 2002: Robert E. Bartholomew and Bob Rickard, *Mass Hysteria in Schools: A Worldwide History Since 1566* (Jefferson, NC: McFarland, 2014).

In Mexico City between 2006 and 2007: Daniel Hernandez, "The Haunting of Girlstown," Vox, May 20, 2020, www.vox.com/c/the-highlight/21242299 /outbreak-girlstown-chalco-world-villages-villa-de-las-ninas.

Starting around 2009 in Afghanistan: Matthieu Aikins, "Are the Taliban Poisoning Afghan Schoolgirls? The Evidence," *Newsweek*, July 9, 2012.

In Malaysia in 2019: Heather Chen, "The Mystery of Screaming Schoolgirls in Malaysia," BBC News, August 11, 2019.

At the Starehe Girls' Centre in Kenya: Nancy Agutu, "Starehe Girls Diagnosed with Mass Hysteria," *Star* (Nairobi, Kenya), October 4, 2019.

12. SPEAK AGAIN

Deepak Chopra (once sued for sexual harassment): Rich Juzwiak, "A Decades-Long History of Hollywood Getting Away with It," Jezebel, October 10, 2018, jezebel.com/a-decades-long-history-of-hollywood-getting-away-with-i-1829536822.

Her rationale (fn): Anne Carson, "The Gender of Sound," in *Glass, Irony, and God* (New York: New Directions, 1995), 126.

Author bell hooks had to change her name: bell hooks, *Talking Back: Thinking Feminist, Thinking Black* (New York: Routledge, 2014), 9.

"laws were passed specifying the location": Carson, "The Gender of Sound," 132–133.

"a brief decade men of science listened to women": Judith Herman, *Trauma and Recovery: The Aftermath of Violence—from Domestic Abuse to Political Terror* (New York: Basic Books, 2015), 11.

events like 9/11 are "less likely to cause trauma": Ezra Klein and Bessel van der Kolk, "This Conversation Will Change How You Think About Trauma," *New York Times*, August 24, 2021.

"The first systematic test of the power of language": Bessel van der Kolk, *The Body Keeps the Score: Brain, Mind, and Body in the Healing of Trauma* (New York: Penguin Books, 2014), 241.

"In most studies of emotional-awareness": Eleanor Cummins, "Is the Pain All in My Head?" The Cut, January 25, 2022, www.thecut.com/2022/01/pain-reprocessing-therapy.html.

"exorcising a diary's worth of negative feelings": Juno DeMelo, "A 30-Year-Old Best-Selling Book Might Hold the Key to Curing Chronic Pain," *New York Times*, November 9, 2021.

"even remembering an angry experience results": Soraya Chemaly, *Rage Becomes Her: The Power of Women's Anger* (New York: Atria Books, 2018), 53.

"Women must write her self": Hélène Cixous, Keith Cohen, and Paula Cohen, "The Laugh of the Medusa," *Signs* 1, no. 4 (1976): 875.

there's even the term "rejection violence": Lily Katherine Thacker, "The Danger of 'No': Rejection Violence, Toxic Masculinity and Violence Against Women," master's thesis, Eastern Kentucky University, January 2019.

"screen our jokes, our laughter": Tressie McMillan Cottom, *Thick: And Other Essays* (New York: New Press, 2019), 194.

13. RECLAIMING WOMEN'S VOICES

"a poem works if it lives": Suzanne Juhasz, *Naked and Fiery Forms: Modern American Poetry by Women* (New York: HarperCollins, 1976), 185, 201.

"playing catch-up after centuries": Hilarie M. Sheets, "Female Artists Are (Finally) Getting Their Turn," *New York Times*, March 29, 2016.

"the extraordinary sense of shedding": Adrienne Rich, "Conditions for Work: The Common World of Women," *Heresies* 3 (1977): 53–54.

"Without models, it's hard to work" (fn): Joanna Russ, *How to Suppress Women's Writing* (repr.; Austin: University of Texas Press, 2018), 117.